SEX AND MEDICINE
Gender, Power and Authority in the
Medical Profession

Professional medicine has often been seen as a field that discriminates against women as doctors and patients. Yet women are entering medicine in increasing numbers. This book explores the position of women in the medical profession in Australia and the UK, asking the key question: do women doctors make a difference? Based on an extensive survey of general practitioners and specialists, the book evokes the culture of contemporary medicine by describing the experiences of doctors themselves, often in their own words. Pringle employs a distinctive theoretical approach, but writes accessibly and with insight about a profession that is slowly being transformed. She notes the success of women in entering medicine and describes the ways in which they have challenged medical authority and practice. This is an original and important work that contains new visions for medical practice.

Rosemary Pringle is Professor of Women's Studies at Griffith University. She has written widely on gender and work, feminist theory, family and the state. Her books include *Gender at Work* (with Ann Game), *Defining Women* (with Linda McDowell), *Transitions* (edited with Barbara Caine) and *Secretaries Talk: Sexuality, Power and Work*.

SEX AND MEDICINE

Gender, Power and Authority in the Medical Profession

ROSEMARY PRINGLE

CAMBRIDGE
UNIVERSITY PRESS

PUBLISHED BY THE PRESS SYNDICATE OF THE UNIVERSITY OF CAMBRIDGE
The Pitt Building, Trumpington Street, Cambridge, United Kingdom

CAMBRIDGE UNIVERSITY PRESS
The Edinburgh Building, Cambridge CB2 2RU, UK   http://www.cup.cam.ac.uk
40 West 20th Street, New York, NY 10011–4211, USA   http:/www.cup.org
10 Stamford Road, Oakleigh, Melbourne 3166, Australia

First published 1998

Printed in China by L. Rex Printing Company Ltd.

Typeset in New Baskerville 10/12 pt

A catalogue record for this book is available from the British Library

Library of Congress Cataloguing in Publication data
Pringle, Rosemary.
Sex and medicine: gender, power, and authority in the medical
profession/Rosemary Pringle.
Bibliography.
Includes index.
p.   cm.
Includes bibliographical references and index.
ISBN 0-521-57093-X (hardcover: alk. paper).
ISBN 0-521-57812-4 (pbk.: alk. paper).
1. Women in medicine. 2. Sexism in medicine. I. Title.
R692.P74 1998
610.69'52'082–dc21   97–46532

Contents

Tables

Acknowledgments

I should like to acknowledge the support for this research from the Australian Research Committee (1992–94) and from Macquarie and Griffith Universities. The BMA, the Medical Women's Federation and Women in Medicine helped me to get the project going quickly in the short periods that were available to me in England. In Australia, I was fortunate to be invited to be a member of the AMWAC Female Medical Workforce Working Party. An earlier version of Chapter 8 first appeared in the *Journal of Gender Studies,* 1996 5 (2), pp. 157–68.

Many people have contributed to the outcome of this book. My promise of anonymity prevents me from thanking directly the one hundred and eighty doctors who agreed to be interviewed, many of whom spent a lot of time with me explaining medical history and terminology, providing background material and facilitating contact with colleagues. As a visitor to the United Kingdom I received great hospitality and support as I struggled to find my way around the system.

I should like to thank Jenny Mann, Susan Lewis and Jo Alley who worked as researchers on the project at various times. They set up meetings, collected data, carried out some of the interviews with individuals and focus groups and indexed the vast amount of transcript material that emerged. Jenny discussed the questions that I should ask, read all the transcripts interpreting their medical content, and spent long hours talking medicine to me. Stefania Siedlecky read the entire manuscript with great care and attention to detail.

A number of key people discussed ideas with me, read drafts, suggested references and helped me to construct my field. I should like to thank the following:

In the United Kingdom: Susan Bewley, Jos Cornwell, Rosemary Crompton, Melanie Davies, Lesley Doyal, Ruth Gilbert, Sam Hall, Jeff

Hearn, Clare Moynihan, Jane Salvage, Susan Schonfield and Irene Weinreb.

In Australia: Christine Alavi, Pam Benton, Robyn Brown, Barbara Caine, Bob Connell, Steve Corbett, Lorraine Dennerstein, Frank Forster, Pat Game, Ghassan Hage, Liz Jacka, Jo McCubbin, Linda Mann, Warren Murphy, Owen Dent, Margaret Philp, Caroline Quadrio, Beverley Raphael, Kathy Sant and Deidre Wicks. I should like to thank my publisher, Phillipa McGuinness, for her enthusiasm for the project and her faith that I would complete it.

Sophie Watson helped me get this project off the ground, discussed ideas, read drafts, and gave me a great deal of encouragement and support. To reread my field notes and transcripts is wonderfully evocative of time spent together, in both countries.

Above all, my thanks go to Elspeth Probyn. At a point when I was still searching for an intellectual framework she persuaded me to go back to Bourdieu and discussed his ideas at length with me. She read carefully through my early scratchy drafts, made detailed and careful suggestions about how to turn them into chapters and about how the book should be structured. She helped me through the stressful period of rewriting, and read each subsequent draft with an unfailing eye for the gaps in the argument. Without her intellectual, emotional and practical support this book would not have happened.

ROSEMARY PRINGLE
Brisbane

Abbreviations

AIHW	Australian Institute of Health and Welfare
AMA	Australian Medical Association
AMWAC	Australian Medical Workforce Advisory Committee
ANZCA	Australian and New Zealand College of Anaesthetists
ASA	Australian Society of Anaesthetists
BJME	*British Journal of Medical Education*
BMA	British Medical Association
BMJ	*British Medical Journal*
DA	Diploma of Anaesthesia
DPM	Diploma of Psychological Medicine
ECT	electroconvulsive therapy
ENT	ear, nose and throat
FFA	Fellow of the Faculty of Anaesthetics
FPA	Family Planning Association
GP	general practitioner
GPI	general paralysis of the insane
HO	house officer
HRT	hormone replacement therapy
HSC	Higher School Certificate
IVF	in vitro fertilization
MBBS	Bachelor of Medicine, Bachelor of Surgery
MI	myocardial infarction (heart attack)
MJA	*Medical Journal of Australia*
NHMRC	National Health and Medical Research Council
NHS	National Health Service
NPC	non-patient-centred
PSA	Public Service Association
RACGP	Royal Australian College of General Practitioners

RACOG	Royal Australian College of Obstetricians and Gynaecologists
RACP	Royal Australian College of Physicians
RACS	Royal Australasian College of Surgeons
RANZCP	Royal Australian and New Zealand College of Psychiatrists
RCGP	Royal College of General Practitioners
RCOG	Royal College of Obstetricians and Gynaecologists
RCP	Royal College of Physicians
RCS	Royal College of Surgeons
RN	registered nurse
SHO	senior house officer
SMH	*Sydney Morning Herald*
VMO	visiting medical officer
WIGO	Women in Gynaecology and Obstetrics (UK)
WIST	Women in Surgical Training (UK)

1

Introduction

> Surprisingly little has been written on the careers of women
> doctors; the triumphant story of their entry into the
> profession is enthusiastically chronicled, but nobody analyses
> their achievements on arrival.
>
> *(Harrison, 1981: 53)*

Many feminists have been profoundly suspicious of the medical profession, seeing it as serving the interests of contemporary patriarchy.
Male doctors, they argue, have acted virtually on behalf of men as a
group to maintain the social subordination of women by controlling
their bodies and reproductive capacities. Modern, professional medicine
snatched healing out of the hands of women (its traditional practitioners) and turned women into the main objects of its practices,
subjecting them to new forms of humiliation and surveillance. In particular, some feminists have been furious that male obstetricians and
gynaecologists took control of childbirth, an area of great symbolic
power for women, and claimed a near monopoly of knowledge about
women's bodies. The women's health movement has been anti-
professional in its philosophy, believing that knowledge and skills should
be widely dispersed, and that doctors should hold no special authority as
health practitioners.

Women doctors have therefore been regarded ambivalently by some
feminists. There is the heroic past, when they played a key part in the
history of feminism, scaling the heights of patriarchal power to gain
entry to the profession, enduring ridicule and hostility from male
doctors and medical students. And then there is the present, when
women doctors, in the main, are seen as a conservative group with little
sympathy for feminist causes. Where militant feminism had once been of

1

assistance to women doctors, some women who trained in the 1970s thought that, if anything, it had hampered them, since male colleagues were likely to hold them personally responsible for what they saw as the excesses of women's liberation. For those doctors who do identify as feminists and place their skills in the hands of the women's health movement, sisterhood is still conditional on their renunciation of special privileges and their willingness to work on an equal basis with other health workers. For some hardliners they are 'honorary men', sometimes 'worse than the men', a position which is often echoed by nurses, whether or not they have had much experience of working with women doctors.

To some feminists it is easier to accept women doctors if it can at least be shown that they are still exploited and oppressed within the medical profession: there is something almost reassuring about the surveys that continue to provide evidence for this conclusion. Since the late 1970s there have been literally dozens of surveys of sexual divisions within the medical profession, carried out by governments, by the various colleges, by national medical associations and unions, by university departments and by independent researchers. Everywhere the same factors are identified as problematic: the difficulties in combining family and career; the high stress levels and suicide rates; the lack of part-time work and training; sexism in the syllabus; discrimination in appointments and promotions and in relation to training positions; the clustering of women in the lowest status positions and their absence from key specialties like surgery and obstetrics and gynaecology; difficulties in getting partnerships in general practice. Medicine, it is said, has failed to adapt to the presence of women by adopting more flexible patterns, providing part-time training and career opportunities or positively encouraging women to be surgeons and high flying consultants.

While there is some truth to this, the very fact that it has been so amply documented indicates that a major shift is taking place. To paraphrase Foucault (1980), what is interesting here is not just that women doctors are oppressed but that they are now so loudly and urgently saying that they are oppressed. Medicine, the occupation which above all has required a vocational commitment, a readiness to be available twenty-four hours a day, seven days a week, is being called upon to restructure. Through all these surveys, emphasis is placed on the need for change, on the importance of women practising in all areas of medicine, not just those that have been defined as gender appropriate. There is an awareness that unless medical work as a whole is restructured (or men miraculously take on a full 50 per cent of responsibility for child care) women will continue to be disadvantaged. The growing number of women graduates suggests a degree of democratisation and creates pressure for stronger representation across all specialties.

The purpose of this book is deconstructive. I have treated the interview transcripts themselves as texts, and I have read them for what they do not say as well as for the repressions that make possible what they *do* say. Women doctors are simultaneously a part of (patriarchal) medicine and placed outside it, their presence in large numbers necessarily a destabilising one. Their speech both affirms and undercuts medical authority. If the masculinity of the medical profession rests on a binary opposition between 'women' and 'medicine', then 'women doctors' constitute the third term which undermines its functioning. Jane Flax (1990: 37–8) suggests that deconstructive readers should be disrespectful of authority, attentive to suppressed tensions or conflicts within the text and suspicious of all 'natural' categories. Rather than reinforcing women in a position of marginality or victimhood I have chosen to emphasise their success. In doing so I have been sceptical not only of medical authority but of the 'truths' of many feminist theorists and social scientists.

The book is intended not just as a description of women doctors but as an intervention into feminist theory and especially into the sociology of work and health. Social scientists have been attacking the pretensions of medicine and the professions for a long time while denying the force of their own criticisms. They continue to write as if nothing has changed. What if it can be shown that, after a century of marginalisation and downright hostility, women are having a major impact on medicine? It would then be difficult to go on conceptualising medicine as the linchpin of patriarchy or to assume western cultures are still patriarchal in a systemic sense. The presence of women doctors points to the need for a rethinking of many conventional assumptions about medical power and privilege, the operations of medical 'fields', the status of the professions, of 'patriarchy' and gender inequality. It provides an important opportunity and context for a substantial revision of feminist categories, concepts and strategies. Some readers may think I am naive, overly optimistic or cavalier in my treatment of the ongoing realities of male medical power. But it is possible to overstate the power and glamour of medicine in ways that unwittingly reinforce medical authority. Rather than dwelling on the realities of male medical power I can point towards its vulnerabilities and cracks.

A study of women doctors provides a window into some of the major changes of our times which have been characterised as 'postmodern'. While doctors are not about to be 'proletarianised' *en masse*, they need to be recontextualised in the shifting class relations of the postmodern world. With the restructuring of medical work and the shift to group practice doctors have had to rethink their relations with patients, with each other and with the health professionals who work alongside them. People want more egalitarian relationships with their doctors, and have less respect for medical authority. As every occupation seeks to 'professionalise' itself the distinction between professions and occupations becomes blurred. Middle-class professionals are less protected than they used to be from the exigencies of the market and, while some doctors continue to work 120-hour weeks, others, especially in cities, are having trouble finding work except as locums or, in the case of specialists, as sessionals. Even the 'glamorous' end of medicine has become bureaucratised and routinised as surgeons spend their time doing standard hip and knee operations. Often they work through the night not because they are dealing with an emergency, but because, as resources become more limited, this is the only time they can book the theatre.

The movement of women into medicine is unsettling both to medical authority and to the overall organisation of work, to the relation between public and private worlds, and to the conditions of 'modernity'. The demand that women be accepted on equal terms with men, I will suggest, may no longer be able to be accommodated within a 'modern' package of reforms and points towards a world in which work, medicine and gender relations are dramatically repositioned.

Gender and status

Everybody 'knows' that in the former Soviet bloc the majority of doctors are women while in the United States they are men: 70 per cent in the old USSR as compared with 10 per cent in the USA in 1982 (Day, 1982: 103–4). Any number of binaries are invoked to explain this: men and women, socialism and capitalism, East and West, and public and private health systems. But the bottom line is that at the primary care level Soviet medicine had limited training and prestige and this is associated with the fact it was done by women. The wealth and prestige of American medicine is associated with the fact not only that it is private but also it has largely been the monopoly of men. Now that Western medicine appears to be falling off its pedestal, the question is inevitably raised, what is the relationship between the status of medicine and the proportion of women in it? Do women lower the status? Does their appearance indicate that medicine has already nose-dived? If there is a relationship between gender and status, what are its mechanisms?

The trends everywhere in the West are very similar. Women are concentrated in general or family practice and community or public health. They have made some impact on paediatrics, psychiatry, pathology and anaesthesia and a large impact on small specialties such as dermatology. They are moving into newer specialties such as geriatrics, rehabilitation medicine and genetics. Even in the former Soviet bloc they have been notoriously absent from surgery. In most countries they remain a tiny minority of surgeons and are seriously under-represented in the more prestigious (and lucrative) procedural specialties within internal medicine. Their distribution has been explained in both individual and institutional terms. The first emphasises gender-related preferences: for example that women are better at people work or emotion work and choose those areas. The second suggests that women have made long-term 'investment' decisions about their human capital by balancing their domestic and occupational roles (Day, 1982: 105; Riska & Wegar, 1993: 79–80).

Rather than locating the discussion at the level of the social system as a whole, I shall concentrate on the aspects of the medical culture that make it resistant to adapting to the needs of those who have others to care for or, indeed, who would like to be able to care properly for themselves! Caring for children will always be difficult to combine with occupations where dedication and competence are seen to reside in full-time commitment and long working hours. Medicine has evolved as a global culture with rigid conceptions of what constitutes good practice and huge reluctance to 'water these down'. But it is changing. While it is not inevitable that, because more than 50 per cent of students or graduates are women, they will come to be more evenly spread across medicine, it seems unlikely, given the strategic concerns of these women, that they will not make further major inroads over the next few years.

Medicine and modernity

As a child growing up in the 1950s I believed that I had been born at the precise moment when modernity came of age. While much of this can be put down to childhood megalomania there was some basis to my belief. It was the beginning of the space age, of jet travel, the triumph of science and technology, medical miracles, television, rock music, and all kinds of new electrical goods along with truth, justice and the American way. I was less aware of the underside: Hiroshima, Belsen, the nuclear threat or the damage being done to the environment. I believed that things were going to get continuously better, that progress was endless.

'Modernity' in all these senses is something that we now look back on as a world we have lost. What we lost, and when we lost it, are open to debate, for modernity has always had within itself the seeds of its own demise. From contemporary vantage points, modernity is generally understood to signify fluctuation and change as industrialisation and the growth of cities swept away the traditional social order and established social relations, leaving in its place the isolated individual and a sense of fragmentation and chaos. But there was another side to modernity which derived from the Enlightenment faith in objective science and reason, the possibility of affirming universal values of morality and justice, accumulating and expanding knowledge to be used for the emancipation of humankind. Scientific advances seemed to guarantee freedom from scarcity, want, and the effects of natural calamities. Enlightenment thought embraced the idea of rational progress and knowledge in place of the irrationality of myth, religion, superstition. Science would put people in charge of their own destinies, no longer subject to the whims of nature or the dictates of tradition.

Scientific medicine was a key aspect of modernity since it seemed to promise triumph over pain, suffering and disease. By the 1950s it was delivering very impressively. Developments in anaesthesia had made possible more daring surgery, while 'magic bullets' seemed capable of striking at just about every disease. Where medicine had previously been able to do little more than diagnose it was now able to cure. The arrival of chemotherapy and radium and drugs ranging from aspirin and paracetamol to salvarsan, insulin, penicillin and streptomycin, to name a few, all contributed to the rising prestige of medicine in the first half of the twentieth century. The discovery of sulphonamides in 1935, the first antibiotics suitable for mass use by non-specialists, marked the beginning of a golden age of uncritical faith in the social value of applied medical science (Hart, 1988: 18). In all countries, the period after World War Two saw a vast expansion of the hospital sector and the proliferation of specialties and sub-specialties. The development of relaxants turned anaesthesia into a complex science and made longer and more complex operations possible, culminating in transplant surgery. In internal medicine it looked as if infectious diseases could be eliminated and there would be miracle cures to deal with every problem. The remaining killers, cardiovascular disease and cancer, would soon be brought under control.

Many writers have observed how often women are located outside of modernity as its 'other' (Morris, 1988; Johnson, 1993). Women are represented as more traditional, closer to nature, limited by and to their bodies. Women's bodies are routinely presented as objects of sexual consumption for Western modernity. And women are seen as *consumers* of the fruits of modernity rather than as producers and as part of mass culture as opposed to the scientific elite. In relation to modern medicine, women have been positioned both as its objects and its chief beneficiaries. Their presence as healers was relegated to 'traditional' times, their skills denigrated because they worked 'with' nature and lacked mastery over it. If doctors were normatively male, patients became normatively female. In fact medicine was seen as of particular benefit to women in freeing them from their bodies. Modernity saw the superstitious fears of women's bodies evaporate and created a basis for replacing female bonding against male brutality with heterosexual solidarity.

Thus, argues Edward Shorter, the major health changes of the first quarter of this century actually made possible the first great wave of feminism 'in alliance with men rather than in the context of traditional women's culture' (1984: 296). If women are the objects and consumers of masculine medicine, women doctors are placed symbolically in between. Since they are not properly either the subjects or the objects of medicine, they may challenge this dichotomy between subject and object on which modern medicine rested.

Since the 1970s the euphoria with the power of medicine has begun to evaporate. In a book and BBC television series entitled 'The Trouble with Medicine' Dr Melvin Konner describes how we were lulled into a false sense of security. 'We enter an illusory world in which anything that is broken can be fixed, in which anything that is wrong with us has its own private molecular magic wand that, when waved over us, will make it go away' (1993: 49). The so-called magic bullets not only had side effects but led quite quickly to the development of new strains of drug-resistant bacteria. The AIDS virus appeared at a time when medicine was already being forced to withdraw its claims to have permanently won the battle for infection control and to recognise that it was instead locked into something more like permanent guerrilla warfare. Doctors have to some extent been humbled and, Konner suggests, the community should withdraw the godlike expectations it has had of them and take more responsibility for its own health. While medical discoveries continue at a rapid rate, the mood has changed. Developments in reproductive technology, for example, have brought mixed responses, and the Human Genome Project, with its potential to create 'perfect' human beings, and another round of miracle cures for every thing from cystic fibrosis to homosexuality, inspires as much fear as optimism.

Part of this 'trouble' with medicine has to do with gender. Both medicine and modernity have been linked with masculine power and domination (Davies, 1996). The reversals to medical triumphs can be seen as a colossal blow to the masculine ego. Women have to some extent caused the 'trouble' in attacking patriarchal medicine and demanding new forms of health care. But they can also be represented as part of the solution, the new 'human' face of a humbler form of medical practice. What is going on here is a recasting of practice and priorities as medicine engages in diverse ways with the heritage of 'modernity'. The outcome of these processes is not foreclosed and is unlikely to be linear. On the contrary, it will be diverse, local, temporary and shifting. It is a world in which opportunities open up but may just as quickly close off again.

The story of western medicine's resistance to women and of women's struggles to gain entry has often been told. Having overcome the educational barriers, women had great difficulty getting hospital appointments or setting up practices. They were accepted in a limited range of work on condition that they behaved as 'lady doctors'. While the occasional brilliant surgeon or physician was tolerated, most women doctors before World War Two worked in community and public health or family planning. A surprising number from the UK and Australia sailed off to India as missionary doctors in a country where women could not see male doctors. A few were able to set up general practices either in remote areas or catering to a female clientele. Others went into practice with their husbands. By the early twentieth century women doctors were no longer a feminist *cause célèbre* and their numbers declined or at best remained static. Nursing, with its shorter training period and lower entry costs, began to be promoted as the more appropriate health profession for women. In England and Australia the proportion of women doctors grew slowly in the 1950s as women became more accepted in general practice and in some of the shortage specialties. Quotas remained in force at British and North American universities until the late 1960s (Crompton & Sanderson, 1990). In the United States the numbers lagged behind and it took the revival of feminism to force changes. In 1970 the Women's Equity Action League filed a class action complaint against every medical school in the US and shortly afterwards Congress passed Title IX legislation prohibiting sex discrimination in educational programs (Walsh, 1979: 450–4). The numbers of women medical students immediately increased but are still well behind Britain, Australasia and Northern Europe, not to mention the old Soviet bloc.

In the 1980s doubts were still being expressed about the level of community support for women doctors. Since then a sea change has taken place. Women have moved from being 'oddities' within the profession to perhaps its most valued members, the 'human' face of medicine. Doctors have been impelled to embrace a more feminine style, more holistic, and more concerned about communication. Even conservative governments have taken steps to ensure that women are represented in every branch of medicine. In 1991, for example, as part of Opportunity 2000, the British Department of Health established a goal to increase the percentage of women consultants to 20 per cent by 1994 and to accelerate the rate of increase in the surgical specialties to 15 per cent per annum. While these figures have yet to be reached, a few years earlier the project itself would have been inconceivable. Quotas, which had previously been used to *limit* the number of women admitted to medical schools, came to be used for the opposite purpose, to *increase* their representation in what had been male bastions.

Women doctors are in high demand, no longer perceived as anomalous but as 'family' women who understand everyday problems. Surveys have consistently confirmed the shift of public opinion since the 1970s in favour of women doctors (Schlicht & Dunt, 1987). They are thought to combine the good qualities of male physicians and female nurses – assertiveness and initiative combined with tenderness and nurturing (Waller, 1988). When I was first researching women doctors the topic that came up repeatedly on the computer was Pap smears. It was clear that many women experience Pap smears as a form of invasion verging on rape; they preferred to go to a woman doctor at the very least for this purpose. The most publicised contribution of women doctors to women's health undoubtedly *is* in relation to breast and cervical cancer. Certainly the government likes to measure women's health by the growing numbers of Pap smears and mammograms which, it argues, have improved rates of both cure and quality of life.

Members of the medical establishment now publicly welcome women doctors, seeing in them their best hope of reclaiming some of medicine's lost public esteem. Policy makers talk about the 'right' to see a woman doctor. 'Right' functions as a kind of code word for a safe place to seek help with a range of issues from menopause and gynaecological problems to domestic violence and sexual abuse, suburban neurosis, minor tranquilliser addiction, misery, desperation, poverty and despair – all of which are believed to be a result of living with gender inequality. Given that the medical component of many of these is quite small, it begs the question of why the appropriate first port of call should be a doctor. But whether we like it or not, women doctors *are* typically the first port of call for a great many women scarred by emotional, physical and sexual violence.

Even lip-service support for women doctors would have been significant but more than that has been forthcoming. Health ministers and deans of medicine also speak not only of equal opportunities for women but of the community's *right* to have access to women doctors and express a vision of medicine in which women take an equal place. Dame Rosemary Rue, an ex-president of the British Medical Association (BMA) argued in an editorial in the *British Journal of Hospital Medicine* (1992: 287–9) that a mixed profession was desirable at every level of education and training and in the practice of all branches and disciplines of medicine. Professor John Chalmers, President of the Royal Australian College of Physicians (RACP) and Dean of Flinders Medical School, told a graduation ceremony (1992: 726–7) that '. . . it is vitally important for the future of Medicine that it find ways to attract the brightest and best young women available into every avenue of professional medical practice . . .' He called on male colleagues, friends, partners and husbands to give their full support.

For Chalmers, women's entry is important because they are 'so well endowed with the characteristics of caring, of altruism and selflessness which our profession so particularly needs . . . Many of the difficulties facing the medical profession as a whole arise from perceptions that doctors have become too self interested, self centred and selfish.' Whether or not women do actually display the characteristics that Chalmers outlined (and there are studies which suggest the differences have been hugely overstated – see Miles, 1991: 145) their success in medicine demands that they situate themselves in this way. It offers many short-term advantages in competing with their male colleagues, especially when the public is demanding doctors with better communication skills. But it may also restrict them, as surely as the injunction to be 'ladylike' restricted earlier generations. Chalmers went on to speak of the 'biological realities' of child bearing and motherhood, which impose a different structure on a woman's career, as well as the 'social obstacles arising from the social structure as a whole and not merely professional problems'. He did not foreshadow any reorganisation of medicine beyond an extension of part-time work specifically for women with children. Modernity in this version implies the continued existence of distinct full-time and part-time patterns.

Medical time

Medical resistance to women doctors now centres on the issue of part-time work. It is argued that part-time work interferes with continuity of care and inevitably reduces its quality. Women's demands for a restructuring of medical time strike at the heart of the medical sublime. Doctors like to think that what differentiates medicine from other occupations and gives it a priestly dimension is its 24-hour on-call responsibilities. The profession suspects that those who do less cannot be real doctors or are not being serious about their careers. Not only do women challenge this but they do so in the name of a modernising force, seeking to sweep away the irrational, traditional and outdated work structures and teaching methods. It will no longer be good enough to learn simply by hanging around and 'doing the work'.

Medical time is a complex mixture of industrial and pre-industrial time, of clock time and body time. The rhythms of biological time are not necessarily consistent with the order of clock time. The ability to follow the 'course' of a disease through time, and to vary clinical procedures as it changes, is essential. Medical interventions become internalised by the organism as part of its own internal rhythms. Medical skill is acquired in the process of watching a disease progress, literally minute by minute, acquiring the judgment that enables the doctor to know instinctively when and how to intervene. 'Timely' interventions must intersect appropriately with body time, and will always be subject to a degree of uncertainty. But waiting is built into the structure of our society as an expression of power. The powerless wait on the powerful. Waiting is therefore the task of the more junior staff, the residents and registrars who must keep the consultant informed.

Scientific medicine aims to predict more accurately the course of disease and to shift from watching and waiting to active intervention and the imposition of linear or clock time. It is not uncommon for hospital doctors to log up more than 100 hours per week. It is a standing joke that 'half time' in medicine means 40 hours per week, that is, more than the average full-time working week. These long hours, Frankenberg suggests, can be seen as a 'symbolic initiation into their opposite, the sacred, inviolable time of the qualified physician' (1992: 1). He has pointed to the different relations to time that doctors have at different phases of their careers. They have the longest period of training of any professional and during that training they work longer and more irregular hours than any of their fellow students. They have the shortest vacations and during postgraduate training their time is literally not their own. Senior doctors can work fewer hours but they gain cultural capital by choosing to forgo private time. They may appear at the patient's bedside at any hour of the day or night. Such a choice is not available to nurses who, despite their caring functions, come to work at fixed times and go off duty at the end of their shift, whatever crisis might be in train. Where for the hospital patient the disruption of the boundaries of private and public space and time marks a loss of status, for the doctor it is 'a symbol of almost sacred power and powers' (Frankenberg, 1992: 5). Medical time comes to be valued as a precious commodity, the most valued cultural capital that doctors have.

At first glance the time spent on housework and child care looks as if it has much in common with medical time. As caring work it requires long hours and permanent on-call which is encapsulated in the phrase 'women's work is never done'. In this case there is nothing to mediate between the incompatibility of such work with a work time that can be measured, exchanged for money, accumulated for 'time out' or delimited against leisure time. Women's time is not regarded as sacred and they do not typically have a choice about forgoing private time. Ann Forman comments that 'to be female is to have an uneasy relationship to time' and asks if it is fair to say that for women 'time is an enemy, albeit domesticated and familiar?' (Forman, 1989: 1). Women have often been associated with a traditional order that is outside clock time and associated with the rhythms of the seasons and of the body. In particular, the experience of giving birth is claimed to be 'outside' of time, and much of the hostility to obstetricians is linked with their attempts to impose linear time, to monitor pregnancy and determine the moment of birth either through induction or Caesarean, in ways that reduce it from an 'archetypal and eternally recurring act to a mechanical and time bound process' (Fox, 1989: 126).

As Barbara Adam has pointed out, body time, as in the 'outside time' sensation of childbirth, is as much a discursive construction as linear time (1994/95: 99–100). Pre-industrial rhythms were not superseded by industrial ones but continue to permeate our present. And housework, though it appears flexible, is heavily structured by the demands of the clock (Vanek, 1977). All of us experience time in a subjective as well as a clock sense and are well aware of the ways in which it can speed up or slow down in relation to emotional intensities. Particularly important here are patients' subjective experiences of time. Not only are their normal lives disrupted by illness but, if they are very ill or dying, time may come to have starkly different meanings for them, which doctors have to heed.

Women doctors are not just mediating between women's and doctors' time but performing an extraordinarily complex juggling act of many kinds of time both at home and at work. One writer has suggested that their success depends entirely on their skills of time management (Hantrais, 1993: 145). They have first to confront the assumption, from families, patients and colleagues, that as women they have 'more' time or that their time is less valuable. Women are said to listen more and to spend more time with patients (Waller, 1988). They tend to work harder and longer than the men and take off extraordinarily little time for the birth of their children (Hantrais, 1993: 148). They also have to work out ways of running their households efficiently while fighting off assumptions that they are less well fitted to the rigours of medical time. Time for them is actually a scarce commodity. A consultant psychiatrist described how she timetables her day so that she can go home to the children at 3 p.m.:

> I make all my own appointments which involves a little extra work but gives me control over my time. I don't let my secretary see my diary at all. You just have to be very efficient really. You have to be a good manager. There is no point in leaving at 3 if there is stuff that needs to be done. I just have to make sure I have done everything. I have to concentrate very hard when I'm at work and think about it when I'm at home.

Within the workplace, time may open up ambiguous possibilities. An Australian GP pointed to the 'subtle inheritance' of the idea that women's time is not as highly valued, but suggested that it could also free women to offer a different kind of service. While general practice in England is tightly structured around the five to seven-minute consultation, in Australia, 'if you are not out to make a heap of money, you can practise any way you want'. She suggested that the men must 'flip out at the number of women being willing to practise that way'. While it placed women in a 'double bind' it constituted a significant challenge at the level of primary health care.

Where men tend to pursue linear career paths, women's career paths are more likely to be cyclical as they adapt to changing family situations. They juggle time not only on a daily basis but in terms of their life's career plans, developing strategies about when to marry, when and how to have children, how to take care of their babies, and how to manage their household responsibilities as well as their jobs. Men value the 'traditional' work schedules as part of a process of building up cultural capital. Women are less concerned about cultural capital and just want to get the job done as quickly and efficiently as possible. Hence there is a fear that, should the profession become female dominated, medical time will be less valued and medical work demystified. It is women doctors who threaten to impose the rationality of clock time on medical mystiques about time. They are no longer satisfied with a few part-time opportunities, for which Medical Women's Federations campaigned for decades, but a much more fundamental restructuring of working hours. Medical establishments were happy to accept a few part-timers on the margins of general practice, family planning and public health, but fear that any fuller incorporation of part-time work undermines both the quality of medicine and its status.

England and Australia

The material for this book was collected in two countries, England and Australia, which often find themselves locked into a binary relationship. This is a tale of two islands, at opposite ends of the world, and as far away from each other as it is possible to get, which function as each other's cultural 'other', the mirror of possibility, a projection of envy or fear. To the English, Australia represents the working class that escaped into vulgar hedonism, forgot its place and now expresses itself in crass republicanism. But it is also the land of sunshine and opportunities, a more open and relaxed lifestyle. To Australians, England is the land of oppressive class relations, of snobbery and restriction, but it is still the parent, there to be alternately shocked or impressed. In discourses about cultural difference England and Australia are set up as 'opposites' yet the opposition is based on taken for granted family resemblances.

Drawing a sample from two countries makes the task of writing much more difficult and sets up an expectation that comparisons and contrasts will continually be drawn. However, taking two countries makes it possible to reflect on the global as well as the local dimensions of medical cultures. Despite regional differences between the two countries, it is the similarities that stand out. A large number of British-trained doctors have emigrated to Australia looking for more lucrative futures and, until the 1970s, it was usual for aspiring Australian specialists to spend time training in the UK and even to take their exams there. The Australian medical journals report the workings of the British National Health Service in some detail. Britain and Australia are the closest of all countries in their doctor/patient ratios and in their proportions of women doctors, despite their different public health systems. In this way they provide a different kind of comparison from the more hackneyed generalisations about the United States and the Soviet Union. Their health systems have evolved from broadly the same conditions of possibility, with similar economies, class structures and shared history and culture. Australia has retained the system of colleges with the physicians and surgeons setting up chapters in the inter-war period and becoming independent in the 1950s. The Australian Medical Association (AMA) remained a part of the BMA until 1961.

There is therefore some justification for treating them as part of a continuous medical field. While each has a particularity it is also obvious that each has evolved in very similar ways. A national health system was a priority for social democratic parties in both countries, while conservative parties along with the British and, later, Australian Medical Associations favoured a subsidised private system based on fee for service. For British readers, Australia represents a path that their own health system could have taken and may yet take. Even before the Thatcher years private medicine and private health insurance had made substantial inroads in Britain. By 1990, 10 per cent of the population were insured for private treatment, a shift which helps to legitimate the running down of the public system (Mohan, 1991: 42–3). Hospitals are now able to secede from the NHS and become self-governing trusts, which can set their own wage rates, borrow money, acquire and dispose of assets and generate surpluses. A strong element of competition has been added within the public system which raises questions about whether quality will be maintained. Australia, on the other hand, saw an expansion of its national health system with the move to universal health insurance under the Whitlam and Hawke Labor governments, the increased use of bulk-billing by GPs (which means that a high proportion of the population can avoid up-front payments for consultations), the establishment of community health centres, and initiatives like the 1994 Better Practice Program.

Each country therefore represents a set of possibilities that may just as easily have taken place in the other; each is a different resolution of very similar political debates, subject to ongoing political struggles; and, given that both parties have had periods in power in both countries, there has been ample opportunity for a kind of tinkering that ensures that they have run on parallel but connected paths. A comparison of the UK with Australia provides an opportunity to study some of the contexts in which these tensions are negotiated and opens up a different range of insights from the ones drawn from the persistent comparison with the United States. While the question of public or private health systems is of fundamental importance to the consumer, it appears to be of only marginal relevance to the question of how and why men and women doctors are distributed through the system in the proportions that they are.

Until after World War Two England and Australia had broadly similar health systems. As in North America the bulk of health care was carried out by general practitioners who were essentially small businessmen. They were paid directly by the client or by unions or friendly societies. For an annual fee to the friendly society people could insure themselves and their families for medical expenses. Friendly societies in turn paid the doctors a per capita rate to treat the people on their books. Because they had large numbers of subscriptions the friendly societies were able to negotiate favourable deals for their clients and were often greatly disliked by doctors.

Hospitals remained a relatively small part of national health expenditure. People went into hospital for surgery but wherever possible the sick were nursed at home: hospitals were not thought to be of much assistance. Specialists held honorary positions at the large teaching hospitals and treated the poor for nothing (on condition that they could use them for teaching purposes) and on condition that they were also allowed to admit private fee-paying patients. Australia has a long tradition of state financial support for private hospitals but Queensland was unique in having a free public hospital system from 1912. Most consultants were general surgeons or general physicians. Further specialisation was rare before World War Two and a good deal of obstetrics, anaesthesia and minor surgery was taken care of by GPs. Hospitals were a ramshackle collection, owned largely by churches and charity organisations. Hart notes that when in 1948 the British Government took over the hospitals it found that three-quarters of them had been built before 1914 and a third were former workhouses, while only 8 per cent of doctors were hospital-based specialists (1988: 80–2).

The 1950s saw a huge expansion of the hospital sectors and a proliferation of specialties and sub-specialties. In the UK, the introduction of the NHS increased the power of all consultants. It transformed them from a scattered body with primarily local interests into a single group, regionally organised with a national income structure and considerable influence on national hospital policy which they used to subjugate their rivals, those GPs who had previously carried out much specialist work (Pfeffer, 1993: 138). UK specialists were for the most part happy to give up their honorary status and restrict their private practice in return for high salaries, and a considerable degree of professional autonomy and control. More recently, under the terms of the *Health Services Act* of 1989, their contracts have been altered to enable them to undertake significantly more private practice without forfeiting their privileges in the NHS (Pfeffer, 1993: 167).

In Australia a constitutional amendment gave the Chifley Labor Government wide powers to deal with hospital and medical services and it did briefly establish free public hospital treatment and a free pharmaceutical benefits scheme. However, a series of High Court challenges prevented it from bringing in a national health service. Instead, the Menzies Liberal Government, after it came to power in 1949, poured money into the hospital system, set up free health care for pensioners and subsidised voluntary health insurance by meeting part of the cost of the rebates for medical expenses. The Australian system was in this way more heavily subsidised by the state than was ever the case in the US. In 1975 the Whitlam Labor Government set up a national insurance scheme, along similar lines to the Canadian one and, despite tinkering by subsequent governments, this basic structure remains in place. Like the British, Australians have access to basic hospital and medical care at no additional up-front cost (though since 1997 high income earners have been forced to take out private insurance or pay an additional levy). Through Medicare, the government pays a rebate on the scheduled fees charged by doctors in private practice, and it also subsidises private nursing homes and pharmaceuticals provided by the private sector (Palmer & Short, 1989: 17).

Most consultants combine private practice with sessional work in public hospitals. In return for treating public patients, they have the right to admit private patients to the public hospitals to which they are attached. Since sessional payments replaced the honorary system in the mid-1970s they have come to constitute a major source of income for some doctors, often women with at most limited private practices. There are also increasing numbers of salaried doctors working in hospitals and community health centres. The latter, as well as women's health centres, are based on a perceived need to foster health promotion strategies and to experiment with multi-disciplinary teams.

The biggest differences between the two countries are probably in the area of obstetrics. England has relied heavily on midwives and obstetric nurses while Australian women are more likely to be attended by obstetricians even for routine deliveries. This is made possible because a large proportion of the population takes out additional private health cover, mostly in relation to hospital insurance which gives them the right to be treated as a private patient and some degree of choice in selecting their doctor.

In both countries general practitioners remain the first port of call and it is they who control access to specialists. Despite endemic debate about their future, GPs have played an important gatekeeper role in curbing health costs and providing high quality primary care to the whole population. A similar feature in both countries is that GPs, usually now in groups, operate as private businesses. In Britain their main source of income is capitation payments derived now from the government instead of the old friendly societies. Everyone is registered with one practice and the practice receives a payment on the basis of the number of patients registered.

Australian GPs, on the other hand, derive most of their incomes from fee-for-service. Australians are more likely to shop around for doctors and second opinions. This places pressures, especially on GPs, to be responsive to customer demand. It may lead to over-servicing, and governments have not been slow to blame GPs for the health budget 'blow-out', but it ensures a more thorough diagnosis and treatment than the busy British GP is usually able to offer. The extension of the direct billing option under Medicare has given the government greater in-fluence over the fees charged by doctors and places a strong competitive pressure on those who do not bill directly. The centralising of the processing of medical claims has made the administration of health insurance more efficient and has also generated a comprehensive set of profiles of the practice patterns of doctors, which has considerable potential for detecting fraud and over-servicing (Palmer & Short, 1989: 65). Ironically, because they do more Pap smears, women doctors have found themselves being watched very closely for an over-use of pathology services. Until Helena Britt's recent work (Britt et al., 1996) the govern-ment was unable or unwilling to recognise the distinctive profiles of women practitioners.

The current study

This study is based on semi-structured life history interviews with 150 women doctors (fifty in England and one hundred in Australia) ranging in age from twenty-four to ninety-two. The Australian sample was gath-ered in Sydney, Melbourne, Adelaide, Brisbane, Newcastle, Wollongong and Wagga Wagga in rural New South Wales. The British sample was drawn from London, Manchester, Birmingham, Bristol, Cambridge and Hastings. The interviews lasted between forty-five minutes and about two hours and were transcribed and taped. Where possible, transcripts were returned to the participants for further written comment.

While I did interview a few friends and acquaintances the majority of contacts were made more formally via a 'snowballing' process. Starting from an initially small group in each country, I was 'passed on' through various networks until I had filled the categories I was seeking. I wanted to construct a sample drawn from a wide range of specialties as well as general practice, to talk to women in large and in solo practices, in academic and public policy positions as well as clinicians, and to include a range of ages, ethnicities and social backgrounds. In England I went to the BMA and was given a list of women from various fields and various parts of the country who had been active committee members. The Medical Women's Associations in both countries facilitated access to their members. In Australia I briefly employed two women doctors who drew on their own networks to help locate suitable subjects. Further assistance was gained from the colleges. Explicitly feminist doctors were found through the Women in Medicine group in England and women's health centres in Australia.

For comparative purposes I interviewed thirty male doctors drawn from across the range and followed a similar schedule to that used with the women. I did not wish to attribute to the women perceptions or problems that are shared by both sexes. I spent time observing doctors in action in hospital wards, operating theatres and GPs' surgeries. I visited women's health centres in several states of Australia and conducted interviews and focus groups with a full range of workers as well as female health service managers. In addition I conducted focus groups with nurses specifically on the subject of their relation with women doctors.

People interviewed for this book were assured both confidentiality and anonymity. While the first has been scrupulously maintained, the second is more difficult, since in many specialties the number of women is tiny and they are easily identifiable to colleagues. Changing minor details, or using initials and *noms de plume* does not by itself solve the problem but I have done all in my power to honour the promise. Care was taken to identify the areas which participants regarded as sensitive and, where possible, transcripts or drafts have been returned to individuals for comment. It is my hope that many women will identify with the figures in the text, and that these figures represent more than individual experience (see Table 1.1 opposite).

It is not a random sample of women in medicine for, as Bourdieu suggests, 'if you take a random sample, you mutilate the very object you have set out to construct' (Wacquant, 1988: 38). To establish the contours of the field it was important to speak to people in positions of authority and to seek out women in each of the surgical and physician specialties. In some of these, their numbers are so small that sampling was never an issue. While thirty of my subjects defined themselves

Table 1.1 Sample of women doctors interviewed

	Australia	Britain	Total
Obstetricians and gynaecologists*	9	4	13
Surgeons*	13	8	21
Physicians (including dermatology, radiology and pathology)*	22	11	33
Anaesthetists*	10	4	14
Psychiatrists*	6	6	12
GPs	17	10	27
Women's and community health	10	2	12
Academic medicine/public health	5	5	10
Medical administration	2	–	2
Interns and residents	6	–	6
Total	100	50	150

* Specialist groups include registrars and senior registrars

predominantly in relation to general practice, the sample is biased towards consultants. The remainder were registrars, residents or worked in public or community health areas or in academia. Ten of the women had retired while the rest were currently in the workforce or on maternity leave.

Participants were asked to describe their childhood and social backgrounds, their initial decision to study medicine, their experiences of medical education and the crucial decisions about hospital postings, postgraduate training and job applications. They described their trajectories through a myriad of mix and match training positions, who had influenced them, both positively and negatively, and who had acted as mentors. I asked them what in their work they felt passionately about and what they found tiresome. I wanted to know how they had succeeded and what compromises they felt they had made, what alternatives had been considered and rejected. I explored with them the extent of their social networks, their interests outside medicine and their level of participation in medical politics. They were asked to talk about what feminism meant to them and about their religious and political beliefs. While they were asked to describe their most likely scenario for the future of women in medicine they were not asked for their views as 'women' doctors. Many were keen to deny that they were in any way different from the men although their subsequent remarks often contradicted this. I took the view that if there was anything distinctive about their approach it should be allowed to emerge in the general way they talked.

Whether they were telling 'the truth' about their lives is of less relevance than the discursive frameworks on which they drew and the ways in which they chose to represent themselves. In some ways the surfaces are more interesting than the 'inner' self since this is where they interface with the rest of the world. The personas they presented to me were probably not dissimilar from those they used in other contexts. I appeared as someone of equivalent professional status to themselves but from an entirely different background. I stressed that I was researching 'work' rather than 'health', in this way distancing myself from the branches of sociology with which they were most familiar. Most had thought about what they would say and frequently challenged me about the relevance of my questions. It was particularly difficult to get them to describe their practice rather than provide me with opinions on the range of topics they expected me to cover. Yet that is the element that most clearly differentiates my data from that produced in other studies.

On a number of occasions I was in a position to check the 'authenticity' of their stories and to realise that they were misrepresenting themselves to some extent. But it would be surprising if they did not also do this in other contexts. Undoubtedly I missed the arrogant and intimidating sides, the displays of temper that nurses often complain about. Just occasionally, there were hints of it, when my line of questioning did not correspond with their expectations, or appeared to be off track.

Some, realising that this was a one-off encounter that would remain entirely confidential, chose to treat the interview as a free therapy session and poured their hearts out, often telling me things that they said they had never told anybody else. I will not forget the psychiatrist who expressed surprise that I did not 'throw her out' after fifty minutes. Or the harassed GP with an overflowing waiting room who went well beyond the allotted hour because she felt a need to sit with her unresolved feelings about her father, who had died suddenly when she was still very young. Or the lesbian who described what it was like to maintain silence about her lover at the two places that really mattered to her, the hospital and her church. Having once before been rejected as a church elder, she now felt that keeping silence about her sexuality was the lesser pain. When I asked her why she was spontaneously telling me about this she laughed and said, 'you are a sociologist aren't you!'

Frameworks

Reference has already been made to 'agents', 'strategies', 'discourses' and 'fields', indicating my debt to Foucault (1977, 1980) and Bourdieu (1989, 1990, 1993a, b) for the broad contours of this study. Both provide a dynamic sense of the ebbs and flows of power, of struggles, victories and reversals, of contested knowledges and shifting subjectivities which contrast with the static world of the surveys, with their emphasis on 'patterns' and the 'factors' that produce them. Ultimately what matters are the processes that produce the differential distribution of men and women across different specialties and different parts of the medical hierarchy. Foucault suggests that we need an ascending analysis of power that starts with its smallest mechanisms and explores how they have been 'invested, colonised, utilised, involuted, transformed, displaced and extended by ever more general mechanisms' (1980: 99). In relation to medicine this provides some encouragement for giving attention to the apparently trivial, the strategies and resistances of the apparently powerless rather than the pyramidal structures imposed by the dominant. It will be at the capillary level that shifts will take place that may eventually challenge or transform these structures.

I have been less directly concerned with Foucault's work on the history of medicine than with his account of the ways in which discourse constitutes social subjects. 'Doctors' come into being as subjects through the discursive practices that structure teaching and learning, their interactions with patients, with doctors and other health workers, and with all whose acknowledgment confers on them the position of 'doctor'. The meanings of 'doctor' are created not just in medical discourse but in the wider culture. By the late nineteenth century novelists were treating doctors as princely figures in whose hands lay the progress and well-being of humanity (Rothfield, 1992). These meanings range from the saviours of humanity in late nineteenth century novels (Dr Lydgate in *Middle-march*) to the romps of *Doctor in the House* and the handsome perfection of Dr Kildare. Contemporary soap operas like *Chicago Hope* and *ER* show doctors as opportunistic, competitive and power-hungry, as making mistakes and yelling at each other. It is a flawed but still largely a masculine culture.

Women doctors appear occasionally but it is difficult to tell them apart from the nurses unless they are very clearly attired in the regulation white coat and stethoscope. In series like *E Street, General Practice, Heartbeat* and *Surgical Spirit* women doctors have been central figures, but they are presented as 'ordinary' women who have the same dilemmas and relationship problems as anybody else. Medical discourse has been obliged either to degender the meanings of 'doctor' *or* to define certain areas of practice as 'appropriate'. For women doctors, therefore, much is at stake in the discursive practices that constitute doctors.

As doctors are well aware, they are not merely the effects of discursive formations but flesh and blood people who make day-to-day decisions about how to live their lives. Their actions, based on the constraints of their own subjectivities and the knowledge of structures that they are able to produce, are in turn constitutive of ongoing structures. Though he does not apply his insights specifically to medicine, Bourdieu offers a helpful balance between seeing individuals as merely bearers of structures or of overemphasising their capacity to act outside them. For him the agents (collective or individual) of social interaction do not simply follow rules but are strategists who have the potential either to reproduce existing structures or to bring about shifts. As a sociologist he too is engaged in strategies that involve exposing strategies of domination and altering the ways in which we see the world. In his account structures do not exist separately from the knowledge we create of them and that knowledge is fluid, shifting and manipulable.

In place of the closed systems that characterise many other sociologies, Bourdieu talks about a range of 'fields' in which social relations are conducted. These are market-like structures which constitute players with the capacities and the motivation to play the game. The stakes are the accumulation and deployment of the various forms of economic, cultural, social and symbolic capitals that are constituted by the field. Capital is used here virtually interchangeably with wealth and power as the capacity to exercise control over one's own future and that of others. The strategies open to any individual will depend on their *habitus*.

Bourdieu has described the habitus as a set of dispositions, a 'feel for the game', or a 'second sense' which is treated by the initiate as a matter of natural talent, of personality, of the 'virtuality' of practitioners though it actually derives from a person's particular family and educational background (R. Johnson, 1993). For Bourdieu, the habitus is embodied capital, the 'past which survives into the present', the basic beliefs, values, norms and ways of being in the world which are taken into the body at a very deep level, and will reproduce class domination as apparently natural and effortless. It is the conceptual bridge between capital and field, the mechanism that 'propels' agents to take up particular strategies. While sheer technical brilliance has allowed some women and members of subordinate classes to build spectacular careers in medicine, perhaps more frequently the appropriate class background and bodily presence have been permitted to make up for intellectual limitations. Those who start off well-endowed 'have only to let their habitus follow its natural bent in order to comply with the immanent necessity of the field and satisfy the demands contained within it' (1993a: 75–6). Those who do not can only bring about change if they are prepared to act against the grain and to identify the relations of domination. Where the first group generally opts for conservatism and the status quo, the latter might attempt partial revolutions in order to strengthen their hold on the various forms of capital.

'Habitus' is a central concept for this study for it directs attention to the ways in which inequalities are inscribed on the body and lived through the body. While Bourdieu largely ignores sexual difference, it may be argued that the possession of a male body was, for a long time, taken for granted as part of the medical habitus. Miles describes the legacy of this in the following terms:

> That women in medical schools are no longer a minority makes it the more interesting to observe that they often behave as though they are. Like female students in engineering and other numerically male-dominated university courses, they feel a greater sense of insecurity than do the men students; they feel that they must try harder to show that they are equal to the demands made upon students, demonstrate a greater commitment to the cultural norms of the institution and, above all, obtain higher results in order to gain status similar to the men. (Miles, 1991: 134)

The reasons, she suggests, can be located in the sex stereotyping of doctors and nurses, which is absorbed in childhood, and reinforced in adolescence and adulthood through soap operas, parents and teachers. In all kinds of ways women students are given to understand that they are not expected to rise high in their chosen career. Many respond by feeling that they have to work harder than the men if they want to be taken seriously, a pattern that they carry forward into their future professional lives. They may pay for this with health problems, feelings of isolation and loneliness and greater difficulty making new friends (1991: 138).

Lacking the habitus, women have rarely been at ease in the medical field. But they have also been pushed to act in ways that often go against the grain of their conservative inclinations. This book, therefore, is not (only) about women as victims, or as the proletariat of medicine, but about what has propelled them to push for change and to launch the series of 'partial revolutions' which are beginning to transform the practice of medicine.

2

Women Take the Field

People are at once founded and legitimized to enter the
field by their possessing a definite configuration of
properties . . . forms of *specific capital.*

(Bourdieu, 1989: 7)

Medicine has a long history but it became a profession in the modern
sense only in the mid-nineteenth century and the generic term 'doctor'
was not widely used until the end of the century. Women's struggles to
enter the medical profession may therefore be linked with the formation
of the field in all its complexity. This chapter traces both their movement
on to the periphery of the medical field and their attempts to occupy
some of its more central points. The field itself should be understood as
rugged and uneven, with hills and gullies, dangerous booby traps and
tracks leading nowhere, as well as bunkers, lookout points and safe
passages. Its external boundaries have expanded enormously as it
claimed territory from traditional healers and from the Church, while
it has also become more internally differentiated. Power circulates
throughout this field, in some places thinly and in others in thick
coagulations which are represented by the teaching hospitals, the
colleges, the academic departments and representative bodies such as
the BMA and AMA.

The outfield: 1858–1948

In Britain the *Medical Act* of 1858 established the first clear boundaries to
the field of medicine and spelt out what its entry qualifications would be.
The Act required that a national medical register be set up listing all

those who were regarded as qualified to practise medicine. This brought together three groups that had previously been quite separate. There were several hundred gentlemanly physicians and wealthy surgeons who had been to Oxford or Cambridge and were members either of the Royal College of Physicians or the Royal College of Surgeons. They dominated the London teaching hospitals and served the needs of the upper class. Alongside them were several thousand provincial surgeons, apothecaries and surgeon–apothecaries who were to become the first general practitioners. While they had gained their training largely through apprenticeship, new entrants would in future be required to hold a university degree before being admitted to the register and entitled to practise. The Act was automatically extended to the Australian colonies which passed their own legislation shortly afterwards.

Women were not formally excluded from the register but, since they were not admitted to any university medical schools, they may as well have been. The field of professional medicine was defined as masculine territory. While this is often portrayed as an attack on women healers, such a position rests on somewhat romantic notions about the place of women in medicine *before* 1858 (Ehrenreich & English, 1972; Blake, 1990). While women were not prohibited from practising (no one was) they did not have any significant presence in commercial medicine (Walsh, 1979: 448). Women's healing activities were largely undertaken in the domestic and community areas and were already being reduced in significance. As the market for medical services grew, fuelled by the expansion of the middle classes and the growth of their incomes, even midwives began to be displaced. The image of the midwife as the dirty, drunken 'Sarah Gamp' circulated widely. Any woman who wanted to study medicine would have had to be apprenticed to a male practitioner, an intimate relationship which would have compromised her sexual reputation. In practical terms, therefore, few had access to training unless it was with family members.

Women who wanted to practise medicine were treated as oddities. Anxieties were aroused when in 1865 one James Barry, who had gradu-ated from Edinburgh in the early part of the century, joined the military and risen to the rank of hospital superintendent was discovered after death to have been a woman. Blake records that she had a reputation as a lady-killer and also notes that the scandal surrounding her death meant that her considerable achievements in preventative medicine were ignored. Not even the feminist Sophia Jex-Blake was prepared to claim shared sisterhood here (Blake, 1990: 89–90). The case prompted the editor of the *Medical Journal of Australia* to write that 'there is little fear that in any British community women [doctors] will exist as a class. They will occasionally be imported like other curiosities, and the public will wonder at them, just as it wonders at dancing dogs, fat boys and bearded ladies . . .' (quoted in Goldberg, 1984: 16–17).

The new licensing laws at least enabled women to prove their competence more clearly. It was easier to overcome known obstacles than to tilt at shadowy spectres. Once entrance requirements were established a woman could attempt to meet them and, if rejected unfairly, raise the cry of injustice (Walsh, 1979: 449). The pioneers specialised in finding loopholes in the new regulations and then challenging the establishment by showing that women fulfilled the laid down requirements. This often meant going off to the Sorbonne or to the Swiss universities which had opened their doors to women in the mid-1860s (Blake, 1990: 73).

Elizabeth Blackwell, the first woman to be placed on the British register, graduated from Geneva Medical College in New York State in 1849. She had managed to enrol there under highly unusual circumstances. The faculty treated her application with such derision that they handed over the decision to the students with the understanding that even one negative vote would be enough to reject her. The students, regarding this as a practical joke, promptly accepted her application (Walsh, 1979: 449). It was a long time before a second woman, Elizabeth Garrett Anderson, was placed on the British register in 1866 and a further eleven years before Sophia Jex-Blake and three others were granted a licence (Blake, 1990: 43). The first Australian woman, Constance Stone, was not admitted to practice until 1890. A century later she was commemorated with a postage stamp but at the time she had been refused entry to the University of Melbourne and been obliged to study abroad at the Women's Medical College in Philadelphia (Williams, 1990).

It was only at the point when women challenged gendered exclusionary practices that their precise mechanisms became clear and it was then possible to identify the institutional arenas within which male power and privilege were most effectively organised and defended. The obstacles included the hostility of male medical students, the persistent refusal to admit women by medical staff on the committees of medical schools, and the examining bodies themselves. Given that most medical schools were closed to women, the earliest strategy for meeting the entry requirements was to establish separate schools. In England, the London School of Medicine for Women which was set up in 1874, and the Royal Free Hospital which from 1876 provided clinical facilities, were to make a remarkable contribution to medical training. By the 1890s the United States had seventeen such schools while a further forty medical schools had a female enrolment of 10 per cent or more (Walsh, 1979: 450). These institutions were important in a number of ways. They enabled women to bypass the quota system. They also addressed the specific difficulties that women faced in getting access to education in physics and chemistry at secondary school level. And they gave women some sense of a critical mass, the opportunity to acquire confidence through mutual support and solidarity.

The first phase, the battle for entry to the field, was inextricably bound up with the rise of feminism and the suffrage movement. The entry of women into the professions was seen as a key aspect of the claim for citizenship and had strong public backing from women's organisations. Many chose medicine because they regarded independent, self-supporting careers as a positive alternative to marriage and not as a necessary fall back in the event they failed to marry. Some married women also embraced the ideology of financial independence and self-reliance. At a time when salaried jobs for married women were almost impossible to obtain, there were great hopes that medicine would offer more flexibility and permit women to combine family and career (Moldow, 1987). In 1911 80 per cent of UK women doctors were unmarried (Blake, 1990: 160). But they should not too readily be stereotyped as spinsters who sacrificed personal lives to careers. Alison Mackinnon (1997) has documented the ways in which this first generation of professional women sought to transcend simplistic choices between love and freedom, creating new subjectivities and reshaping relationships. Many had lifelong friendships with other women which sustained important professional identities, enabled them to maintain households, and met deep emotional and, perhaps, sexual needs.

When Dr Lillian Cooper arrived in Brisbane in 1891, having trained in Edinburgh and London, she brought with her a companion, Mary Bedford. The two women lived together for many decades, with Lillian gradually building up a practice and becoming Honorary Surgeon to the Mater Misericordiae. Both served with distinction in Serbia during World War One when Mary was in charge of an ambulance unit and people came from far and wide to watch Lillian operate, such was her reputation as a surgeon. On no occasion was the sexuality of these two 'companions', or others like them, scrutinised. While care needs to be taken about defining such relationships as 'lesbian' before the discursive category was fully available, a woman like Sophia Jex-Blake could thumb her nose at marriage and have intimate relations with women as well as a circle of intense female friendships (Blake, 1990: 196–8). In later periods single women would find that their sexuality and their relationships were much more closely monitored.

Medical qualifications did not guarantee women anything more than a provisional place in the field. They had difficulty getting appointments to the large teaching hospitals even when they had graduated near the top of their year. Clara Stone and Margaret Whyte, the first women to graduate from Melbourne in 1891, topped the honours lists in medicine and surgery and yet were refused positions at the Royal Melbourne Hospital (Neve, 1980: 30). Constance D'Arcy graduated sixth at Sydney University in 1904 and had to move to Adelaide when she was refused positions at both Sydney and Prince Alfred Hospitals (Neve, 1980: 75). Jessie Aspinall was appointed to Prince Alfred Hospital and then prevented from taking up her position. It was a common story. Some women went to the tiny country hospitals and practices where there was a great shortage of doctors. Ellen Kent Hughes, widowed and with a small child, left Melbourne for Kingaroy in outback Queensland and established a successful practice and a long career in local government. At the age of seventy-seven she sat for the examinations of the Royal Australian College of General Practitioners (RACGP) and gained her fellowship (Williams, 1992: 240–50).

The drive to standardise medical training undoubtedly created difficulties for women. The legendary Canadian physician, William Osler, who probably had more influence on medical training in England and North America than any other physician at the turn of the century, actively prevented women from entering medicine. He was the most influential advocate of the professional model, aiming to bring clinical medicine into association with laboratory science, and instilling in students both a clinical inquisitiveness and a passionate belief in the application of science to the solution of diagnostic puzzles (Hart, 1988: 45–6). It was he who demanded that students totally immerse themselves in the illness on a twenty-four-hour cycle (the term 'resident' was first applied to his students at Johns Hopkins who were expected to stay overnight). Osler also defined the professional ideals of doctors in terms of *aequanimitas* – equanimity – the capacity to remain cool, precise and confident in all situations (Konner, 1993: 22–6). He apparently believed that women were not up to these professional demands and joked with his students in the 1890s that 'humankind might be divided into three categories – men, women and women physicians!' (Moldow, 1987: 16).

In the United States, the separate schools were progressively shut down after the influential Flexner Report of 1910, and stringent quotas restricted women's participation in the coeducational schools. By 1911 there were 495 women doctors in England and Wales. While this was impressive in absolute terms it was still less than 2 per cent, and had failed to keep pace with the growth of the medical profession as a whole (Harrison, 1981: 51–2). While entry to university was less of a problem, graduates had difficulty in getting internships. Opportunities expanded during World War One but most of the places made available at the London medical schools were subsequently withdrawn and in 1921 women were still only 5.4 per cent of the total medical workforce (Day, 1982: 27). They were concentrated in marginal fields – as missionary doctors in India and the colonies, in the thirteen hospitals for women, and in the developing maternal and child welfare services at local level (Elston, 1980). However, medical careers for women became to some degree normalised during the inter-war years and the numbers climbed slowly to be around 15 per cent at the outbreak of World War Two (Day, 1982: 29). Women consultants were few and their work and training opportunities were largely restricted to the women's hospitals.

Where the pioneers had the support and, in many cases, played an active part in the women's movement, the second generation had to fend for themselves. Harrison suggests that the feminist connection was largely lost and that 'far from transforming the ideas and methods of the medical profession, the American and British woman doctor seems to have accommodated herself quickly to the ethics of her male-dominated profession' (1981: 55). Given the level of hostility to women moving into 'masculine' territory, it is not surprising that they emphasised their ladylike qualities, apparently denying any direct challenge to men. But the price was high. Michael Belgrave (1990), writing about New Zealand, has noted that the barriers preventing women from entering medical school were more easily overcome than the subtle obstructions that frustrated them from competing in the medical economy. It became acceptable for women to study medicine as long as they practised within the stereotype of 'lady doctor', which implied that they continued to fulfil roles consistent with late nineteenth century norms of behaviour acceptable for middle-class women. In contrast, 'medical men' were free to set themselves up as aggressive entrepreneurs. The early women doctors, he suggests, lent medicine the virtues of their sex as compassionate healers but by emphasising respectability they created difficulties for those who came later.

State intervention: 1948–75

By the end of World War Two, British women were about 25 per cent of medical students and 15 per cent of civilian doctors. Their student numbers were soon reduced to 20 per cent as ex-servicemen claimed university places. At the same time, the 1944 Goodenough Report, the first national review of medical education, created a precedent in arguing that the number of medical students should be a matter of public policy rather than for individual schools to decide. It insisted that no barriers other than aptitude should operate in the selection of students and that coeducation should become the norm. Accordingly the Royal Free was opened to men (to the trepidation of many women doctors whom it had served well) and the male strongholds of Guy's, St Bartholomew's and Middlesex were finally opened to women. With the end of separatism women had a more established place in the mainstream of medicine but it did not immediately make their lives any easier.

A doctor who had commenced her studies at the Royal Free in 1945 recalled:

> We got a rocket on the medical school and we were dispersed as refugees to various other London schools . . . We were the first women ever to cross the threshold of St Mary's, and it was absolutely appalling. There were about twenty of us and we were plunged into the utmost misery and deprivation. If we ever put our noses into the main medical school we were boo-ed and hissed all the time. They never let up, the whole year we were there . . . It was the students – the staff were incredibly kind.

Secondary school teachers were still advising female students against medicine, as a British psychiatrist recalled:

> Our headmistress told us she thought it was more ladylike for girls to be nurses or teachers. She sent most of our year to teacher training college, not even university, and they were really under-educated as a result. I did Latin, Greek and History knowing I could still apply to medical school. I was also aware that you could make good money in medicine for a woman. It was a career that paid better than most women's jobs that I could see. It wasn't very obvious that being a classics teacher, which is what the school had in mind for me, was anything more than a kind of recycling.

As women came to compete directly with men, the hostility shifted from sex to sexuality. In the earlier period their womanliness was seldom questioned: they were placed as celibate spinsters or their husbands' helpmates. Back in the 1890s a doctor like Frances Dick, who worked in England, Australia and later Germany was described by Dame Mary Gilmore in the following terms: 'When everyone else was dressed in floral or other soft materials, Dr Dick wore tailor-made tweeds, as like a man's, without aping man, as possible' (Neve, 1980: 145).

By the 1950s this kind of presentation was given sexual connotations, as indicative of a woman who had trouble with her gender identity. My subjects frequently recalled such women, especially consultants, in tones of awe or revulsion. When I sought out the women to interview, they rarely struck me as particularly masculine. The mystique had been built on the basis of their having chosen a career ahead of marriage and children and the fact that they might not trouble themselves with creating a 'feminine' appearance. Gail Young, looking back on her training in the 1960s, reflected that 'a woman doctor, whatever her job, is essentially in our culture an honorary man, simply by virtue of society's concept of what a doctor is, and she will therefore have a lot of difficulty in integrating her self concept as a woman with her doctoring' (Young, 1981: 19).

Women in medicine were frequently perceived and judged as 'masculine' and/or 'sexless'. A 1962 graduate recalled: 'There were two sorts of girls, the rather plain ones who did not get married in those days and became whatever they wanted to be, consultant physicians and things like that; and the ones who obviously wanted to get married and who usually went into general practice'. A number of women, including the speaker, did both, but the stereotype may well have deterred some women from pursuing the most desirable specialties for fear of being defined as plain or masculine. Men, by contrast, were never divided into the handsome and the ugly, and certainly it would be difficult to guess much about their marital status on this basis. They were, however, divided into bright and dumb, with the 'dumb' ones destined for general practice. In an interesting turn, women GPs were thought to be brighter than the men since they had chosen it for different reasons, and this may ultimately have contributed to their popularity.

Women who fitted the male social definition of female attractiveness were 'suspect' in the sense that their appearance was interpreted either as 'just a front' or, if not a front, taken as evidence that they were not very bright or not serious about medicine. Ulyatt and Ulyatt claimed, on the basis of their 1973 survey, that it was possible to predict from the attitudes of women medical students which ones would give their all to medicine and which would try to combine medicine and family. The authors actually suggested that 'special interrogation should be devised to detect those applicants who are likely to prefer to care for their own children rather than employ a nanny' (Shaw, 1979: 282).

Women faced anxieties about their sexual attractiveness and marital prospects that were largely unknown to the men. As an anaesthetist put it:

> The minute a sixth year male medical student puts Dr in front of his name he becomes hot property. They have a wonderful intern year. Women are faced with the reality of their career choices. You look around and you think, I can choose from about 0.5 per cent of the population for a mate. That is really soul destroying and you see examples of women who have compromised on both fronts and that does not make them happy either. I suddenly thought, this isn't going to be easy.

The majority of women doctors did marry. As Rosemary Rue has observed, 'they have always followed the social trends and always had the average number of children. At a time when there were more spinsters in society, there were spinster doctors. During my career, nearly all of the women doctors I know have actually been married.' But there was hostility towards women who tried to 'have it both ways', as a 1950s graduate recalls:

> I went and did a year as a trainee in general practice and then I started applying for jobs and I found nobody wanted a married woman with two small children, so while I was looking I got a job in what was called Public Health doing Infant Welfare and Maternity Clinics. I had an obstetrics diploma so I

got that quite easily, and it was quite well paid and more or less office hours, so it seemed sensible to stay in that sort of job and bring home money. I also did a lot of evening locums in general practice. But neither the men nor the women wanted me as a full-time. That generation of women had given up everything to become doctors and thought what was this woman with two children expecting?

In the 1950s no one imagined that large numbers of married women would want to work full-time or that women would take anything other than a minority role in medicine. The BMA remained hostile to women but restricted its attack to the wastage of medical training to marriage and motherhood, letting go of the arguments about modesty and delicacy that had preoccupied it in pre-war days. In the London schools, the pre-war average of 15 per cent women was regarded as a reasonable maximum quota. But the provincial schools began to take in a larger proportion and the national average climbed steadily to around 25 per cent by the 1960s (Elston, 1980: 106–7). In Australia (where quotas did not apply) applications from women grew at a similar rate. This was in contrast to the United States where significant increases had to wait for sex discrimination legislation (Walsh, 1979: 450–4).

Since the 1960s women have steadily increased their presence in general practice and could well come to dominate it. Hospital appointments have been a tougher nut to crack. As the earlier generation who had trained in the separate women's hospitals retired, the proportion of women specialists actually dropped. In Britain, surgery, medicine, obstetrics and gynaecology and anaesthetics all had fewer women in 1985 than in 1963 (*Lancet*, 30 May, 1987). Dame Rosemary Rue recalled:

> We had got down to only eleven consultant general surgeons in England who were women. I knew them all and I knew they were all getting on a bit. Where were the role models going to be compared even with my youth? They had really fallen out of surgery . . . and obstetrics was virtually closed down to women. It was one of the specialties that almost became lost to women completely.

It was in this period that the pattern of women's involvement in the specialties was laid down. In order to understand these patterns something needs to be said about the ways in which the medical field has structured itself since the 1950s.

Mapping the contours

In Australia and the UK medicine has retained its tripartite division between general practice, surgery and internal medicine, each of which has a college to coordinate its interests and to manage its training programs. Surgery and 'physick' are both divided into a number of specialties which, in turn, have their own sub-specialties. This has spawned a large number of organisations, some of which operate under the umbrella of the original colleges, while others have become colleges in their own right. There are separate colleges, for example, for paediatrics, psychiatry, anaesthesia, pathology, radiology and dermatology. Obstetrics and gynaecology, while grouped with the surgical specialties, has strong links with internal medicine. The growth of specialisations around particular organs and functions makes the surgery/internal medicine division to some extent archaic. Cardiologists and cardiac surgeons, for example, share more with each other than with other physicians or surgeons, and the Cardiology Club may be more of a focal point than the colleges. But the colleges still determine the training programs and thus ultimately decide who will become consultants and on what terms.

Until the 1950s, it was not uncommon for general practitioners to sit for the membership examinations. GPs often became general physicians or psychiatrists as they clarified their areas of interest. GPs can still move into some of the less popular specialties which have difficulty filling places or where broader community experience is seen as desirable: rehabilitation and geriatrics are obvious examples. But such moves are becoming rare. Instead, general practice has become a specialty in its own right, with its own college, a postgraduate training program, and diplomas in areas such as obstetrics and paediatrics for those who wish to specialise within general practice. General practice is no longer the 'default' category and is effectively closed to those who have not completed the three-year vocational training program, whatever their hospital experience might be.

Hospital medicine is organised around tight hierarchies. Doctors work in teams or 'firms' which have a consultant at the top and a range of 'juniors' under them. At the bottom are the interns (or house officers) who must complete a pre-registration year covering both surgical and internal medical fields. Those who decide to specialise work in positions known in Australia as resident medical officers (RMOs) and in the UK as senior house officers (SHOs) for a minimum of two years and only then move into accredited training positions. The time taken to reach consultant status varies with the popularity of the specialty and the length of training. It is rare to go 'straight through' unless it happens to be a specialty in which training positions are difficult to fill. To be eligible to enter accredited training a doctor must already have completed two resident years. He or she may then have to spend several years in non-accredited positions before a training place becomes available. This means that the time from graduation to becoming a consultant is at least eight years and may be nine or ten. Further sub-specialist training may take another three to five years. A specialist may not finish training until the age of 38. A past president of the RACOG (Royal Australian College of Obstetricians and Gynaecologists) joked: 'At times I think the Entry to Fellowship application form should contain a box for the candidate's pension number!' (Hinde, 1990: 94–5).

In Australia, specialist training typically takes six years. The first three are usually in 'general' medicine or 'general surgery' and involve circulating through a series of jobs that are accredited as part of the training program. By the end of the three years, at the latest, the student will be expected to have passed the Part One examination administered by the relevant college. This combines multiple choice with some clinical examination. After completing the exam and the three years of generalist training, the student is qualified to enter more specialist training for a further three years. In some cases specialisation starts earlier. Ophthalmologists, for example, no longer do general surgery, and paediatricians take a modified version of the Physicians' Part One. Membership of the relevant college is gained after passing the Part Two examination. In some cases this involves continuous clinical assessment and completion of specified research projects rather than a formal exam.

In Britain, until recently, registrar and senior registrar grades constituted distinct positions in the hierarchy. Only after becoming a senior registrar could a doctor be reasonably sure of progression to consultant status following completion of a further four years. The Part One exam was the formal requirement for entry to a training program as a registrar and the Part Two was required for progression to senior registrar. Because of heavy competition, doctors have increasingly needed the Part Two even to gain registrar positions. What had been intended as an exit exam effectively became an entry requirement. The Calman reforms of 1996 set up a unified training grade known as the 'Specialist Registrar' to replace the old registrar/senior registrar grades. The clear intention was to reduce specialist training to five years when a CCST (Certificate of Completion of Specialist Training) is awarded by the Specialist Training Authority of the Medical Royal Colleges. This should benefit women who wish to complete their training before child bearing. But the entry criteria and the duration of training remain in the hands of the various colleges, and some have tried to subvert the spirit of the reforms by making it difficult to achieve consultant status. All the women who participated in this study went through under the old system.

In both countries, consultants' work is divided into sessions, each a nominal three and a half hours. Eleven sessions per week is regarded as a full-time load. Consultants are responsible for their patients 24 hours a day and they have rotas to cover for each other. While much hospital work is done by junior doctors there is always a consultant on call. Training is largely based on an apprenticeship system. Doctors are supposed to learn by actually doing the job, with the more experienced ones supervising those below them. Residents typically spend their time organising admissions, arranging for tests, taking medical histories, checking drug dosages and improving their diagnostic capacities. They assist with procedures and operations and develop the practical skills they will have had little opportunity to acquire as students. They go on the ward rounds with the consultant and the registrar and watch while they make decisions about the medical management of the patient. They may be doing drips, giving chemotherapy, and giving injections under strict supervision. Registrars are required to be on top of every detail relating to the patients for whom they are responsible, and to present case histories to the consultants when they do their rounds. They are expected to take the major responsibility for all but emergencies or the most complex cases and not to call on the consultant out of hours unless it is absolutely necessary.

How quickly an individual gains proficiency will largely determine whether he or she is singled out by the consultants as 'specialist' material. Some of the essential skills are never explicitly taught because they are thought to be already part of the habitus of anyone with the makings of a good doctor. Women often complain that they are not shown techniques; they tend to do better at book learning than at tasks that require attention from senior doctors. The lucky ones will find registrars and nursing staff who are willing to show them techniques. Women's greater difficulty in acquiring technical skills may be interpreted as failure to behave in ways which reveal their mastery of the indeterminate, that is, their failure to share the habitus. This sense of 'not belonging' in turn limits their options.

Intern and house officer positions are allocated on the basis of results at graduation. Those with the best results have first choice of hospitals and rotations. Teaching hospitals differ in their status, and so do training positions within them. These positions carry a cultural capital far beyond the acquisition of specialist qualifications. Those fortunate enough to land one or more such positions will move quickly through the medical field. The top students may get positions as professorial assistants which mark them out as being in the fast lane. After the first year, students have to make their own way but it is usually thought desirable to spend at least two years in the original training hospital. The only guarantees of continuity in training are informal ones. It is left to the individual to organise a series of rotations that will give them the necessary experience to prepare for their exams.

In Australia, where positions are allocated for a year at a time, trainees are usually based in one city though they may be expected at short notice to spend time in regional hospitals. In England, positions are allocated for six months and trainees have to be prepared to travel to other parts of the country. At each step doctors must compete for positions. It is a world in which not only examination results, but subjective judgments from those more senior, about developing clinical skills, confidence, and capacity to 'fit in' are constantly being made. Although it seems like a kind of 'mix and match' situation to the outsider, for those in the know there are very clear paths towards medical distinction. Having mentors, and building up the right sorts of contacts, are of great importance, not merely in getting short-listed for jobs but in knowing which are the most appropriate jobs to pursue. Those who have reached the top have invariably been taken aside and given advice on how best to conduct themselves. Mentoring is not just about confidence building but about imparting crucial information about which jobs to apply for and providing the kind of sponsorship that will ensure the candidate is successful. Selection procedures, interviews and written references are often little more than a formality in the medical world where the real decisions are taken elsewhere. While women are not excluded from this world they do not compete on equal terms. It is a world in which only a minority will feel at ease.

Towards a level playing field?

In 1974 Melbourne University changed its entrance requirements for medicine to incorporate an English mark. The proportion of women in the first year shot up radically. One of these women recalled that the dean, an obstetrician, 'made a speech on the first day, in which he said, "I notice a huge number of women have got in. I have worked all my life with women and I know this is not a good thing!" And we all boo-ed. It was an amazing first day.' Such remarks were no longer publicly acceptable and were to become increasingly rare. Medical education was coming under scrutiny and the English requirement itself was a limited recognition of the need to improve doctors' ability to communicate.

In the 1970s commentators from a variety of perspectives and political persuasions developed critical accounts of medicine which contributed substantially to a destabilisation of medical power and a certain erosion of its cultural capital. Earlier in the century the tradition of Emile Durkheim celebrated the professions as the saving grace of modernity, a means of balancing rampant individualism and ruthless profiteering. Professional men had been praised for their sense of vocation and selfless altruism. For Talcott Parsons the emergence of the professions, and above all medicine, was 'the crucial structural development in twentieth century society' (1968: 545). Because they were neither capitalists nor workers nor bureaucrats, they were, it was argued, well placed to care about the society as a whole. The professions were supposed to balance tendencies towards fragmentation and help maintain social order through a humane application of reason and accumulated knowledge. Until the 1960s, commentators wrote approvingly of the professions and tried to identify their distinctive traits. These were claimed to be in the existence of abstract, complex and specialist knowledge which was applied for the benefit of humanity.

Sociologists have revised these earlier adulatory frameworks and begun to question the value of trying to generalise about the professions or discover the 'essence' of professionalism. Medicine, far from being a homogeneous 'community', was shown to be racked by internal divisions. A new generation was sceptical of the claims of altruism, community interest and commitment to the service ethic and concerned with the more mundane aspects of professional work which it perceived as essentially similar to other jobs. Attention was drawn to the ways in which doctors had consolidated their own status and prestige at the expense of other groups (Freidson, 1970a, b; Johnson, 1972; Foucault, 1973).

Illich's *Medical Nemesis* (1976) accused the medical profession of being a danger to public health (just as he had claimed in *Deschooling Society* that teachers were a barrier to education), and sold over three million copies (Hart, 1988: 19). Far from liberating us from illness and pain, Zola argued that medicine was becoming a major institution of social control, 'nudging aside, if not incorporating the more traditional institutions of religion and law . . .' He contended that under certain conditions almost any human activity can become a medical concern (Zola, 1972: 70). Far from being detached from the class struggle doctors were denounced as part of a new middle class whose privileges rested on state patronage and the support of strategic elites (Ehrenreich & Ehrenreich, 1977; Willis, 1983). The neo-Weberians (Freidson, 1970a, b; Walby, 1986; Crompton, 1987; Witz, 1992) presented the rhetoric of service and altruism as strategies for closure which enabled doctors to dominate other groups. Professional credentials were seen not just as a guarantee of competence but a means of exclusion and empowerment.

These sorts of critiques have caused many to question the cultural capital embodied in medicine. Men have begun to wonder whether the lengthy training period, the long and irregular hours and the 'lifestyle' factors warrant their continuing in the field. In America the number of applications from men for medical school has fallen 50 per cent since 1974–75. The biggest decrease was from white men but the applications from African–American men also fell while those from Asian–American men rose (Relman, 1990: 1540–1). Relman cites the rising cost of medical education and a growing concern about professional autonomy and economic opportunity as the main reasons. He envisions a future with 'a changing younger profession, more broadly representative of American society, with more moderate economic expectations and a greater commitment to the primary care specialties' (Relman, 1990: 1540–1).

Since the mid-1970s the proportion of women medical students has escalated rapidly in most western countries. In Australia and the UK it has reached 50 per cent and in some individual schools the proportion is higher. This could fall back, if the relevant group chose to study other pure or applied sciences or move into some of the hitherto almost exclusively male preserves, such as engineering. But at present the rise continues. It is possible that we are witnessing not merely an equalisation of numbers but the substantial feminisation of large sections of medicine including medical administration which is a coming power base for women.

The significance of this shift may be lost in the mass of reports which stress the subordinate position of women in medicine. Where first-wave feminism demanded rights of entry to medicine, and medical women's groups earlier in this century wanted part-time positions to be carved out for married women, the current concern is with what needs to happen to allow women to take an equal place in medicine. This involves demands for the restructuring of medical education and the reorganisation of medical work and training. It calls for a questioning of medical power and privilege, a rethinking of the medical hierarchy and the establishment of more egalitarian relations between doctors and other health workers. It also implies a shift in medical priorities, an emphasis on preventive medicine and communication skills, an attempt to balance the current fragmentation with a concern with the whole person.

Resistance to women's entry to medicine has virtually disappeared. The surveys have clearly shown that their medical education does not get 'wasted' on marriage and motherhood. Women doctors are more likely than any other professional women to continue working when they have family responsibilities (Silverstone & Ward, 1980). The popular view in the medical profession that there is a pool of women doctors who are not working is grossly inaccurate (Allen, 1988: 26–7). Their drop-out rate is little different from the men's. In fact the men's has only recently been scrutinised: a 100 per cent retention rate was taken for granted, yet it is now being demonstrated that their sickness and mortality rates are actually higher than those of the women (Allen, 1988: 49). If 'wastage' from the NHS is the issue, men have been far more likely to emigrate or to go into private practice, while loss of medical time through balancing family commitments is counteracted by the time that men take out for 'medical politics' (Elston, 1980: 115).

In England the 1980s saw an expansion of part-time opportunities in the physician specialties. As Regional General Manager at Oxford, Dame Rosemary Rue was almost single-handedly responsible for this. Because there was a manpower shortage in the NHS, her proposal to bring back women not currently in the labour force was well received. Initially she applied for £4000 a year to take on four doctors each for four sessions a week. Within a year this had increased from four to forty. It was quickly built up to around 120 and stabilised at around ninety. Similar schemes were established in other regions. The original take-up was largely from women aged around fifty who had not worked for fifteen or twenty years but it quickly spread to younger women. They were employed as associate specialists, which is a sub-consultant grade. 'You were almost independent . . . You had tenure and you could practise the specialty in a limited way.'

Many of the younger women distanced themselves from this development, fearing that it would create second-rate jobs and entrench women in subordinate positions within the hospital. But it did employ a large number of women, in a short space of time, who would not otherwise have had medical jobs. According to Rue, 'what very often happened was that women came in doing just three or four sessions, quickly built up to seven or eight, polished off say a senior registrar training with two full years – because by that time their children were older – and a very high proportion of them became consultants'. Rue argues that because these women spent up to five years in the job they provided greater continuity of care than trainees who rotated through on six-month secondments. Nursing staff supported it 'when they discovered that these women didn't come and go like lightning'. The key to its success was the presence of the right person in the medical personnel department who could interview the applicants, help them make a career choice, stiffen their resolve, and match them with appropriate consultants.

The most detailed assessment of the position of women in medicine anywhere has been Isabel Allen's UK study (1988) which was taken extremely seriously by the Department of Health which commissioned it. It was based on face to face interviews with large numbers of male and female graduates from 1966, 1976 and 1981. It documented the range of difficulties that women have faced including discouragement both at school and university, poor careers advice and inflexible training regimes. Allen found plenty of evidence of women being 'ignored' by older consultants, who thought they were only in medicine 'for a hobby' and could not be taken seriously. Women were still under-represented in the career grades in medicine, as consultants, as principals in general practice and as specialists in community medicine. The increases in the 1980s came in pathology, psychiatry and radiology but there had been no major shift in surgery or gynaecology (p. 59).

What is notable about the report is its evidence about the dis-illusionment of doctors and its insistence on the need for fundamental changes in the organisation of medicine. All three of Allen's age cohorts thought that opportunities were fewer than when they had qualified and that it was becoming harder to get to the top. They said that doctors now had to go straight up the career ladder and that breaks in careers were becoming less rather than more acceptable as the competition for jobs increased (p. 35). They could not afford to change their minds about their specialty, to gain experience abroad or to take time out for any reason. They thought general practice was now as competitive as hospital medicine and they were concerned about unemployment.

Of the 1981 qualifiers, 44 per cent of men and 49 per cent of women said they regretted their decision to become a doctor, citing exhaustion combined with the effect on their family and social lives (p. 73). It was the on-call working and long hours for young hospital doctors in training that were found most intolerable (p. 85). Allen vividly described the frustration of young doctors of both sexes with the current realities of medical life and the 'humiliation' they had encountered at medical school. The report attacks the 'intimidating and humiliating manner of some consultants or other teaching staff', particularly surgeons and gynaecologists towards both men and women students (p. 14). It also criticised the absence of equal opportunity principles, the secrecy of selection procedures, and the patronage system. 'Friends in high places', it was claimed, were becoming even more important as the climate became more competitive (p. 22). At job interviews women are still asked very personal questions about their private lives with questions designed to root out homosexuality, unstable marriages or unacceptable social behaviour as well as to identify their child-rearing plans (pp. 39–41).

Allen found strong support for career posts with full clinical autonomy but without the full departmental responsibilities of the present consult-ant post. There was also a fear that women would be sidelined into these jobs (pp. 51–3). Bottlenecks at the point of entry to accredited training programs make people wait longer to complete specialist training. As entry becomes more competitive, part-time opportunities tend to dry up. In any case, part-time training provides no easy solution. Two-thirds of the men and more than half the women thought that some specialties were unsuitable for part-time training: acute hospital specialties which need continuity of care, on-call commitment and night and weekend duties (p. 44). The medical profession is seriously divided about whether medicine can be learned or practised part-time, though the debate has so far been informed more by ideological position statements than detailed work on how medical knowledge is acquired or practised.

The report concluded that there must be a change in the structure of medical careers so that different types of career paths and flexible lengths of time in grades and jobs are considered acceptable. It also called for a review of promotion procedures and patronage. It argued that there should be more coordinated and well-publicised provision of part-time training and career posts, a concerted drive towards fostering job-sharing and a general openness to the idea that the present way of organising medical jobs may not be the only or necessarily the best way of doing it (p. 93).

Bourdieu observes that 'in order for a field to function, there have to be stakes and people prepared to play the game, endowed with the habitus that implies knowledge and recognition of the immanent laws of the field, the stakes and so on' (1993a: 72). Clearly there are now large numbers of women both willing and able to play the game, who recognise its value and have practical knowledge of how it works. The Bachelor of Medicine, Bachelor of Surgery (MBBS) degrees measure the minimum human capital required in order to play. Having won the battle for entry in the late nineteenth century women then faced a range of subtler and more difficult obstacles. Along with direct discrimination there was the relentlessness of a system of training which demanded not years but decades of complete immersion and tolerated no breaks for childbirth. This is a field that is difficult for even the cleverest and most experienced to negotiate, and one in which most women and ethnic minority groups can expect only limited amounts of guidance and support. While one might hail the future as the coming to fruition of the feminist ideals of a century ago, as women become fully visible in the public sphere and take an equal place in the practice of the professions, the future is likely to be messier and more fragmented than that. However, governments of all shades have intervened to make medical careers more accessible for women and the colleges are now under pressure to act.

The following chapters identify the state of play in a number of specific medical fields and the tactics and strategies that have been available to women. It will be a central theme of this book that the campaigns around the 'nuts and bolts' issues must be accompanied by a politics of representation that creates new visions of what medicine can be. It is no longer just a question of whether large numbers of women can be absorbed into the medical hierarchy but of how far their presence will change the rules of the game and democratise the profession. Having built up their cultural capital, women doctors are now acquiring symbolic capital as well, and claiming the right, like their male colleagues, to shape the contours of the field. In so far as they have a collective vision it necessarily involves the dismantling of current hierarchies and the movement towards a more tolerant, egalitarian and flexible profession.

3

The Power of Gynaecology

The incongruity of a speciality devoted to women being
almost totally controlled by men has always struck me
forcefully.

Wendy Savage (1986: 59)

In feminist discourse, 'gynaecology' is virtually interchangeable with
'patriarchy', signifying men's domination of women through knowledges
and practices that have given them control over women's bodies, their
sexuality and reproductive potential. Many feminists have described the
processes through which, over several centuries, men displaced women
healers and discovered in modern medicine the most sophisticated
means yet of consolidating their power. The emergence of gynaecology
as one of the most prestigious of the specialties was seen, by them, as a
major victory for the forces of patriarchy. The heroines of this story were
not the women who had struggled to break into gynaecology but the
midwives and nurses who attempted to keep alive older folk traditions. It
is the story of a battle between good and evil, alluring in its simplicity and
as a political rallying cry.

The defenders of gynaecology tell a rather similar tale, merely revers-
ing the values. In their view, modern gynaecology has established the pre-
conditions for gender equality, releasing women from the 'historic
burden of their own ill health and able to think of their femininity as a
positive, life-giving force' (Shorter, 1984: 296). Edward Shorter quotes a
working-class Englishwoman looking back in 1914 on her earlier pregnancies: 'I always prepared myself to die, and I think this awful depression is common to most at this time' (1984: 70). There was, he says,
nothing safe or cosy about giving birth in premodern times, when
women risked fistulas, lacerations, prolapse, haemorrhaging, eclampsia,

puerperal fever and any number of infections after delivery. Shorter believes that feminists have romanticised traditional medicine and chosen to ignore midwives' adherence to the ironclad dictates of custom.

This foundation story has largely outlived its political usefulness for either group. The reality has always been a good deal more complex and the changes of recent years have demonstrated how much is excluded in an account that concentrates on two sides locked in permanent combat. Not least, female obstetricians and gynaecologists have become very popular. Women patients have made it clear that, while many of the feminist criticisms have struck home, they are weary of the battle between doctors and midwives. Women specialists offer a chance to break the circuit, combining medical expertise with a level of sympathy and understanding that the men too often have lacked.

And some feminists, too, have shifted ground since the 1970s, revising their understandings of power and dropping their unmitigated hostility to the medical profession. There is less emphasis on overarching structures of domination and more attention to the minutiae of the workings of power. 'Patriarchy' as a term is less widely used, and strategies of power are of more importance than structures set in concrete. Rather than seeing power as a bad thing in itself, the emphasis has shifted towards identifying the networks and discourses through which power operates. Power is not simply a finite quality to be fought over in battles. It operates through a variety of discourses which are not the preserve of any one group. It is always contextual. Obstetric decisions generally have to be made very quickly and under conditions that are stressful for all concerned. While the specialist is exercising the authority of the expert, he or she knows the decisions will be retrospectively scrutinised and legal action may follow. Patients are not merely powerless victims, and gynaecologists are ever-conscious of the risk of being sued.

Concentrating on the power of doctors leaves the power of other groups, such as nurses and midwives, unexamined. Women have also begun to see that they can succeed as specialists in this field, and turn discourses that construct women as carers to their own advantage. The issue is not simply whether women make 'a difference' to the practice of obstetrics and gynaecology but the ways in which their 'absence' from the area has affected the discursive frameworks within which power operates, contestations take place and occupational identities get constructed.

In short, gynaecology can no longer stand as a metaphor for 'global patriarchy' and the universal oppression of women. While such polemics did create a space from which women's health activists could speak, they now limit the capacity to analyse local and specific formations of power. It is not necessary to evoke a monolithic male conspiracy to say that obstetrics and gynaecology are profoundly structured by gender

inequalities. But women are not powerless, either as patients or practitioners. To write as if they are is to grant the specialty more power than
it has yet been able to mobilise and sustain for any length of time.

In this context, the struggles of earlier generations of women in
obstetrics and gynaecology are being re-evaluated. While these women
shared many of the attitudes of their male colleagues, they were also
aware of their failings. Women in obstetrics and gynaecology have
become more vocal about discrimination, about the inflexibility of work
and training programs, and about the behaviour of their male colleagues
to both female staff and patients. They have done much to put sexual
harassment, lack of patient choice and unnecessary surgical intervention
on the public agenda. The groundwork is there for a major rapproche-
ment between female gynaecologists and women's health activists with
the potential to work together for a major restructuring of obstetrics and
gynaecology.

The fact remains that the specialty has been extraordinarily hostile to
the presence of women. While the small numbers can be attributed to
the long training program (six years on top of an intern year and an
elective year), the long and unpredictable hours, and the absence of
part-time opportunities, the animosity to women goes much deeper.
Students and patients tell stories of obscene remarks and of sexist or
patronising gynaecologists (Bewley, 1991). One of the women specialists
observed that there is still a widely held view 'that gynaecologists are
misogynists and hate women and that is why they do it . . . they have the
women with their clothes off and on their backs in the most powerless
position. And sometimes people do live up to their stereotypes.'

In the 1950s and 1960s the proportion of women gynaecologists in
Britain actually declined, once the more supportive environment of the
women's hospitals was withdrawn after 1948, and as images of gynaecologists as sex symbols began to be promoted in popular culture. The
British obstetrician, Wendy Savage, experienced postgraduate schools in
the early 1960s as unwelcoming. Even at the London Hospital Medical
College, with a strong tradition of service to the local community, she
found herself one of only four women among fifty men (Savage, 1986:
8–9). After 1970 the proportion rose slowly only to plateau at around
12 per cent. In 1988 a Sydney woman was rejected for a public hospital
position even though she was the only applicant and the position was
later given to a man (*SMH*, 28 October 1988). By the late 1980s, however,
twice as many women students as men were saying that they intended to
pursue a career in obstetrics and gynaecology (RCOG, 1987). With larger
numbers now starting the training program, the proportion of women
gynaecologists should increase.

While male hostility may be read as a response of the powerful, it
may also suggest a profession uncertain of its legitimacy. Obstetrics has

worked hard to suppress its non-medical origins. Allowing women in is like the return of the repressed, reminding it of a humbler past. Not so long ago, obstetrics and gynaecology came a poor third to surgery and internal medicine in prestige, and still had to compete with midwifery and general practice. The presence of women is a reminder of the claims of midwifery; but women now lay further claims both on obstetrics and on gynaecology which, as part of general surgery, had been the masculine holy of holies. As they came into their own as the 'third force' in medicine in the 1950s, obstetricians and gynaecologists were only too ready to bask in the glitter and glamour of their achievements. But some feminist historians are now beginning to question whether gynaecology is quite so monolithic and to discover a profession that has been divided in its responses to feminism. They have also begun to explore the rather different demands that women in the past made on the profession in the name of feminism.

Feminist critiques

While there has been debate among second-wave feminists about 'advances' in obstetrics and gynaecology and whether women are empowered or disadvantaged, the dominant approach has celebrated traditional women healers who championed the natural, resisted technology and empathised with child bearing. Feminists were less concerned with getting more women into obstetrics and gynaecology than with a critique that plays down any difference that female practitioners might make. While conceding that some women gynaecologists may be more sensitive to women's needs they had the same indoctrination and were under the same pressure to conform (Daly, 1978: 277).

In the 1970s many feminist writers documented the attack on women healers, the 'witches' of the sixteenth and seventeenth centuries, and the process by which men wrested control of childbirth away from women (Donnison, 1977; Ehrenreich & English, 1978). Though Adrienne Rich stressed the importance of choice, the implication of her influential book on motherhood was that men had colonised women's bodies and that medicalised childbirth encapsulated male control of women (Rich, 1976).

When the American radical feminist philosopher and theologian, Mary Daly, used gynaecology as a metaphor for global patriarchy, she was escalating an attack that had been building up for a decade as women expressed their anger about the medical management of childbirth and the treatment of women's bodies. Gynaecology, claimed Daly, 'was/is not healing in a deep sense but violent enforcement of the sexual caste system . . . mind-gynecologists and body-gynecologists have been . . . combining and conniving to repress and depress female be-ing . . . The various types of psychotherapists are the theologians of gynecology . . . Both function to keep women supine, objectified, and degraded – a condition ritually symbolized by the gynecologist's stirrups and the psychiatrist's couch' (1978: 227–30). The fact that most gynaecologists are males, she said, is in itself a colossal comment on 'our' society, 'a symptom and example of male control over women and over language, and a clue to the extent of this control' (1978: 9).

In the 1980s concerns were expressed about the exploitative potential of new reproductive technologies. Participants in FINRRAGE (Feminist International Network of Resistance to Reproductive and Genetic Engineering), which was formed in 1984, argued forcefully that these technologies inevitably involve the patriarchal exploitation of women's bodies. They claimed that, far from providing women with choices, such developments as in vitro fertilisation (IVF), egg donation, sex selection, embryo transfer and genetic screening merely provide gynaecologists with an exciting, high status area of research and a complex high-tech practice (Minden, 1987; Pfeffer, 1987). They saw a danger that these developments would become standard practice. Already, they said, obstetric procedures ranging from Caesarean sections to foetal monitoring, which had first been introduced for 'high risk' cases, had come into routine usage. The female body and its products were providing living laboratories for the technological production of human beings.

Robyn Rowland (1987) refers to 'technopatriarchs' and 'technodocs' interchangeably to indicate that through gynaecological experiment men are systematically increasing their power over women. In her view, gynaecologists operate on behalf of men in what she describes as 'a new stage in the patriarchal war against women'. For those who share this analysis, increasing the numbers of women gynaecologists will do nothing to solve the problem and may be counter-productive.

Another contentious area for feminists has been hormone replacement therapy (HRT). Many take the view that HRT is extremely risky, and that it is being pushed not because it reduces menopausal discomfort, offers protection against osteoporosis and heart disease, or promotes good health, but in order to ensure that women retain their femininity and their sex drive.

For Germaine Greer, 'the medicalisation of everyday life is here taken to its absurd extreme. The husband has become the wife's health problem, and testosterone in her body the treatment for him' (1992: 204). Greer rails about medical ignorance and the failure of doctors to address the emotional issues associated with menopause in our culture. While no one should underplay the risks of endometrial cancer and so on, this agenda derives not so much from risk assessment as from a set of assumptions about letting 'nature' take its course. In Greer's version women should be acting out their anger and hostility about how women over fifty are treated, rather than turning the clock back to construct a more youthful femininity. Not everyone shares Greer's set of problems with turning fifty and, for many women, HRT has brought a new lease of life. Anecdotally, it would seem that male doctors have been more cautious about prescribing it than females who are, perhaps, more attuned to the needs of their patients.

Obstetrics has, for good reasons, been the centre of much feminist concern. British sociologist, Ann Oakley, has given graphic descriptions of what the birth process was like in England in the 1960s and 1970s. For public patients, antenatal checks involved travelling long distances and then being subject to cattle market conditions. When the time came to give birth, the pubic region was shaved and enemas were given. If a woman was late she was induced. She was placed flat on her back with her feet in stirrups. As the infant's head appeared in the vagina she was given an episiotomy in two-thirds of cases. Forceps were routinely applied if there was any delay in the head popping out. If there were complications, like a breech, she was delivered abdominally. While this was usually argued as being for the sake of the child, it may also have been for the convenience of the doctor. Not surprisingly, a home-births movement emerged which argued that the risks to the few did not justify the removal of women's autonomy and control.

Wendy Savage has linked natural childbirth most clearly with contemporary feminism. She believes that most women prefer to put up with pain (which she dismisses as short-lived and quickly forgotten) in order to have control:

> I think that men, who are not going to actually physically give birth, but are onlookers and bystanders, have the feeling that they have got to do something about the pain, about the way labour is progressing, whereas women . . . understand that . . . there are worse things in life than pain, and that to go through the process of pregnancy and labour and be in control of it is a very important part of a woman's self-esteem. (1986: 137)

The implication is that if they want to have control over the process women should choose natural childbirth.

But the politics of pain and power are complex. Some women are now bitter that they went through the pain of natural childbirth because they thought it was the correct 'feminist' thing to do. For them, the remarks of comedian Joan Rivers, 'Just knock me out at the first twinge, and then wake me up at the hairdresser's', strike a chord. It can be argued that women have a right to control the resources of medicalised childbirth to their own advantage (Saul, 1994; Stanworth, 1987). Women who have previously had an unpleasant labour are increasingly demanding Caesareans (Welford, 1993: 25). Some choose an elective Caesarean in order to be able to plan work schedules and child care commitments (Saul, 1994).

Women gynaecologists have criticised the way in which natural childbirth came to be regarded as a test of womanhood, the equivalent of machismo. One said, 'they feel that somehow they're a better woman if they've done it even if they didn't enjoy it. It's now put up as the standard to aim for.' Another objected to the way in which the ability to have a normal vaginal delivery has become the hallmark of what it means to be a woman and believed strongly that patients should not have to prove themselves in this way. This new orthodoxy effectively prevents women from taking advantage of options for pain relief (Crouch & Manderson, 1993). By focusing on 'natural' birth as the 'solution' to inequalities of power, ways of improving the vast majority of births may be ignored. Even where forceps are used, it is possible to include people, by getting them to touch the baby as it is coming out or by cutting the cord. Even with Caesarean births it is possible to make the mother feel she has been actively involved.

Midwifery cannot be contrasted with gynaecology as, automatically, a form of feminist praxis. Sections of the homebirth movement are drawn from anti-feminist groups whose simple lifestyle draws on Christian fundamentalism, the will of God and traditional notions of the family (Rothman, 1989: 170). It is also difficult to point to a state of nature, when women approached birth instinctively and without fear or pain. Childbirth is socially controlled in all societies and we cannot simply counterpoise masculine technological childbirth to women's 'natural' ways, 'as if unmedicalised birth has the authority of 90,000 years of human history' (Saul, 1994: 2). What we understand as 'natural' is very much a social construction. As Saul puts it, 'there is patently no precedent in nature or any other culture for a woman standing naked under a hot shower embracing her partner and sucking ice cubes' (1994: 6). Midwives do not stand outside of power and their ability to construct natural birth in opposition to the medical model has enabled them to retain control of clients who want a 'more natural' experience (Treichler, 1990). Some of the tension and anxiety experienced by patients is generated by the rivalry between professional groups.

Recent feminist historical research has demonstrated that the earlier campaigns for painless childbirth using the anaesthetic 'Twilight Sleep' were led by middle-class women for whom pain relief was an explicitly feminist demand (Leavitt, 1980). These women saw nothing empowering in putting up with the pain of childbirth and would have been astonished by the contemporary emphasis on enduring pain in order to be fully in control of an event that was crucial to their feminine identities. Physicians have also disagreed over these questions and certainly did not uniformly declare a war on nature or decide on a strategy of intervention and subordination of women (Treichler, 1990). If some feminists have underemphasised the importance of pain relief, and oversimplified the relation between pain and power, they have also been dismissive of women with infertility problems. Women's desire for children and interest in high-tech programs cannot simply be reduced to false consciousness.

While feminist critiques of gynaecology have characteristically been directed at high-tech intervention, the underlying criticism is of the power assumed by the doctor. Sandra Coney's revelations (1988) about the 'unfortunate experiment' on cervical cancer at the National Women's Hospital in Auckland concerned the *failure* to provide access to advanced technology. For experimental purposes, the gynaecologists had taken a stand of minimum intervention, resulting in horrendously drawn out deaths for a lot of women. Coney discusses the hierarchical relations in the profession itself and within the hospital which made it difficult for anyone to speak out. Professor Green, the main culprit, tried to use the presumed hostility of feminists to gynaecology to discredit the revelations. He produced in his defence a letter from a woman expressing her 'deep concern for the way some very dangerous bitter women are endeavouring to ruin your wonderful reputation', and another which called the inquiry a 'carefully orchestrated feminist plot'. That this seemed to him like a helpful strategy says much about the kind of relationship that has existed between gynaecology and its feminist critics.

Shaky foundations

Obstetrics and gynaecology had to struggle to achieve respectability let alone prestige. The practice first had to overcome the contempt of the older specialties and then to mark itself out from both general practitioners and midwives. No sooner had it achieved this than it found itself under widespread attack from consumer groups. The fledgling College of Obstetrics and Gynaecology was established in London in 1929 (with an Australian chapter in 1933) to organise the interests of the new specialty which was committed to dealing with the unsatisfactory perinatal and maternal mortality rates, and improving the standard of gynaecological surgery. The two parts came together largely for practical reasons, since both were concerned with the reproductive organs and both were regarded as too small on their own for a full-time practice. Much of gynaecology at that stage involved the repair of the 'accidents of childbirth'. But the two words, separated by 'and', imply a large area of contested or ambiguous territory. Rather than being a single field the specialty was carved out of two existing fields, both of which resisted the loss of their territory, and the earlier boundaries have not been entirely erased.

Many who practised gynaecology preferred to remain with the Royal College of Surgeons (RCS) or the Royal Australian College of Surgeons (RACS) rather than identify with the new college. General surgeons fought hard to keep gynaecological surgery within their own sphere. When in 1938 the new college claimed 'Royal' status this was fiercely contested by the RCS and the Royal College of Physicians (RCP) in court battles stretching into the 1950s. Surgeons sneered that it was 'no occupation for a gentleman' and regarded gynaecology as a second-rate specialty for men who could not make it into general surgery. Few gynaecological operations take more than an hour, which is a stark contrast to the six or seven-hour complicated abdominal operations. Gynaecologists still call in a surgeon when their patients require bowel surgery.

Stories about gynaecological incompetence abound. Iza Segal recalled a man who put every patient he saw into hospital to have an ovarian cyst removed. 'He'd look at their ovaries and there'd be a little bulge somewhere and he'd stick a diathermic needle into it and say, we've removed the cyst, we'll sew her up!' Another had removed a bladder instead of a cyst and refused to stop when challenged by junior staff. A third had taken out the uterus of a woman who came in to have her appendix out. This patient was only 26 and about to be married, but the specialist said, 'look you can see how mottled that uterus is, I'll take it out' and neither the registrar nor the anaesthetist was able to stop her.

If gynaecologists acquired an unsavoury reputation, obstetricians were regarded as inferior within the profession. The Melbourne obstetrician and historian Frank Forster recalled that a sharp distinction between the two remained until the 1960s and that men who concentrated on obstetrics were still regarded as 'a bit funny'. What gave obstetrics respectability, and broke the hold of the midwives, was its incorporation within a surgical specialty. As a result childbirth became more surgically oriented and there was a new emphasis on the 'active management' of labour.

Men's attempts to enter obstetrics have historically been linked with new technologies. The first of these was the speculum with its potential for visual diagnosis. Lynne Tatlock (1992) has described the discursive struggles that took place in Germany in the early eighteenth century over the rival claims of touch and vision, understood as feminine and masculine respectively, in the practice of midwifery. Tatlock examines two famous treatises on childbirth, one written by a man, the other by a woman. In Johan Ettner's version four men plot to throw out the female relatives and helpers and professionalise the birthing room. In the women's story, Justine Siegemund, a famous midwife in her day, has one midwife explain to another that she chooses not to use the speculum because it causes unnecessary pain: 'my gentle hand could lie where the hard iron lies . . . I think that the people who use the speculum are those who use instruments to remove the child from the mother in pieces'. She links the speculum to the greater 'knowledge' of those who remove the child in pieces, thus simultaneously deferring to and sneering at the male monopoly of theoretical knowledge and use of instruments. By asserting the superiority of touch she retains her privilege as a woman to touch the genitals of her patients and marginalises male practitioners. Tatlock concludes:

> Once male practitioners established their right to look and thus to know by seeing what the midwife knew by touching, the field of obstetrics and gynecology was changed forever . . . And what had once been women's own probing tactile inquiry, yielding its own informed answers, would eventually also enter the field of male knowledge as male doctors appropriated even women's own prerogative of touch. (1992: 759)

In the 1730s, when Simpson developed the obstetrics forceps, male midwives became more numerous, again by association with the new technology. While they earned more than the women and were often called in for emergencies, they were not popular. Before anaesthetics, the forceps were greatly feared and those who wielded them were regarded as, at best, a necessary evil. Female midwives generally dissociated themselves from the brutality of the forceps and those who used them. The medicalisation of childbirth in the late nineteenth century extended men's involvement. The medical schools were, by then, turning out large numbers of general practitioners who were keen to add obstetrics to their work. Though poorly trained, they quickly took over 50 per cent of home births in England (Shorter, 1984: 152–3). The midwives then made a comeback, and succeeded in throwing off the drunk and dirty 'Sarah Gamp' image and establishing their own professional identity in the first half of the twentieth century. But they were no match for the new hospital-based specialties.

In Britain, the shift from smaller lying-in hospitals to large public hospitals placed 'management' in the hands of professional male elites (Oakley, 1984). This was justified in terms of reducing perinatal mortality, though in fact the major improvement had resulted from sulpha drugs in the decade before 1946 (Schofield, 1993). The proportion of home births fell from 33 per cent in 1958 to less than 1 per cent in 1980 (Schofield, 1993). Midwives found it difficult to compete as autonomous practitioners, even for home births because, under the

NHS, women could now have a GP. The movement of childbirth into hospitals eventually reduced the role of GPs as well. The shift from the 'classical' Caesarean which the GP could manage, towards the 'lower segment' operation, which was technically more difficult, removed many GPs from obstetric practice. Interventionist procedures steadily increased including Caesareans, forceps deliveries, artificial induction and episiotomy. Midwives increasingly found themselves recast as obstetric nurses, working under the authority of male obstetrician–gynaecologists (Oakley, 1984: 143).

Consultants do not lay claim to all obstetrics. In Britain, they tend to see it as a 'waste' of their time to attend normal births and have generally been content to leave these to midwives or registrars. One confessed, 'I haven't the faintest idea how to look after women in labour and I can't cope with hours and hours of sitting and pain and being nice to people!' In Australia, where a high proportion of the population has private medical insurance, they attend more normal births, but typically turn up just in time to catch the baby. In both countries, the specialists have claimed the right to define what constitutes a 'normal' birth and accordingly to shape the entire field. Whereas a breech delivery would have been normal and so handled by a midwife in 1918, it is now considered the province of the obstetrician. While 70 per cent of childbirths were thought normal enough to be delivered at home in the 1930s, by the 1950s 70 per cent were being delivered in hospital (Oakley, 1984: 142).

A key aspect of the gynaecologists' rise to power was their ability to represent themselves as the third major field of medicine of equal status with the physicians and surgeons (Summey & Hurst, 1986a). This happened first in the United States which was less constricted by the traditions of the colleges and soon had its effects internationally. It challenged the clear division of the medical field between those who cut and those who did not and brought about a restructuring of medicine around a series of specialties based on particular parts of the anatomy. Obstetrics and gynaecology was to claim a special place as the first of these new super specialties. Despite its standing, questions have been raised about its future. The combination of obstetrics and gynaecology is seen by many as arbitrary. Each could easily be linked with other areas like oncology, endocrinology or psychiatry. Far from consolidating its identity as a coherent specialty, obstetrics and gynaecology seems likely to be redivided between obstetrics and 'routine' gynaecology, on the one hand, and the new sub-specialties of uro-gynaecology, oncology, IVF, ultrasound and perinatal medicine, on the other.

Such a split will have important consequences for training. The RACOG has been considering whether the non-operative specialist needs as much surgical training and whether or not he or she would be better off having more exposure to outpatient clinics and even some vocational training in the consultant's rooms. It is also doubtful whether the future gynae-oncologist really needs to do five years of obstetrics before launching into the sub-specialty, or whether 'those features of personality which help to make a person a good radical surgeon – some degree of aggression, boldness, and to some extent impatience' are those which produce the best obstetrician (Hinde, 1990: 95–6).

In Australia, there have been calls to move away from adherence to current British practice and develop a training that is more closely aligned to local needs (Hinde, 1990). The Australian regional council of the college did not become autonomous until 1979. Examiners came from England and reciprocity with the British Part One exam was retained until 1990. But since Australia has a private health system, specialists spend more of their time at normal births and have very different work profiles. Most work in contexts where surgery is limited, and where midwifery (as opposed to complicated obstetrics) and non-operative gynaecological counselling form a large part of the work. There is a strong case, therefore, for shortening the training for those who do not go into the sub-specialties. This could greatly benefit women but, as many are aware, it could also lock them in to the lower, generalist tier of the profession.

Gynaecologists are living with a degree of uncertainty about the future of the profession. They have watched its popularity decline and their medical insurance fees skyrocket as malpractice and negligence cases against them rise. For those who are looking for a scapegoat it is easy to find it in women, both as patients and practitioners. To many of the men, women gynaecologists seem to be having a dream run. Where in the past they were a tiny minority that could be ignored, or a small group of high fliers who could be placed high on pedestals and respected, women now appear to be claiming the whole field. The women are only too aware of the processes that marginalise them but, for some of the men, the dread of having to return to past battles is not far from the surface.

Women in obstetrics and gynaecology

The thirteen women who spoke to me ranged from those who had completed their training in the 1930s to those currently in registrar positions. All stressed their loyalty to the profession and, with varying degrees of comfort, took on its habitus:

> It's a very competitive specialty and a stiff upper lip is all important. You have to look as though you're absolutely unconcerned . . . quite often you are doing a forceps and something is going wrong and your first thought is, oh my god, I've killed this baby. Then you think of the mortality meeting, when you might actually have to get up in front of doctors and say, I did what I thought was right at the time, and somehow defend something – you know – indefensible.

Despite political differences, the thirteen shared the characteristic assumptions of the profession. They identify proudly as surgeons, believe that a normal birth can only be known retrospectively and have a tendency to view childbirth as a risky activity which requires at least some medical surveillance. Germaine Greer has observed that gynaecologists 'are like motor mechanics who have never worked on a car that actually went' (1992: 165). She is not the only one to use the car analogy:

> If I'm driving my car . . . I want to arrive safely. If I'm looking after a mother and a baby, I want that baby to be born safely and I want to give them the best treatment and the best equipment and everything else they can have . . . Now obviously I have never had any argument with a patient as to what I should do for her, never, ever, ever. What I would do is explain to her what I was going to do and why. I don't want dead babies. I want living, healthy babies and I want them to be properly looked after by properly trained staff.

If this woman differed from many of the men it was because she had a capacity to detect, beyond the conscious statements that were articulated about what women wanted, what each was comfortable with in her body. Since she did not give the patient any space from which to argue or consent, I am not putting her up as a model. But she was sensitive to the fact that patients have different pain thresholds and some are willing to exchange 'autonomy' for the security of someone else in charge.

Another commented that 'if the pregnancy is uncomplicated *I am going to allow* her spontaneous labour and normal child delivery'. Like most gynaecologists she stressed the speed at which conditions can change: 'A woman can be having a baby one minute and then she is bleeding to death and has to have a hysterectomy. She is going to wake up and be infertile. But you have to do it and you have to know it is the right thing because you will have to be able to live with yourself.' This woman estimated that only 30 per cent of her clients 'got away without cuts', and they were usually having their second or third child. While defending gynaecology to the hilt, she was also the most explicitly 'feminist' of the group and prepared publicly to attack male gynaecologists for their lack of 'caring'.

The early women in the field were high flyers with a 'surgical bent' who often felt they would encounter fewer obstacles here than in general surgery. The profession was prepared grudgingly, to make space for them, but had little sympathy for the more average women.

My oldest informant, Iza Segal, graduated with first-class honours from Sydney University in the late 1930s and started training in general surgery. She then married and had to leave the hospital but not before completing a Master of Surgery degree. Whether she would have been appointed as a consultant general surgeon was never tested because her husband stepped in and refused to allow her to sit the membership exams. As an obstetrician himself he evidently did not want to be upstaged by his wife being a general surgeon. She continued to do both gynaecology and general surgery and recalled that 'things were very muddled up in the 1940s and 1950s'. As pressure mounted to specialise, she took on obstetrics although she preferred surgical work. One of her fondest memories was of the time when she opened up a woman for an ovarian cyst, found it was an aortic aneurism and, as a surgeon, knew she was fully competent to deal with it. Iza never took membership of the RACOG and always resented the fact that her career as a general surgeon had been cut short. At the same time she was very sensitive to people saying she was not a 'real' gynaecologist and stressed the fact that she had trained in women's hospitals in Philadelphia and London. While she had a reputation among a younger generation as a 'hacker' she also spoke excitedly about the drugs that made much surgery unnecessary, and the developments that enabled surgery to be less invasive.

She identified as a feminist, took a leading role in abortion law reform in the 1960s and was a consultant to Leichhardt Women's Health Centre, though she was at a loss to understand the tensions between herself and some women's health activists. She was outspoken in her criticisms of male gynaecologists, saying she would not trust them 'as far as she could sue them' and was full of stories about their sexual exploits. Throughout her working life she had been a sympathetic ear for women who had run into difficulties with male gynaecologists. She died in 1994 and is remembered with great affection in Australia.

Dr B. trained during the war years when 25 per cent of the first year intake were women. With a less spectacular academic record than Iza's, she was unable to get into a training program and went to England to qualify as a Member of the Royal College of Obstetricians and Gynaecologists (MRCOG). 'This was no mean feat,' Dr B. observed wryly, 'a lot of my colleagues went and didn't get it'. She too aspired to general surgery but felt it was 'more natural' for a woman to do gynaecology. She described herself as a 'surgeon by nature', by which she meant someone who sees things in black and white and can make quick decisions:

> You ask a physician a question and you're left just as bamboozled. You ask a surgeon and they can say yes, yes, done! Surgeons think more clearly and are more decisive.

Dr B. remained a surgeon in spirit, preferring hysterectomy to the more limited operation of uterine ablation: 'I would think they are leaving an organ behind which has a potential malignancy'. Unlike Iza, she was a political conservative, fiercely opposed to abortion and hostile to feminism and to the women's health movement. Yet she had experienced discrimination throughout her working life. She was never made an honorary at a major public hospital though she was employed as a clinical assistant. After having a miscarriage that position too was withdrawn and she was effectively forced into private practice. Unlike Iza, she had a non-medical husband who was willing for her career to take priority over his.

Some women have continued to choose gynaecology as a way into surgery. A 1960s graduate said that although she had had an interest in general surgery she 'thought it would be too hard' and it then became a matter of what else she could do. (She went on to a distinguished career as a gynaecological surgeon in a teaching hospital.) Others have been drawn to the obstetrics side first. While proud of her surgical skills one of these women says, 'I would never call myself a surgeon because I think there are lots of connotations associated with the term . . . the connotations that come to me are male, and a certain arrogance and reservedness that I feel don't fit me'.

Dr C. completed her training in the early 1950s but then, like a number of her contemporaries, dropped out of specialist work. Having started with high ideals about a career in obstetrics, she married a specialist whose own work took him out a lot at night, and decided she was not prepared to hand her children over to live-in nannies and housekeepers. Instead, 'I looked quite carefully at what I could do which would allow me to do sessional and slightly less demanding work and still use my obstetrics and gynae base . . . what was beginning to blossom was family planning'. There are a significant number of women in family planning who might, with more flexible conditions, have worked as specialists.

Dr E. recalled that, in the 1960s so many women dropped out that the college labelled them 'unreliable' and was reluctant to take them on. She herself worked a one-in-two roster through most of her training, which meant that in any 48-hour period she would be at home for twelve hours. Frank Forster, then a young obstetrician in Melbourne recalled, 'In the 1950s, no way! Women's place was still basically seen as not in medicine. There was a tremendous male antipathy.'

The Sydney obstetrics and gynaecology world was so factionalised that the staff at the two main teaching hospitals, Crown Street and King George V had little contact with each other. The Rachel Forster Hospital, though run by women, did not practise obstetrics, had no family planning clinic and refused any women who had suffered a miscarriage.

In Melbourne the Royal Women's Hospital had only one woman on its honorary staff. The men resented the existence of the Queen Victoria Hospital, which was run entirely by women, and refused to invite its staff to clinical meetings. Yet the Queen Vic emerged as a powerful force and, to this day, there is a much higher proportion of women obstetricians and gynaecologists in Melbourne than in other parts of Australia. Dame Ella McKnight, who was strongly associated with the Queen Vic, eventually became president of the college. Even in the 1960s women were strongly in demand. Forster recalled that Lorna Lloyd Green then had the biggest obstetrics practice in Melbourne. But most of the women who got to the top at that time, like Green, McKnight and Margaret Henderson, had a rough road and all remained single.

Despite more flexible training programs, higher recruitment rates, and the obvious consumer demand, the proportion of women working in obstetrics and gynaecology has been slow to increase. Most women prefer to get the first three years and the membership exam out of the way before they think about interrupting their careers. If they have children before they finish their training it is very difficult to come back. In Britain, they can sometimes manage short breaks because the system runs on six-month appointments. A woman can work for the first six months of a pregnancy and then simply not apply for the next six-month job. Men also occasionally take six months off 'to go trekking in the Himalayas or something', but rarely ask for parental leave. The Australian system runs on twelve-month appointments which provides more stability but also makes it more difficult to take time out.

Women's problems do not end when they pass their membership exams. In Britain and Australia, admission to the club 'is not based on expertise or whether you've got the right marks. They are asking whether they want you as a member of their group. You have to look the part and be prepared to continue to look the part.' Having put it on hold, women often have children as soon as they can after completing their membership examinations and then find themselves unable to get senior registrar or consultant positions. Alison Fiander complained that, despite having gained the MRCOG she was unable to get a job in Wales where the budget for part-time training was limited to one person per year (Fiander, 1991: 60). Another woman had worked for seven years as a resident on a one-in-three call in London when she took time out to have her children. She then worked part-time as a senior registrar and, to compensate for her limited availability, took on the hated Friday night shift until it finally wore her down. Having taken a period of leave, she feared that, despite her experience, she would not reach consultant level.

Australian women in a similar position can work in the private sector though they face similar problems gaining public hospital appointments and admitting rights. In Britain, where the private system is small, it is crucial to get a consultant's post and these are highly competitive. Women who have taken time out, or done some of their training

part-time, feel disadvantaged in a competitive job market. The RCOG
(1987) has claimed that the intake of women at senior house officer level
is adequate but found that nearly a quarter of both men and women who
passed the Part One exam did not attempt the Part Two. Of British
graduates with the Part One, 21 per cent of the men and 60 per cent of
the women were single; of those with the Part Two, only 3 per cent of the
men but 31 per cent of the women were still so. About two-thirds of the
women with the Part Two also felt there had been sex discrimination
against them as against one-third of those with the Part One. This suggests that the hostility to women increases as they move closer to the top.

Dr G.'s experiences of discrimination during her training in the 1970s
echo those of earlier generations. After taking first-class honours and
being top of the year she 'did all the right things', working as the
professorial resident and doing the most challenging medical terms.
That she had managed to have two children while she achieved this is a
fairly clear indication of her ability. Nevertheless, the training place she
wanted was given to a man, and he was kept on despite failing his Part
One three times. By the time he passed it, Dr G. already had her Part
Two, having accepted a position at another hospital. There too she had
problems. The hospital had already offered the job to someone else who
was unable to take it up for several months. Because they needed
someone to start straightaway they offered it to her as well and were
presuming that, because she was a woman with children, she would soon
drop out. When she did not, the hospital was in the embarrassing
situation of having only one job. As a result, she had difficulty logging up
the necessary casework which, she was to claim, prevented her from
passing with the highest honours. Despite this, her academic record was
so outstanding that even the misogynists in the profession could not
ignore it, and were eventually forced to give her a prestigious public
hospital appointment.

Since consultants in Australia spend a higher proportion of their time
on obstetrics, they are also more frequently called out at night. They
cannot leave matters to the midwives or the registrars and consult on the
telephone. Though nurses are scathing about obstetricians who turn up
just as the baby is being born, or sometimes miss the birth entirely, for an
obstetrician delivering 250–300 babies a year this makes for an incredibly
disturbed life. Women with families often find the lifestyle impossible
and drop back into general practice or family planning. The pressure is
enormous.

Take Dr H. for example. I arranged to interview her at 5.30 p.m. but it
was after 7 p.m. when we started. For her it had been one of those
'horrendous' but not unusual days. She looked desperately tired and was
clearly longing to get home to her children. I battled with my own guilt

about keeping her there, but decided it was probably always like this. It had taken a long time to set up the appointment and, as I was to discover, her clients had to wait three months. I asked her to describe her day:

> It began very early with a phone call about one o'clock this morning and repeated phone calls thereafter. I had a patient who had come down from the country with ruptured membranes, who'd been in hospital for many, many weeks, who was now thirty weeks pregnant, who'd gone into labour . . . And then I got a call about 4 a.m. to ask me to come in for the birth . . . So I went in, delivered her baby, and it all went very nicely . . . I was looking forward to going home and doing a few things and having a leisurely breakfast, but her placenta was retained . . . in the end I decided to leave her . . . and went home to see the kids. I had a shower, and was just getting ready when I had a call from labour ward again (laughs) to say that one of my hypertensive patients was not very well, and it was clear she would need an earlier delivery. I made arrangements to go back and do a caesar on her and then I found that the first one's placenta was bleeding and I'd have to come back forthwith. So I left with a very rapid breakfast, the kids still weren't up, and I still haven't seen them. I had a busy day the day before too . . . I had been through similar circumstances.

After completing her hospital rounds Dr H. had seen about thirty-five patients in her consulting rooms and still had a string of telephone messages to return. Her practice is very different from most men's, with a lot of second opinion work and a number of patients with psycho-gynaecological problems.

> You know, someone who comes along with pelvic pain who has already had a laparoscopy. If you go into it there's been sexual abuse at ten, the boyfriend has become violent with her, she's not happy at work and there's a lot of other things going on in her life. That probably is the reason for the pain.

It is difficult to schedule appointments with patients like this, which is why she is frequently running late.

Australian specialists tend to move out of obstetrics by their mid-fifties: 'It used to be quite accepted that you established yourself and did an awful lot of obstetrics and worked like a demon but then, as you began to cut off your obstetrics the patients you had looked after in their youth were coming back for their gynae, and you lasted your patients out in a way.' With the trend towards specialising, this transition to a gynae-cological practice with more regular hours will become more difficult.

In England, more women are moving into the gynaecological specialties but these too require exceptional stamina. Dr J. had initially been reluctant to speak to me because she loathes being labelled a 'woman gynaecologist' and avoids seeing 'the types of women who want to see a woman doctor'. She became a consultant at the remarkably young age of thirty-four and then struggled with fertility problems of her own, with a stillbirth followed by twins. The stillbirth is, she says, the only personal experience on which she draws with patients. As well as being a consultant in a major teaching hospital and having a busy private practice, she has been an examiner for the college and spent six years on the College Council. Dr J. has established a major reputation in her sub-specialty and showed me a cv that listed more than 120 published papers in little more than ten years! She expects no special privileges for being a woman but, like the others, has had direct experience of discrimi-nation. At eighteen she was rejected from Westminster Medical School 'because women were a bad bet, they went off and had children and, since my father wasn't a doctor I could not possibly know what was involved or whether I really wanted to do medicine, and I didn't play rugby so there was no place for me.' Later, when she was looking for a research job, a professor told her informally that he did not think she was worth research money because she was a woman. The culture of the profession is still exclusively masculine: she named three well-known gynaecological travelling clubs which refuse to admit women.

Her days are as frenetic as those of Dr H.:

> We get up at about 5.30 and my husband has breakfast with me and then I leave the house by about 6.30 and go in and see my private patients. Then I do a day's work at Q. and I usually leave there in the evening at about 7.30. I get home at 8.00 or 8.30 and I help to bath the children and put them to bed, so I see them at least. And then I get up and feed them in the night so I don't get much time to do any work in the evening. I make a few phone calls and we have a meal. But we usually go out on a Friday evening together and then all Saturday and all Sunday I devote to the children and my husband and seeing friends.

Her hobbies include sky-diving, scuba-diving, horseriding, water-skiing and bridge. 'So when do you write?', I asked, 'do you do that while you're asleep?' She replied that she stayed late at work one or two evenings a week, and otherwise used on-call time and time away at conferences. She acknowledges that obstetrics and gynaecology is 'not a very sensible career for women' and feels that those who take it have to be unusually tough. If they expect special concessions they will not survive long term in a competitive field. She herself worked right up to the day the twins were born and was back at work ten days later. She complains about the women who treat research as a soft option, a time when they will have their babies, and then give women a bad name by failing to complete their PhD or MD. She does not think the provision of part-time work is any solution but concludes that 'maybe I'm a shark'.

Sexuality

That the relationship between gynaecologist and patient is often represented in sexual terms is not surprising, given that it involves vaginal examination and given that pregnancy is taken to represent desire. The uterus is the basis of origin stories representing the key to the mysteries of life and death. Men, it has been suggested, seek to control women and their bodies in order to overcome death itself. The themes of death, desire, and taboo, and the politics of looking and being looked at, are of great importance in comprehending the gynaecologist/patient relationship.

Our culture has placed great importance on visual knowledge and the 'male gaze'. Voyeurism is regarded as a masculine activity and the feminine equivalent is narcissism, pleasure in being looked at. In feminist cultural studies the speculum has been interpreted as the 'masculine' usurpation of the right to look at everything. The glance through the speculum leads man mistakenly to believe himself confirmed in his priority in the creation and thus as the sole contender for knowledge (Irigaray, 1985: 146). The speculum engages us very directly in sexuality and the politics of the gaze. It serves to legitimate the male medical gaze, the right of medical men to examine the interior of the female body and to know what the female patient herself does not know. Ultrasound imaging, it is argued, takes the speculum a step further and discredits and displaces women's own experience of the progress of the foetus and turns them into passive spectators of their own medically managed pregnancy (Wajcman, 1991: 71).

If masculine power becomes organised around vision and knowledge, then gynaecologists are the ultimate voyeurs and their patients 'ideally' the ultimate narcissists. In the broader culture gynaecologists are represented as seducers and their patients are 'expected' to fall in love with them. The relationship between gynaecologist and patient came to be seen as an intensely heterosexual one. It was thought to work best when it could build on the mutual attraction between a pregnant woman and her doctor who, in some sense, stood in for the husband. This was also a convenient way of shutting women out of the profession and marking the boundary between obstetrics and midwifery as a gender division between men and women.

Male obstetricians needed to counteract the perception that there was something a bit strange about a man fiddling around with women's insides. The sexualisation of the relationship suited them because, given the Freudian preoccupations of the 1950s and 1960s, female rather than male gynaecologists could be represented as weird or deviant. It came to be regarded as more 'natural' for a man than a woman to both see and touch women's bodies. While actual sexual contact was not meant to take place the potential for abuse was clearly there and a number of male gynaecologists did take sexual advantage of their patients. Hospitals have been obliged to bring in a 'chaperone' system, with a nurse present and one women specialist said bluntly that students are now taught to be very aware of the clitoris and 'to make sure they don't spend five minutes massaging it during an examination'.

As Paul Komesaroff (1995) has observed, the distinction between the skilled technician and the embodied subject is a fragile one. The doctor's body might be a focus of erotic enjoyment, a cause of sexual harassment or 'a more subtle presence, which participates in communication and facilitates the therapeutic process'. The conventional rules of physical relationships are suspended, the bounds of privacy are shifted and a stranger is granted access to one's most intimate parts. For many women the gynaecological examination is a highly charged emotional situation which may awaken sexual associations, conscious or subconscious, in both patient and doctor. The woman may feel humiliated if she feels the doctor has taken a superior position while she is exposing her most private parts (Areskog-Wijma, 1987: 68). Gynaecologists must formalise the meeting to make it clear that the gynaecological examination is removed from any sexual meaning. The rules that govern the conduct of the doctor are very strict. Both doctor and patient need to establish some level of familiarity with which they are comfortable and this often seems hard to find.

The only contribution that women gynaecologists have been permitted to make here is the negative one of policing the behaviour of their male colleagues and ensuring that sexuality is driven from the scene. Female obstetricians receive numerous, mostly unofficial, complaints of sexual harassment, usually from women who claim that deliberate sexual stimulation has taken place during a gynaecological examination. But where is the body of the female doctor in these encounters? One of the women commented that men wanted obstetrics and gynaecology more than any of the other specialties because it is so full of magical power. 'I mean, it has the power of fertility, the power of sexuality . . . it is full of glittering power.'

Might not the woman gynaecologist also be attracted to the area because of its magical qualities and its sexuality? For a woman doctor, whether heterosexual or lesbian, to love women's bodies or to want to know them is culturally inexplicable. Sexuality in its broader sense has been contained within a bland 'Mills and Boon' discourse and necessarily placed under strict surveillance because of the atrocious behaviour of a minority of men. It excludes from the situation the touch that seeks to understand and to heal, which 'respects but transcends,

otherness' (Komesaroff, 1995: 4). In particular, it places lesbian gynaecologists in a difficult position because they are located as unnatural, as
bad or worse than marauding men. There are a number of lesbian
gynaecologists, drawn to the area perhaps by desire to work with women,
or perhaps simply reflecting the fact that a high proportion of women
gynaecologists are single or childless. Rather than being able to draw on
their sexuality openly and positively, they are obliged to be circumspect.
Since midwifery is outside the Mills and Boon discourse which has
structured the gynaecologist/patient relationship, and is linked with
'traditional' women's business, it is able to celebrate the power of female
sexuality in a deeper sense which does not get reduced to romance or
perversion.

   Gynaecologists have shown remarkably little interest in sexual problems or in broader issues of sexuality. They are, it is said, concerned 'only
with what comes out, not how it gets there'. It is to be hoped that, as they
increase in numbers, female gynaecologists might contribute something
more than an asexual environment free of sexual harassment and create
a specialty which responds more effectively to the sexual concerns of
its clients.

Winds of change

In 1992 the oldest and most prestigious hospital in Sydney for obstetrics
and gynaecology, King George V, dropped three woman registrars from
its training program, replacing them with men who, the hospital claimed,
were better qualified. Outraged nursing staff went public with the story
and a number of female specialists then spoke out. Gynaecologist Dr
Wendy Cox declared that the specialty was 'an exclusive boys' club' which
acted systematically to exclude women (*Daily Telegraph Mirror*, 1 April
1993). To make matters worse, one of the men appointed had been
accused of several instances of sexually harassing staff, including one of
the woman registrars who was sacked. The President of the RACOG
added fuel to the fire, claiming on national television that sexual
harassment charges were irrelevant to the selection of trainees (*Four
Corners*, 7 June 1993).

   The state government appointed a high profile team to investigate the
selection process. Their report confirmed the claims of discrimination
while the sexual harassment complaints were also later upheld. The
review team found that a male overseas doctor had been appointed to a
fellowship without having even the minimum qualifications for work in
Australia and with no interview or reference checks. Formal advertise-
ment and interview processes had been irrelevant to the hospital's
selection procedures. There were no clear selection criteria and, at a

token fifteen-minute interview, the candidates were asked questions which were of dubious relevance to the job and had potential for considerable gender bias. Following extensive interviews with hospital staff the team documented a strong perception that women did not have equal access to training and development opportunities, that they had to perform at a higher standard than their male peers, and that the atmosphere was unfriendly and at times hostile to women both as doctors and patients. They observed a strong cloning process (specialists seemed to have gone to the same schools, trained at the same overseas hospitals and played the same sports) and suggested that, had the merit principle been properly applied, 'it is likely that a much more diverse set of backgrounds and experience would be present'. Although it was too late to overturn the selection, the report amounted to an indictment of the hospital for failing to bring its selection procedures into line with contemporary standards.

The King George V affair was not the first occasion when the issue of discrimination against women in obstetrics and gynaecology has surfaced. But this time the state health minister affirmed 'it is of the utmost importance to send a clear message to women that we will not stand for them being shut out of our hospitals' (*SMH*, 2 April 1993). The hospital was forced to take the accusations seriously and to take steps to protect the three women registrars and to watch over their progress. Women who had previously been reluctant to speak out now publicly aired their complaints on the ABC's 'Four Corners' program (7 June 1993). They criticised the RACOG for its failure to support women and made it clear that the problem was not only the length of the training program but an old-boy network which effectively excluded women from training and visiting medical officer (VMO) positions. It may not be coincidental that a woman, Heather Monro, was elected the next college president.

Male gynaecologists are now on the defensive. Women consultants are not only more popular but also constitute a financial threat in that they are more willing to work as salaried staff specialists as well as VMOs with private practices. On the 'Four Corners' program Dianne Jacubowitz in Sydney and Jude Searle in Adelaide both accused male colleagues of attempting to veto their appointments to salaried jobs in the hope that the positions would be abandoned. Since the 1970s 'O and G' has been more heavily criticised than any other branch of medicine, under attack from those who say that it performs unnecessary surgery, is too interventionist and has robbed women of control over childbirth.

The claims that it has made childbirth safer have been disputed and the new reproductive technologies are more often portrayed as furthering men's power over women than as offering any genuine gains. The men are further accused of being patronising or misogynist, of being too concerned with making money, and of sexually exploiting patients. The women have endorsed many of these criticisms of their male colleagues. They are vocal in their claims of discrimination and are demanding changes to work practices and behaviours. Given the record of hostility between obstetricians and midwives, it was not insignificant that nurses at King George V gave public support to the registrars for it implies at least the possibility of breaking the deadlock between the two groups and finding more cooperative ways of working.

In Britain too, women gynaecologists have been outspoken in their criticism of the profession. There was outrage when the respected obstetrician and academic Dr Wendy Savage was suspended from her post as consultant to the Tower Hamlets Medical Authority in 1985 on the grounds of alleged incompetence. Savage was accused of having failed, on at least five occasions, to intervene quickly enough in the labour process to prevent infant deaths. Three of these cases concerned breech presentation, while in a fourth the baby was facing towards the abdomen and in the last case the baby was stillborn. Some of the women had previously delivered by Caesarean section and were eager to attempt vaginal delivery. Savage admitted that they were not her five best cases but considered her treatment fell well within the acceptable range and had been motivated by her desire to make decisions in partnership with the women after they had been given the fullest information. As she summed it up

> I have come to understand that it is important for some women to feel that they have tried to deliver a baby vaginally even if, at the end of the trial of labour, they end up having a Caesarean section. Ten years ago I would not have understood that, and would have thought that there was no point in a woman labouring in vain. (Savage, 1986: 37)

Savage had strong support from patients, from the community, from GPs and other health professionals, and even from within the specialty. It was clear that many obstetricians were concerned about the rising level of technological intervention in childbirth and recognised that there was a legitimate debate about when intervention was appropriate. Most disagreed with Savage about where to 'draw the line' but they affirmed her right to clinical autonomy. One said, 'I think you've got to recognise as a doctor that you have a risk threshold over which you will not go. I guess Wendy's is further than most people's . . . but everybody, apart from those who are absolutely authoritarian, takes some level of risk.' Savage was finally exonerated having, in the context of a four and a half month inquiry, succeeded in drawing public attention to the 'gulf between what women were seeking in obstetric care and what the medical profession wanted to provide' (Savage, 1986: 71).

Savage felt that the male medical establishment had been out to get her and that the college ought to have supported her rather than taking a position of neutrality. Ironically, she was elected a Fellow of the College right in the middle of her suspension period (Savage, 1986: 59). Before the inquiry she had already been active in setting up the group WIGO (Women in Gynaecology and Obstetrics) and, having been honoured for her advocacy of patient rights, she would go on to become president of the Medical Women's Federation and an important symbol of the rights of women in medicine.

These two cases, the George V incident in Sydney and the Wendy Savage case in London, bring together two kinds of struggle. The women at King George V were operating within an 'industrial' framework concerned with working conditions and relations. They were at loggerheads with their male colleagues and with the hospital authorities over workplace discrimination. Wendy Savage drew her support directly from the 'women's health' model which mobilises anti-doctor philosophies, emphasising the importance of sharing power with patients, and minimising high-tech intervention. Savage had worked with Professor Peter Huntingford, famous for his efforts to make obstetrics more responsive to women's needs, to provide women with genuine choices, and to encourage midwives to take back their autonomous practice. Her own attempt to practise this kind of medicine brought her into conflict with the medical authorities and drew attention to the male domination of obstetrics. These two approaches are beginning to mesh. The demand for workplace equality combines with demands for a transformation in the practice of obstetrics and gynaecology that draws on ideas from the women's health movement to criticise the practice of a male-dominated profession and to assert that women are generally more responsive to the clientele.

Women gynaecologists are caught between their loyalty to the profession, and partial alliances with feminists, midwives, natural childbirth advocates and women's health activists. This 'between' space, though uncomfortable, has enormous potential for the reshaping of the profession in ways that bring it into line with popular requirements.

As a group, women are thought to combine specialist skills with a more patient-centred and less arrogant approach. Women gynaecologists have become adept at deploying feminist discourses to enhance their cultural capital. In a climate of dissatisfaction and confusion about obstetrics and gynaecology, the demand for women is high and they could easily capture a larger share of the market. Not only do they establish successful busy practices more quickly than the men but they attract a lot of gynaecological work, which is viewed with some jealousy. This, of course, may change if the move to specialise enables men to monopolise surgical obstetrics and gynaecology. In England, a post called 'community gynaecology consultant', with no hospital admitting rights, has been designed especially for women with children. Midwives are also making a comeback, as governments increasingly look to cut costs by using non-obstetrician providers. In 1992 the British Government endorsed the conclusions of the Health Committee that midwives were the group best placed and equipped to provide continuity of care throughout pregnancy and childbirth (DOH, 1992).

The attraction of birth centres is that they make it possible to avoid the highly medicalised practices of the labour ward while providing the security of medical support by their location within the hospital environment. They quite literally occupy a space between home and hospital (Sharpe, 1995). What most people seem to want is a safe back-up system if something does go wrong. This might best be provided by midwives and obstetricians working together, in a more equal and respectful way. As one gynaecologist put it bluntly, 'each side talks so much justifying bullshit. I suppose if you are used to complicated obstetrics and you see the occasional unexpected sudden happening that can be dealt with only in hospital, you would think everyone should be there. It is probably true that most would survive quite well without any medical attention at all.' Said another, 'it is not a fight between doctors and midwives. Midwives would be mad to say they want to take over everything and doctors are mad to want to tell women how to deliver women.'

There are a lot of things working to fragment the obstetrics service, with midwives wanting to take back as many clients as they can and obstetricians being sued up hill and down dale. While some midwives feel threatened by women specialists who are able to appeal to the same discourse of caring, the presence of more female obstetricians also has the potential to create new sets of working relations. In Australia, some women specialists are already working directly with midwives in their practices. The men in contrast, mostly employ them as receptionists and draw on their midwifery skills only in an emergency.

There remains a large gap between the 'feminism' espoused by women obstetricians and gynaecologists and that of women's health activists. Savage's work was not primarily inspired by feminism and many feminists have criticised her ways of working. But doctors have been influenced by women's health critiques and, at the same time, feminist approaches have become more diverse and are less intrinsically hostile to medicine. Women's concerns have moved beyond the provision of part-time work and training positions, which preoccupied an earlier generation, to questions about discrimination and the medical hierarchy, doctor–patient relationships, sexuality, and the inadequacies of male gynaecologists.

There are now signs of substantial realignments of the field. 'The profession has finally accepted that it has got to *do something*, not just to increase the proportion of women entering, but to retain them to reach the top' (Bewley, 1991). The haphazard nature of the training has been roundly criticised, especially in Britain where trainees have to move around the country, changing jobs frequently, relying on references and patronage for successive posts (Allen, 1988). It is no longer acceptable to be treated as a 'junior' until you are thirty-eight or so, 'having learnt by osmosis, with little formal assessment of skills, no curriculum, few trained teachers, no critical forum for debate and challenge and no proper support for the emotional turmoil that the work demands' (Bewley, 1991: 237). Women are calling for a shorter training period that would enable them to be appointed as consultants at around thirty. This could be achieved by well thought out regional rotation, clearly stated objectives, better quality lectures and seminars, including videos and simulators. Men, as well as women, want reasonable workloads and remuneration. Intelligent women do not want second-class posts, such as the associate specialist without status or responsibility.

Women active in WIGO have expressed the hope that they might work collectively for change. This is due to their coming in with a different experience from their predecessors and as a result of the women's movement. The fact that WIGO can bring a hundred women gynae-cologists together in one room is a powerful sign for women who are used to being marginalised among groups of men. As more women come into the profession they are more openly critical and will continue to call for changes. They have the support of many of the men who share the concerns but have felt less able to take the initiative. Women appear to be less concerned with power and income, less likely to stand on ceremony, more willing to work in small, group practices which include midwives and more willing to cooperate with GPs in shared antenatal care. Their criticisms of the training programs are finally being heard and it seems likely that there will be larger numbers of women in the profession in the near future.

4

As a Fish out of Water: Women in Surgery

Social reality exists, so to speak, twice, in things and in minds, in fields and in habitus, inside and outside of agents. And when habitus encounters a social world of which it is the product, it finds itself 'as a fish in water,' it does not feel the weight of the water and takes the world about itself for granted.

(Bourdieu, interview with Wacquant, 1988)

In surgery, women feel the weight of the water lying heavily all around them. Whatever their social backgrounds, they will have difficulty taking as theirs the habitus of the surgeon. Seeking to enter a field whose traditions and values are firmly masculine, they find themselves unwelcome, in an area in which all but the exceptional few are presumed incapable of surviving. Writing in the *Lancet*, a leading surgeon, J. R. Benson, denied that women had been unjustifiably discriminated against in surgery:

We live in a world where a policy of sexual equality, especially at work, prevails. However, in reality the sexes differ not only biologically, but also in less tangible, more subtle ways in respect of psychological make-up . . .

Apart from the long and unpredictable hours of work that inevitably involve sleep deprivation, surgeons also sometimes have to operate (often on long and difficult cases) when very fatigued. In my experience, female house surgeons are not as tolerant of sleep deprivation and more prone to succumb to exhaustion than their male counterparts . . .

Some aspects of surgery – for example, procedures for emergency thoraco-abdominal trauma – demand a certain attitude of mind and level of confidence, with a minimum of diffidence and hesitation and absence of any impression of panic. Such qualities may be to some extent gender dependent in favour of the male psychological constitution. (Benson, 1992: 1361)

69

While his letter provoked a number of angry replies, it is an accurate rendition of the habitus of surgeons, as it has been passed on, adapted and celebrated, over many centuries. Surgeons have taken pride in inhabiting a certain kind of manliness. That they have not, historically, been part of the highest social echelons, has contributed to this habitus, enabling them to incorporate an element of roughness and bravado more commonly associated with tradesmen than with gentlemen. Surgeons are the embodiment of what Bob Connell (1987: 183–6) has described as 'hegemonic masculinity'. This image of them is endlessly reproduced in popular television dramas such as *ER* and *Chicago Hope*. Women have encountered greater problems engaging with this group and a field structured through these values, than they have with the milder-mannered physicians.

The successful surgeon of the early nineteenth century has been described as a 'man of remarkable and unusual qualities' who tackled every type of operation including dentistry and dermatology (Cartwright, 1967: 16). Without anaesthesia, knowledge of germs, or efficient methods of stopping bleeding, his work was hazardous: amputation carried a mortality rate of around 40 per cent (Cartwright, 1967: 13). Given such risks, surgery tended to be regarded as a last resort and the number of operations performed was small. Two hundred a year was a fairly typical load in a large London teaching hospital. Every hospital had its weekly operating day when the surgeons performed in order of seniority. Speed was the most prized attribute and the best surgeons could carry out an amputation in less than a minute. With the advent of anaesthetics, huge operating theatres were built to incorporate viewing galleries and operations were attended not only by medical personnel but by members of the public, to whom the surgeon might lecture before and even during an operation (Cartwright, 1967: 279–85). The habitus of the surgeon required 'a case-hardened insensibility to the signs of acute suffering; only thus could he have retained calm judgment when operating upon the conscious patient'. This was no place for women or weaklings because the resistance of the muscles to pain demanded 'strength above the average' along with 'perfect muscular coordination'. This emphasis on physical and mental strength, authority and decisiveness is at the core of surgical tradition.

In the nineteenth century, surgeons were regarded with a certain amount of dread. There was a revulsion at the realities of surgery and a view that those who could bring themselves to operate under such conditions must, by necessity, be coarse and uncouth (Dally, 1991: 53). The association of surgeons with body snatchers, in the days before the 1832 *Anatomy Act* made the corpses of paupers available for dissection, also gave them a disreputable flavour. After the introduction of anaesthesia and the establishment of a fellowship exam in 1845, their status rose but they were not regarded as gentlemen. Even in the 1890s people were willing to speculate that a mad surgeon was responsible for the Jack the Ripper murders. As Judith Walkowitz tells us, these murders took place between the Aldgate slaughterhouse and the London Hospital and the experts debated 'whether the murders exhibited the skill of a butcher or a "scientific anatomist"' (1992: 199). This association with butchery is something that surgeons feel particularly sensitive about. It conveys incompetence, a botched job, but it also evokes a dimension of sexual sadism as well as reminding them of their trade origins.

The butcher and the surgeon are both working at the boundaries of life and death, bodies and corpses. Culturally these are areas of ambiguity and transition which evoke fascination and horror, and threaten the unity of the subject. Body fluids signify danger to our sense of separate identity for they traverse the inside and outside of the body. Menstrual blood is particularly important because it signifies woman's more permeable boundaries and links her with the borders of death and corporeality, fear and loathing as well as pleasure and desire (Kristeva, 1982: 71). The slightly sinister presence, which the surgeon shares with the butcher, arises from his intimacy with death, flesh and blood. The body on the operating table is unconsciously equated with flesh and death, both of which are associated with the feminine which stands in need of being controlled by the masculine. For women to work either as butchers or surgeons can be interpreted as a threat to the inherited symbolic order (Pringle & Collings, 1993).

Ludmilla Jordanova (1989) has identified an explicitly sexual dimension to surgical power and knowledge, observing that far from being neutral or clinical, medical images of the body have been highly eroticised. Until bodies became more readily available for dissection wax anatomical models, especially of female bodies, were popular in teaching. These 'Venuses', as they were called, lie on silk or velvet cushions in passive, yet sexually inviting poses. Many repeat positions and gestures from well-known works of art; Bernini's statue of Saint Teresa, with its ambiguous mixture of sexual and religious ecstasy, was a favourite. The viewer was intended to respond to the model as to a female body that delighted the sight and invited sexual thoughts. They combined the anatomical and the erotic charge of unclothing by containing removable layers that permitted ever deeper looking into the chest and abdomen. It is certainly possible to speak of shared metaphors at work here, such as penetration and unveiling, which are equally apt in both sexual and intellectual contexts (1989: 110).

These sexualised images of penetration have a particular resonance given that the major new surgical techniques of the second half of the nineteenth century concerned the opening up of the abdomen which had previously been regarded as far too dangerous. It was experimentation with ovariotomy, initially for the removal of large ovarian cysts, that led the way (Dally, 1991: 1–34). The anxiety about women in surgery was partly based on fear of competition, and partly because it overturned the custom that women do not wield knives or shed blood. Dally suggests that it was also to do with the fact that middle-class women were the best patients. Surgeons wanted to keep women firmly on the other side of the knife. 'The whole process involved the challenge of crossing boundaries which inevitably provoked a response in the form of rituals, beliefs and taboos in order to clarify, reinforce and maintain the existing social structure' (Dally, 1991: 67).

Surgery steadily gained prestige because it was the only approach that could decisively cure. Physicians were able to diagnose more accurately but until antibiotics and other drugs came into general usage after World War Two their power to cure was little better than that of a traditional doctor (Shorter, 1985: 92). Surgeons took great risks but they produced results. As their techniques became more complex, their aspirations limitless and the research funds poured in, surgery also became glamorous. Christian Barnard, famous for performing the first heart transplant operation in 1967, epitomised this glamour and sophistication. Though it is quite difficult now for outsiders to get access to operating theatres, they are, through media representations, the most familiar part of medicine. Surgeons are the public performers of medicine.

The difficulties that women have had in entering the surgical field are well known and increasingly well documented (Allen, 1988; Dally, 1991; Dillner, 1991; Parkhouse, 1991). All the doctors in Allen's study identified surgery as the area in which women would do least well. Allen comments that as far as most of them were concerned, 'surgery and women were not thought to be compatible . . . it was thought that only the most dedicated and exceptional woman would find surgery a specialty in which she might reach a senior position' (1988: 59).

I shall not dwell here on the facts of discrimination but reflect instead on the strategies available to address it. The preoccupations so far have been with making available part-time work and training so that women will not be forced to choose between children and a surgical career, with providing better careers advice, support and encouragement during the long training years and, to a limited extent, attempting to reform teaching methods, eliminate bullying and blatant discrimination on selection committees. While some equal opportunity measures have been achieved among the medical specialties, they have had little impact on the surgical specialties. Central to my argument is the fact that equal opportunity measures alone will not be effective until there is a shift in the wider cultural and social meanings of surgery which enables it to be seen as an appropriate field for women. Fortunately surgeons do not exclusively control the social meanings of their profession and there is scope for wider public participation. Surgical techniques are changing rapidly and each new development and its implications is eagerly discussed by the media.

Despite the emphasis on brute strength, a certain androgyny has always been a part of successful surgery. The famous early nineteenth century surgeon Robert Liston was said to have had 'the arms and hands of a Hercules, yet he was renowned for the artistic delicacy of his operating' (Cartwright, 1967: 16). But while it has always been acceptable for men to exercise a feminine, 'creative' side (Battersby, 1989) women have been discouraged from expressing 'masculine' qualities. A 75-year-old retiree commented that women surgeons 'should dress like ladies and behave like gentlemen'. (The trouble, she said, is that there are so few gentlemen around these days.) The current struggles to break into surgery may be seen as an attempt to claim for women an androgynous identity. Sandra Bem's message (Bem, 1974), that it is possible to score highly on both 'masculinity' and 'femininity', may have made it easier for women to appropriate the masculine toughness and decisiveness associated with surgery without becoming 'honorary men'. 'Dressing like ladies' may be a strategy for reassuring the men that their masculine prerogatives are not under threat. It can also be argued that more 'feminine' components of surgery are coming to the fore with the less invasive approaches made possible by endoscopic, laparoscopic and radiological technologies. Whatever practical problems women face in moving into surgery, the time is ripe for a redefinition.

Surgery engages a variety of component skills whose delicacy and intricacy can be interpreted as conventionally 'feminine'. In areas such as neurosurgery the skills required are very diverse:

> It is hard, physical work. The brain and the spinal cord are always enclosed in bone. There is the dichotomy of needing to get through the bone, which requires physical stamina, and then to handle the delicate tissues underneath, which requires a light and delicate touch.

Surgery was frequently described to me in aesthetic terms, and compared with art, sculpture and music:

> The whole thing was almost like a symphony in the sense that you began the operation in a quiet way and you built up to the worrying bit and you eased off at the end. And the whole team knows what is happening.

> Some surgery is a really aesthetic experience. The thyroid surgeons I work with do the most beautiful work – it is almost like a painting.

> If you were a concert pianist would you want to practise three days a week?

While women may feel freer than men to talk in this way it is not exclusive to them. Kevin Murray (1993) has reflected on the role of pleasure and judgment in the surgeon's craft. He quotes a urologist on how beautiful it can be to watch a good surgeon: 'the tissues just seem to fall apart', indicating a dexterity that exceeds what is required merely to get the job done. The grace and lightness of touch referred to here are conventionally regarded as feminine qualities – the question is, do only men have them? The habitus of the surgeon/genius apparently requires a male body in order to make a creative use of 'femininity'. The task for women in surgery is therefore, not only to lay claim to those qualities that have been understood as 'masculine', but to demonstrate that inhabiting a female body need not be a barrier to exercising the 'feminine' qualities that have in the past been associated with male genius. The practical problems begin to look like the easy part!

Women surgeons rarely look like men. Contrary to the old stereotypes, they do not dress in lounge suits or have men's haircuts. What is striking about them as a group is their stylish appearance. The consultants dress more fashionably than any other group of women doctors. Their reputed masculinity is entirely to do with the fact that they share a common set of attitudes with their male colleagues about the nature of their work. They share a common surgical identity with the men but counterbalance this with cultivating a feminine appearance. It is a fine balance; they cannot afford to be too masculine or too feminine. Men do not like it when women are tough and ruthless one minute and fluttering their eyelashes and flirting the next. Such a strategy can backfire.

It could be said that my view is coloured by the fact that I have interviewed twenty-one women consultant surgeons and surgical registrars and fifteen consultant gynaecologists and registrars and only a handful of men in these categories. But it is a powerful experience to meet as a large group those who are normally a tiny minority. Collectively these women show what is possible and construct very different images of surgery from the dominant ones. Eleven of the women were married. Six had children but only three had more than one child. Four were married to doctors. Only three came from families in which at least one parent was a doctor. While most came from middle or upper middle-class backgrounds, five had parents who were skilled manual workers or lower middle class: a much higher proportion than for the sample generally. In addition to the interview data I ventured into the theatres of a Sydney public hospital to familiarise myself with what my subjects were describing and to observe working relationships. I gained access through the nursing staff and went in dressed as a student nurse. My guides were nurse educators and, at times, I experienced quite directly the venom of male surgeons, questioning my presence and demonstrating their total control of the space.

The initial objections to women being allowed entry to medicine were based on the propriety of their presence in anatomy classes; for decades they were isolated from the male students, permitted to dissect only female cadavers and only in single sex groups (Belgrave, 1990; Blake, 1990). This now seems quaintly prudish in the same way that the current concerns that are voiced about whether they are strong enough to do orthopaedics or neurosurgery will doubtless sound ridiculous in another decade or two. Mrs M. recalled the odd male colleague who would say, 'what does a nice girl like you want to do surgery for?', in a very condescending way as if women should be protected from direct contact with blood and guts. Yet all medical students do surgery as part of their undergraduate training: a Bachelor of Surgery is one of their first degrees. Interns are obliged to do at least one surgery term before they can gain their medical registration. It would be misleading to conclude that women have no experience of surgery, for they spend quite a lot of their junior years watching and assisting.

Fragmentation and feminisation

General surgeons, capable of responding to any emergency, are a disappearing species. Although in the UK nearly a third of all surgeons still do a lot of paediatric, vascular and abdominal surgery, the trend everywhere is towards specialisation. Ophthalmology, orthopaedics, ear, nose, and throat (ENT), plastic surgery and urology have separate training programs and vascular and gastro-intestinal surgery are expected to follow. Doctors joke that general surgeons will soon do little more than ingrown toenails and varicose veins.

Using optical fibre technology surgeons have developed tools to look into knee joints and abdomens without the need for large incisions. With precise instrumentation and video technology which produces images directly on screen, they can operate on many organs and parts without even putting their hands inside the body. Endoscopes can be used to operate on joints, hernias, Fallopian tubes, chests and abdomens (they are less effective so far on appendixes). Almost all urinary stone surgery is performed endoscopically. Surgeons talk excitedly about cholecystectomy, the removal of the gall bladder. Where it once took ten days to recover from this operation and patients spoke of the endless pain, the difficulty moving or breathing, the huge cut and scar and the long recovery period, it now involves three days in hospital, two days off work and four very tiny scars. It is safer and faster and has fewer complications than the earlier method. At the same time, as operations become standardised, surgeons fear they are being deskilled. Newcomers barely know how to remove a gall bladder any more, or to do gastrectomies, which used to be routine for ulcers.

These days it is orthopaedic surgeons who are the main bearers of the macho tradition but their techniques and working conditions are also changing. As surgery tends towards the minimal and becomes less invasive, the dividing line between surgeons and physicians also becomes less clear. What exactly is the difference between an 'operation' and a 'procedure'? Colo-rectal surgeons and gastroenterologists, for example, compete for lucrative procedures like colonoscopy which can be easily learned and performed by either. Most patients with inflammatory bowel disease can be managed with drug treatment but a certain proportion need surgery. Physicians tend to believe the surgeons are too quick to operate, while surgeons believe that physicians often treat patients for too long with drugs when surgery would be more appropriate. Given the surgical skills involved in the removal of the colon, they resent the physicians' move into the procedural area and claim they are just as capable of doing the preliminary investigations. Of course much of this is friendly banter between two groups who enjoy articulating their traditional differences and who, for the most part, negotiate perfectly amicably about which of them is more appropriate for any individual patient. But it does have an edge to it, an edge which indicates that the boundaries between medical fields are being redrawn.

Without doubt, surgeons are losing some of their work to other specialties and, in so far as these specialties have a higher proportion of women than the surgical specialties, it is possible to argue that women are moving sideways into surgery, or at least to parts of the field that surgeons have been forced to vacate. Plastic surgeons and dermatologists, for example, find large areas of overlap in the treatment of skin cancers and it may not be accidental that they have among the highest proportions of women in the surgeon and physician specialties respectively (in Australia, 10.8 per cent and 29.9 per cent).

Another important area of overlap is with radiology, a specialty which, in Australia, has 14.4 per cent women. In the past, radiologists performed a handmaiden role, providing diagnoses for surgeons. Increasingly they are able to treat people without recourse to the surgeon. Under the guidance of X-rays and ultrasound, they drain abscesses, take biopsies, inject drugs into obstructed bile ducts, free blocked arteries, inject chemotherapy directly into tumours and treat malformations of arteries in the brain and spinal cord. This has brought dramatic changes to cancer and vascular surgery, since it is possible to find and treat cancers earlier, and often without the need for surgical intervention. There is no need now for vascular surgery in the periphery of the leg. As one surgeon comments, 'we can see the blood flow in the legs. If there is an area of narrowing we can put in a dilator under X-ray control and dilate it.'

Table 4.1 Proportion of women consultants in surgery and related specialties: Australia

	%
General surgery	3.0
Cardio-thoracic surgery	6.3
Neurosurgery	2.9
Orthopaedic surgery	1.2
Paediatric surgery	7.0
Plastic surgery	10.8
Urology	0.7
Vascular surgery	0.2
Otorhinolaryngology (ENT)	3.4
Ophthalmology	11.0
Diagnostic radiology	14.4
Radiation oncology	16.1
Accident and emergency	12.2
Obstetrics and gynaecology	11.4

Source: AIHW (1996). These figures do not include South Australia or Western Australia.

Table 4.2 Proportion of women consultants in surgery and related specialties: England and Wales

	%
General surgery	1.6
Cardio-thoracic surgery	2.8
Otolaryngology (ENT)	4.1
Neurosurgery	1.8
Ophthalmology	12.2
Paediatric surgery	14.8
Plastic surgery	5.4
Traumatic and orthopaedic surgery	1.6
Urology	2.3
Radiology	22.9
Radiotherapy	19.4
Accident and emergency	10.5
Obstetrics and gynaecology	14.9

Source: Wilson and Allen (1994: 75).

Fragmentation within the field, and its shifting boundaries with other fields, open up new possibilities for women, who once had very limited opportunities to succeed as general surgeons. This is not to say that all areas are opening up equally, as tables 4.1 and 4.2 above demonstrate.

The figures are remarkably similar in the two countries both of which now have around three per cent overall of women surgeons.

Women are extremely aware of being channelled into some areas rather than others. While some bitterly resent this, others are finding ways of building careers around it, recognising that for most people, men as well as women, medical careers involve chance and compromise, being in the right place at the right time and being able to take advantage of those opportunities that present themselves. There is a cultural reluctance to let women operate on men while it is acceptable for them to work with women and children. Thus there are only two female urologists in the whole of Australia, but larger numbers of women in breast and paediatric surgery. Plastic surgery is now thought appropriate, doubtless because of its cosmetic associations, as well as the delicacy of its operations. The 'nimble fingers' discourse holds that women will be better at intricate hand surgery than they will dealing with gastrointestinal systems or orthopaedics. Women have also made headway in ophthalmology, where they have been able to take advantage of a shorter training program.

Surgeons have been criticised for their excessive and unnecessary use of procedures. Melvin Konner (1993) has charted the fashions in the removal of appendixes, tonsils, ovaries, gall bladders and in the use of forceps and Caesarean sections, and concludes that far too much surgery is done without any evidence of its effectiveness. In the face of such criticisms, some feminist writers have been able to argue that women will be more discriminating in their use of the knife and more aware of the feelings and anxieties of their patients. A female breast surgeon, for example, will understand the implications of the surgery for her client's sense of herself as a woman. There are powerful equal opportunity concerns here as well as the cultural and symbolic dimensions of what surgeons represent. Getting more women into surgery became an emotive issue in the early 1990s.

Surgical identities

We generally think of surgeons as domineering, confident, decisive, practical people, rugged individualists, doers rather than thinkers. They like to contrast themselves with physicians who they see as tentative, unable to make quick decisions, rarely involved in immediate life and death situations, introverted and intellectual, even effeminate. Hospital inefficiencies, they say, are often the result of management being too much in the hands of physicians and/or bureaucrats. If surgeons ran the show things would be a lot more streamlined. It is a matter of finding the problem and excising it as quickly as possible. Surgeons are prepared to take risks, they are full of bravado, thrive on drama, and are in their element in the operating theatre.

Most women surgeons had no difficulty in claiming an identity within these recognised contours. They are tough, but not incipiently feminist. They tend to support conservative political parties, are hostile to what they describe as 'positive discrimination', and believe that women can make it by themselves, since that is what they did. Their idea of 'equal opportunity' involves being treated in exactly the same way as the men; most consultants have little interest in any radical restructuring.

They share enough of the world views of their male colleagues for the term 'honorary men' to strike some chords. But they do not operate in the same discursive territory as men; their relation to the public and private spheres is different; neither in work, personal or domestic life can they call on the same support systems that men take for granted. Even those who remain single, or choose lesbian relations are not on the same footing as men. There are expectations that they will behave as 'women', that they will respond differently and in particular, will communicate better with patients.

The point therefore is not to draw lines of absolute difference but to suggest that the same characteristics and views are given slightly different meanings depending on whether they are attributed to men or women. Despite my distance from their worlds, I enjoyed their humour and directness, their resilience and, above all, their capacity to bounce back, their refusal to see themselves as victims whatever sacrifices they had made to get where they are. When asked to describe what gave them the most pleasure in their work, several enthused about the joys of wielding the knife:

> I have this theory that the only doctors who don't want to be surgeons have never had a knife in their hand! I really just love operating. It is something you get addicted to. It is wonderful.

> I love major surgery . . . removing a bladder or a kidney. Not to do that stuff would be very difficult.

They clearly enjoyed recounting tales of heroism and crisis:

> Oh I was Sheila Sherlock's can opener. That's what I called myself. She wouldn't have anybody else so I was on call for 15 years day and night. It was a terrible strain . . . It was a liver unit and there were a lot of emergencies . . .

> What I really like is emergency surgery . . . People who come in with some dreadful emergency and you try and work out what is wrong . . . then you open up and find out if you are right and you fix it and you go and see them

tomorrow and they are better. That sort of instant stuff. Yes I have to admit I like that.

One particular week I was up three nights and the fog was so thick I had to walk three or four miles to the hospital and back. That's in the middle of the night and you have got to work the next day, you don't have a day off.

They happily conceded that a surgeon needed to be decisive and to have a very strong sense of being in charge. Like the men, they believed they were dealing with 'perfectly normal' people who had one small thing wrong with them which could be put right. And they liked a quick fix:

I realised I wasn't the sort of doctor who wanted to remember great lots of detail about diseases . . . I was more interested in trying to fix a problem as quickly as I could.

My need was for concrete ways of dealing with things: you've got right iliac fossa pain . . . you do an appendicectomy, or you've got a gangrenous leg, you do an amputation. Maybe it satisfied some deep need inside me to have clear answers to things.

The women did also claim that they brought additional skills to surgery, particularly communication skills. They see themselves as more patient and tolerant, spending more time talking to the patients. Miss P. believes that people get over an operation more quickly if they trust their surgeon and communicate with them:

You have got to realise that surgery is only an incident in returning the patient to their normal health. The actual operation is only an incident. Some surgeons, I think, make the mistake of thinking that's all there is to it. Perhaps the female approach is slightly different.

However, lest one jump to any hasty conclusions she quickly modified this apparent concession to femininity:

I don't mean in an emotional sense because that mustn't be allowed in any way. You mustn't care emotionally whether somebody gets better but you must be able to communicate with them and care a lot in a theoretical way . . .

Patients want to be able to discuss the implications of surgery on their lives and general health and may be drawn towards women because their practice is more likely to be holistic in this broader sense. At the same time, patients spend much less time with their surgeons than with psychiatrists or physicians. A physician laughed that 'what people remember about their surgeon is the scar!' It is usually a one-off relationship, not an ongoing one.

Beyond the solid and unified appearance, surgery is subdividing rapidly. The idea that the best solution is necessarily to chop out the offending body part seems outdated, out of tune with the current move towards less invasive forms of surgery. The image of the surgeon is softening. There is a world of difference between the carpentry of a hip replacement and the exquisite microsurgery involved in restoring an amputated finger. Even orthopaedics has seen a shift of emphasis away from brute force. Weight is not universally recognised as a problem since there are always assistants to help pull the hip out or do heavy lifting. As nurses pointed out, no one expresses concern about their capacity to hold up heavy limbs for long periods. What is most required to see it through a six-hour operation is not so much strength as endurance and tenacity. Women surgeons felt that they had greater stamina than the men in that they often combined the same long, tiring days with care for young children.

Gender and masquerade

As a group, surgeons are extroverts and surgical identities incorporate a great deal of display. If gender is also essentially about performance, the concept of masquerade is a useful one for thinking about the 'gender' of surgery. Bob Connell has discussed the performance of masculinity by various groups of men including young working-class men on the margin of the labour market (1991). In obvious ways they are diametrically opposed to high status women. They lack any of the institutional benefits of patriarchy and are unable to lay any credible or permanent claim to 'hegemonic masculinity'. The masculinities they do construct are fragmented, contradictory and often over-acted. Connell draws on Alfred Adler's notion of the 'masculine protest' to explain how, in response to their powerlessness, they make an exaggerated claim to the potency that our culture attaches to masculinity. In this account masculinity is seen as a social, largely collective, practice and as a masquerade which hides their lack of power.

Masquerade is a term rich in implications, suggesting not only acting and duplicity, but the veiling of something prior and so more 'true'. While it is used more frequently in discussions of femininity I have deliberately introduced it first in relation to masculinity. It could be argued that all versions of masculinity, including the surgeon's, are to some extent masquerades, which may stem from a sense of lack or fragmentation and lay claim to an omnipotence which is impossible for anyone. Precisely because masculinity is performance, there seems no reason why women cannot participate in it. In their case, however, this must be carefully balanced with a performance of femininity.

The psychoanalyst Joan Riviere (1986) used the term masquerade earlier this century to denote the masking that constitutes all womanliness. She saw 'the wish for . . . masculinity' as being at the heart of the masquerade. In her case study, an intellectual woman assumed a feminine disguise after public performances in which she displayed masculine behaviour, in order to remain unthreatening to men. The necessity of 'flirting and coquetting in a more or less veiled manner' was to avoid punishment for effectively castrating the father (substitutes) by rivalling his possession of the penis. This mask always involves acting 'as if' one were a helpless, foolish woman; pretending that one's (masculine) competence and intelligence are merely a game and not the 'real' thing. Women symbolise both the threat of castration for men and the value of the penis, as approximation of the phallus. But there is always the danger they will steal the phallus if they haven't done so already; masquerade, which is supposed to avert that threat, simultaneously evokes it.

While this has a general cultural relevance, it has particular application to a group of women working in an area that not only has a history of male domination but also a profound significance for masculine authority. What struck me in my interviews, especially those with high powered specialists, is a particular usage of femininity which I think is meaningful to talk about in terms of masquerade. It is a manner that makes light of their talents, career struggles and personal sacrifices. Miss C. comments:

> I don't think it ever occurred to me that it was a silly career for a woman . . . I mean, it IS a silly career, because of the years when you're climbing the tree, every six months or every year you're changing jobs, working every other night on call, every other weekend, long hours, irregular life. Unlike men, who can usually get women to wait for them, I don't think most women can get men to wait for them . . .

Discrimination is laughed off: 'There's often people that say to me "Why don't you do hand surgery or something, that's delicate." Well, I mean, it's just not my particular interest.' Her style is light and breezy and feminine. Yet she remains in control of the conversation and I can sense her authority. Describing her work she says laughingly:

> It's a power phenomenon isn't it? I'm the one with the knife. You submit to my power, I with my skill will make you better . . . You come to me a cripple. I do the operation. You walk out of the hospital carrying your bed or whatever it is . . .

Miss C. attributes her own success to the fact that she does not feel good about herself and work makes her feel better. Her older sister had always been regarded as the intelligent one – who would go to Oxford and who later became a barrister. When she became a consultant herself, she remembers her mother saying, '. . . we never expected *you* to be a consultant. We thought you'd just be a GP!' It is hard to imagine a male surgeon talking in this way. At forty, Miss C. has given herself entirely to her work, believes it could not have been combined with children, and is conscious of the sacrifices. A close relationship with her sister and nephews compensates to some extent. She describes her affairs, and her recent marriage, at thirty-eight, to the man upstairs. It would seem she had little time to look further afield and he, at least, had ample opportunity to become acquainted with her work routine. She commented that men 'are very threatened by women in medicine . . . and the way to success is actually to make them feel comfortable'. Miss C. has so effectively defused the aggression of male surgeons that some of her old bosses, 'are now very proud that they have been seen to foster a successful woman'. Unlike some of her colleagues, Miss C. has gone out of her way to encourage more women into surgery.

Social meanings

Nicholas Fox, a social scientist, has focused quite literally on the management of masks in the operating theatre to examine the ways in which surgical power is confirmed in the everyday activities of surgery. His work is based on ethnographic data collected mostly in operating theatres and on ward rounds. His primary informants are anaesthetists and it was as their associate that he gained access to the theatres. Fox (1992) argues that 'surgical authority must be understood not as a once-and-for-all given, but something which is continually negotiated through social strategies in the interactions which go on in the daily surgical enterprise' (p. 6). Surgeons employ discursive strategies to convince other groups – patients, anaesthetists, nurses, managers – of their own criteria of success. While surgery is hardly unique in doing this it has, says Fox, accrued a number of 'rhetorical markers' concerned with unconsciousness, purity, and the breaking of barriers between outside and inside the body. Low status specialties tend to lack such markers (p. 132).

Fox argues that the surgical mask is a rhetorical device which marks out what is being done as legitimate activity, and the right of the wearer to be involved in the enterprise. The aseptic routines of the theatre are technical procedures to guarantee a sterile environment. But they also establish that what is being done is surgery, and not butchery, and mark out certain rights and statuses. Despite the need to wear masks in operating theatres, there are a number of situations where the requirement is dropped. When the theatre does not contain a patient or when surgery on a patient has been completed the masks tend to be dropped although logically they should be retained (p. 24). Even when surgery is in progress, consultant anaesthetists often drink coffee in theatre although no one else is allowed to do so. If the usefulness of the mask were questioned, the authority of the surgeon could be undermined. Consultants, therefore, wear their masks idiosyncratically, in a way that only covers their mouths and not their noses. Student nurses, by contrast, must wear theirs perfectly straight (pp. 24–6).

My own observations confirm that it is possible to identify the hierarchy in the operating theatre by observing how people wear their masks. The sister in charge may use this as an occasion to assert her authority over residents and medical students. A registrar confirms, 'you know you have crossed over to the club when no one tells you how to wear your mask'.

Fox has begun the process of identifying 'rhetorical markers'. He discusses the making of anaesthetic judgments which establish that the patient is 'fit' to undergo surgery. To proceed without such an assessment would, again, be akin to butchery. Finally, he describes the ward rounds through which the surgeons manage their status as healers. They move from one patient to another, accompanied by registrars, sisters and students, with whom they hold court on issues of wound condition, recovery and discharge. Beyond recognising that doctors and nurses may be of either sex, he does not pursue the gender dimensions of this behaviour. In this way he assumes that female surgeons use exactly the same techniques as the men to establish their authority and that these techniques are equally available to them. He can only do this by concentrating on discourses that appear relatively neutral. As a result, he ignores the wider cultural meanings that link surgery specifically with masculinity. While women surgeons obviously share a great deal with their male colleagues, they have additional problems in establishing their authority.

A number of other markers can be identified which have a more specific reference point for gender relations in surgery. These are largely to do with the construction of surgery as an obstacle course. Only those who continue over the final hurdle qualify to join the club. The main hurdles are: passing the Part One, getting accepted into a recognised training program, surviving bullying, completing the Part Two and, finally, being accepted into the club by being appointed to a VMO or consultant's position. Not only women, but most men, stumble at one or other of these hurdles. The 'hegemonic masculinity' of surgeons triumphs not only over women but over those men who have had to settle for something 'less' than a surgical career.

The Part One

The Part One is a formidable three-hour multiple choice exam in basic sciences which any aspiring specialist must pass. Each of the colleges sets such an exam tailored to its own specific requirements. In the case of surgery it is heavily weighted towards anatomy, physiology and bio-chemistry. The Part One has taken on a new significance because it is now required of a candidate before being accepted on an approved training program. This will exclude the kinds of people who have managed to pass only after many attempts. Back in the 1970s Mrs F., having still not passed after three years on the training program, took up the traditional year's lectureship at the anatomy school to give herself time to retake the exam. Now she would probably not even get an unaccredited registrar's job at that stage and people would typically be three or four years older than she was when she finished her training.

Passing the Part One is a major rite of passage. Candidates receive very little help, though most training hospitals run some courses and lectures. A usual strategy would be to try and get a non-accredited surgical roster in such a hospital. The quickest way to get through is to take time off to swot but to take more than four to six weeks implies weakness. People would say, 'oh they had to take a year off to pass. It would go against you.' Registrars generally prepare for the exam while carrying out a gruelling work load: 'Surgeons think you are only worthwhile if you have worked hard and long hours. They hate it when RMOs take the rostered days off introduced into their awards. They think, how can they possibly learn enough surgery if they take rostered days off?' Having a baby might legitimate taking study time, but in the long run makes it more difficult to get an accredited job afterwards.

It is a rare achievement to pass the Part One at first attempt and in the past it was common to fail the exam six or seven times. Most of my sub-jects initiated conversation about how long they had taken. There was no particular shame in taking it several times over (as long as you got it in the end). It was viewed as a matter of book learning, not the essence of what surgery is about. The most successful surgeons are not necessarily the academic achievers. In some circles, passing first time round is viewed with some suspicion, as a sign of bookishness over practical competence. Some of the women had been subjected to scrutiny rather than praise:

> I was a good resident. I got my primary first off . . . it looked as if that was going to be my path . . . but as time went on . . . I was unable to cope with the personal attacks, and I think they were personal attacks.

As a registrar this woman was routinely humiliated by consultants, who had decided that she was no good at operating and told her so,

constantly, over the operating table. While similar abuse was dished out
to the men, there is little doubt that this was a deliberate attempt to keep
women out of surgery. While the men managed to take the abuse in their
stride, perhaps having developed coping strategies during their school
days, she had no emotional resources to deal with it. Having come top all
her life, she was unable to cope with being undermined in this way. While
she may not have been brilliant technically, she was sure she was perfectly
competent. A female colleague, who had to work harder to pass the Part
One said 'I don't think she had been as downtrodden as I had, and so
when it happened it was a bigger shock.' She dropped out a few months
short of becoming a consultant and moved into an entirely different area
of medicine.

Another woman topped the Part One but was refused an interview for
a position on the training program in her own hospital: 'They said, our
surgeons don't believe a woman can do surgery.' She had wanted to be a
general surgeon but changed her mind when she realised that she would
only get work as a breast surgeon: 'While I like my fellow women I did
not want a career of removing breasts because people think it would be
nice to go to a lady doctor.' She contemplated plastic surgery only to be
patronised: a woman wanting to do plastics must be 'artistic'. Eventually
she found the range and challenge that she wanted in paediatrics. But
even here, people are constantly saying to her either: 'Isn't it nice for a
woman to look after babies?' or 'You don't cut up little babies do you!'

Before the Part One can even be attempted, getting started on a
surgical career requires being noticed by the consultants. Miss P. had the
advantage of training during the war years when there were more places
for women. But quite early she was singled out:

> When I was a junior student one of the surgeons . . . said one day on a ward
> round, one day you are going to take your fellowship Miss P. He just picked
> me out and said, you will do it.

Miss P. is one of those exceptionally gifted people who are likely to
succeed under any conditions. But she also put in the work. As an intern
she impressed the consultants with her enthusiasm by turning up for
6 a.m. ward rounds that she was not required to attend. As a result she
was very soon allowed to do simple cases under supervision. After that,

> I did a six months Dip Obs and by that stage I was starting to get positive
> feedback from surgeons . . . And when I got to do the odd appendix I got a
> real buzz from it. Real adrenalin.

She was offered a lectureship in anatomy while preparing for the
primary, moved smoothly through a sequence of registrar positions and

got her fellowship at the age of twenty-eight. At that stage, 'one of my old chiefs rang and said he had a job coming up, did I want to put in for it?'

It is important to have such encouragement to verify that you have the 'natural' ability. But most women have to survive without such feedback. A survey of female medical students at Oxford indicated that the key reason for the lack of women in surgery was the discouragement they received at undergraduate level. Of those women who responded to a questionnaire, 70 per cent had considered a career in surgery and 83 per cent claimed to have been actively discouraged (Clarke, 1992: 994–5). Consultants assume women do not want careers in surgery and do not bother to show them basic techniques. It was a common complaint that women are singled out for blame but rarely for praise. A number of the women had had discouraging experiences with surgeons who would not address them by name but called the men by name. Getting on to first name terms with superiors is an important preliminary to being accepted into the club. While men can do it by playing golf or rugby, and going out for a drink the women have to find other ways. The most successful ones had male supporters and had often been able to appeal to the fatherly or brotherly sentiments of the men with whom they worked. Glamour does not seem to be a plus at this stage, since it can be a cause of suspicion or undesirable attention. Warmth and an ease with men are more helpful in gaining acceptance. Several women spoke of the advantages in this respect of having grown up with brothers.

Bullying and bravado

In many hospitals bullying seems to be a deliberate part of the training, apparently designed to elicit the kind of bravado that is taken as evidence of surgical competence. Orthopaedic surgeons have the reputation of being the biggest bullies and since the specialty is almost entirely made up of men this is directed at male trainees. Bullying often takes the form of expecting registrars to be competent in procedures as a result of having read about them in a book, and perhaps having seen them done once. This makes for a nerve-racking life for the trainee (and one has to wonder how it affects patients) and seems a highly ruthless way to discard those who do not have the necessary confidence and decisiveness. One consultant recalled:

> I had a lot of trouble with one particular surgeon who wrote me a really bad report, who would leave me to operate on things that I did not feel confident to do on my own, would not come and supervise major cases . . . He has also been a problem for some of the guys . . . but apparently he said before I started there that he did not want the woman to be his registrar. If a complication came up he would say, that woman did it.

Fortunately for her, two men on the scheme, who had become 'mates and mentors' stuck up for her and said, 'She did not. She wasn't even there.'

How much a surgeon or surgical registrar chooses to teach their resident varies according to their assessment of how interested that person is and how much talent they have. Female residents get very little, whereas a male resident may be taught to do an appendicectomy at the end of his first or second year. 'While they cannot always keep women out of things that can be learnt from books they can easily keep them out where you have to physically be shown something.' It starts early when, for example, women interns are not taught to tie knots properly. Senior doctors will then become impatient and they will always lag behind and fail to impress the people who could give them a job.

Consultants may systematically ignore women residents. A GP recalled times in theatre when the surgeon and the surgical registrar would be talking about cricket or football. The male registrar was not remotely interested in these subjects but would check the paper so that he could talk to the surgeon about it. She actually was interested but when she tried to participate he made it clear that this was man's talk.

Consultants are in a position to intimidate their registrars by writing poor reports on them. While this is not restricted to women, it can be an easy way of pushing them out:

> I got this terrible report saying I was incompetent, I couldn't operate, I didn't know how to manage trauma, that I couldn't communicate with the nursing staff and the other residents . . . I got called up for an interview and they put me on probation for six months.

It is a characteristic of bullies that they single out their victims and women are easy targets. Some women attempt to deal with it by denial, while others, like the woman quoted above, build supportive relationships around them. Those who risk a confrontation are often not troubled again (but this is a high risk strategy and the stories that get repeated are always the successes rather than the times when someone was fired on the spot). A lot of women are deliberately deferential in the belief that it is the more 'aggressive' (i.e. independent or feminist) women who get bullied. Some go out of their way to distance themselves from feminism, and even build up a repertoire of dirty jokes, to demonstrate that they are part of the crowd. It is not clear that these latter strategies offer much protection since the trainee needs not just neutrality from the consultants but their enthusiastic support.

The women who have been most successful tend also to be the most gregarious and tune in better to support networks. They do not need to be sexy but to make friends with a wide range of their colleagues. This is good for self-esteem and means that bad reports or individual bullying are countered. The ones that come a cropper are more likely to be relative loners, particularly if they are single. To have had good relations with their father seems significant – especially where he has treated them a bit like a boy. Some have working-class backgrounds and parents who care about education. Others have professional, and often medical, backgrounds which seem to reassure the medical hierarchy that they are serious. Those from middle and lower-middle backgrounds seemed the most brittle and least able to cope with bullying and criticism.

Joining the club

Since women are thought to work harder and be less 'cavalier' than the men, they are often welcome at junior levels but are not expected to last the distance. They are seen as a separate breed, 'not part of the club', or there principally to be nice to patients' relatives (Laurance, 1993). If they drop out half-way, it reduces the bottleneck at senior registrar level. But if they continue, they are likely to run into more serious opposition because they are not thought to have the necessary attributes to join 'the club'. The teamwork that is required of surgery is thought to be fostered as much on the sports field and in the locker room as in the operating theatre (Laurance, 1993).

To become a Member or Fellow of the RCS or RACS, one must complete the appropriate number of years in training, have a satisfactory logbook of operative cases and pass the second part examination. In Australia this is an exit exam taken four or five years into accredited training while in England it is usually taken about two years after the Part One. Before even starting this, a candidate is likely to have spent time in non-accredited positions waiting for a vacancy. British trainees may spend five years or more moving between different cities. Australian trainees usually stay in the same city but often have to do some country service. Mrs W. was summoned by her consultant and told that one of the four registrars was to be transferred to a country branch for six months and he had decided that she should be the one to go. She was given a month to prepare and told that if she did not go she would not get an advanced traineeship. Her three male colleagues had been allowed to stay in the city because they had 'domestic responsibilities'. It was the last straw for a marriage already strained to its limit by the demands of her work.

Although the Part Two is regarded as a lesser hurdle, only 10 per cent of those who pass the Part One go on to complete, a drop-out rate that gives some indication of the difficulties encountered in the training years. The Part Two is clinically based, including short answer and essay questions and probing clinical tests and interviews. In order to pass, it is necessary not only to demonstrate one's knowledge but to show that one is capable of leading a team and taking final responsibility. For anyone, this involves a psychic leap. But women have to find ways to communicate authority and confidence in a situation where they are likely to be under particular scrutiny. As one woman commented:

> The orthopaedic surgeons recognise fellow citizens when they see someone sitting in front of them who happens to have been in the first football team and the first cricket team, went to Melbourne Grammar and they think, oh there is a soul mate there. They see you as being, you know, of the right mould to be a good orthopaedic surgeon. Now maybe they are right, maybe that means you have a fairly strong personality and you will be able to make decisions because you really don't want to be wishy-washy about decisions when you are a surgeon. But it is hard for them to put the women in that sort of category. When a woman says she was the captain of hockey they don't get the same sort of feeling that they do with the man who was the captain of the footy. I guess they must have the same problem sitting across from someone who happens to be Vietnamese who wouldn't care a stuff about football.

Becoming a fellow of the college in itself did not guarantee a public hospital appointment. A neurosurgeon recalled that in the 1970s:

> The last jump to consultant was quite emotional and tough in terms of just gritting your teeth and saying, I'm going to stick in there and apply for every job and take it through to the end. I applied for an enormous number . . . It was difficult to keep one's morale going.

While waiting for a consultant's position, people often work as clinical superintendents and press on with further research. Publications are increasingly important in the competition for jobs. In Australia it is technically possible to set up in private practice but it would be unwise to do so until one also had operating and admission rights at a public hospital. Indeed, it would be seen as poaching. In this way senior surgeons retain very considerable power to determine where a new fellow will be allowed to practise and even if they will be allowed to practise at all. It is not unusual for women to be relegated to the least prestigious hospitals.

Beyond the breast

Miss P. was discussed earlier as a high flier who had a very smooth path into surgery and wanted to become a general surgeon. With such early recognition of talent and the support of his consultants, a man would have taken it for granted that the future was his. In Miss P.'s case a number of people tried to talk her out of her choice, suggesting that she think about gynaecology or eyes. She decided quietly that 'it may be difficult but I will have a go until I can't get a job and then I will switch courses . . . I may as well have a go for something I want'. Even then, she included breast surgery in her areas of expertise because she thought it was 'sensible for a woman'.

Though breasts are not regarded as particularly interesting or challenging surgically, this is the main area into which women surgeons are moving, some reluctantly, some willingly. No less than three of my subjects had taken time out, at senior registrar level, to do research in this area in preparation for their future careers. Mrs M., however, was not so keen. She spent five years as a senior registrar in biliary surgery but when she set up in private practice she was sent only haemorrhoids and breast problems. She built up a reputation in the latter because she became interested, and because she has to make a living, but she resents the fact that she gets no other work. Ninety per cent of her current patients are female and 80 per cent are sent by female GPs.

All women who go into surgery have to negotiate the pressures and the expectations that they will specialise in breast surgery. A registrar training to be an endocrine surgeon took the risk that she would 'not get many thyroids and I'll get a lot of breasts'. A colo-rectal surgeon recalls:

> There was very much pressure on me to do breasts. But I don't like breast surgery and don't think that I'd do it particularly well.

If women are not channelled into breasts, they are directed to other areas that are regarded as suitable. In Australia, where public hospital work is combined with private practice, this is linked to the problem of getting referrals:

> When you tell people you want to do surgery, they say, do you want to do ophthalmology? And when you say you want to do urology, they say, oh are you really interested in paediatric urology? An anaesthetist said to me, you will starve, who is going to go to you?

Ophthalmology has a higher proportion of women than any other surgical specialty. Until the 1970s it was a quiet backwater in which nobody took much interest and much of the specialist's time was spent in darkened rooms examining eyes and testing vision. Because of its low prestige there was not much competition for places and it was relatively accessible to women. It provided a broad spectrum of patients, a lifestyle that was seen to be compatible with having a family, predictable hours and relatively little night work. Though their training is entirely separate from other surgical programs, ophthalmologists are members of the surgical college as well as their own, and they identify as surgeons. But there is more overlap with physicians' training than in most other surgical specialties, and those working in areas such as paediatric ophthalmology might be doing very little surgery at all.

Mrs F. confessed that she had intended to study medicine but opted for ophthalmology to avoid a clash with her boyfriend. They broke up and she was stuck with ophthalmology. It turned out to be the right choice because it was 'something you could do for two hours a week or a hundred hours a week' and you did not have to be there all the time. All of this was said in frivolous tones reminiscent of Miss C. the orthopaedic surgeon. But Mrs F. is a serious person extremely committed to her work. What she enjoys most about it is its dramatic results:

> I've done thousands of cataract operations but I still get a joy like it's the first one every time someone comes back and says, 'It's terrific, I can see again. All the colours are bright and I didn't realise my husband had so many wrinkles!'

Mrs F. had thought long and hard about how to structure her practice into what for her was a balanced and satisfying life. She believes most men have a different mentality. All they can think of is how to scramble for the most prestigious specialties and try to get to the top of the ladder. Women have broader concerns and in some cases have set up group practices which enable them to cover for each other.

What changed ophthalmology from its backwater status was the arrival of the intra-ocular implant. Previously, people were given big, thick glasses which distorted their vision and made it hard for them to walk around. Now an implant replaces the lens in the glasses and each eye can be treated separately. The implants are getting smaller and smaller. They needed a 6 mm incision but this has been reduced to 2 or 3 mm with the introduction of foldable implants. In addition, lasers are now being used to correct short-sightedness and astigmatism. Glasses could become obsolete, as more problems are able to be corrected surgically. But this is highly delicate work in which there is no room for error.

Ophthalmology has now become highly competitive. In Australia, even those who have the Part One may have to wait two years for a training program and the length of training has been increased from three to four years. There is a tendency to sub-specialise and, though it is not formally stated, people are expected to get some overseas training. In Australia, 32.5 per cent of the workforce is aged over sixty, making it urgent that the number of trainees be increased. The numbers entering training programs in any one year are so small that it is difficult to gauge trends. In Mrs F.'s year, six out of seven trainees were women, but in the years on either side of her there were never more than one or two. In

1995 there were only five female registrars, representing 6 per cent of trainees (AMWAC, 1996: 21). It remains to be seen whether women will retain their current toehold.

The other area with a growing proportion of women is plastic surgery:

> I realised general surgery was becoming a bit dead. And I didn't really want to be a surgeon that was going to be doing varicose veins and haemorrhoids and toe nails for the rest of my life, so I decided that specialising would be a good idea and plastic surgery was really the only thing I wanted to do.

Plastic surgery also has a high proportion of women patients. It is an expanding field which is creative, has variety, and is visually very satisfying. The hours are generally more predictable than general surgery since it does not usually involve dealing with life and death situations or a lot of night work.

> Plastic surgery is definitely more friendly to women. When I was first scouting around, I had much more positive encouragement from plastic surgeons than I did from other surgeons. Maybe they are a slightly less aggressive lot because surgeons in general are very aggressive, very dominating people, there is no doubt about that. Plastic surgeons may be a bit more lateral thinking.

But it does not suit everyone. Another woman who had changed her mind after a term:

> You see the very socially deprived in acts of self-destruction come into cas in the middle of the night with slashed faces and tendons. And you think, crikey, this is plastic surgery. I felt a bit disillusioned by that . . . and I started down the path of general surgery.

Very few women venture into the 'masculine' specialties of urology and orthopaedics, but some have been drawn to these areas despite the difficulties:

> Urology is an incredibly high-tech specialty which I think alienates some women . . . I'm not a high-tech person by nature . . . but I evolved that way. I think that's maybe the difference that has enabled me to break new ground. Some women have said to me they cannot stand tubes . . . If you are doing things that simulate dressmaking people feel comfortable – and that is what plastic surgery is all about. Whereas we do a lot of endoscopic surgery . . . we use these very fine two to three millimetre telescopes that go up the ureter and we use a laser fibre to break the stones.

This woman also claimed to bring a feminine touch to the area, priding herself on her ability to examine people well and to put them at ease.

Several in the group had been attracted to orthopaedics but been discouraged. The few who stayed were not obviously bigger or stronger than their colleagues and neither had they had it as their lifelong ambition. Miss K. was devastated when she was rejected for plastics training and only very reluctantly applied to do orthopaedics. The law of surgery appears to be that people rarely end up with their first choice.

Part-time surgery

Both the British and Australian governments have become concerned to get more women into surgery. In Australia, the 1994 Baume Report criticised the absence of women from surgery on both equity and efficiency grounds:

> It is neither sufficient nor credible for those in charge of surgical training to claim that the figure represents simply limited applications from women. While some surgical training programs were making efforts to improve the proportion of women, these had not been universal or far-reaching enough. (1994: 104)

Perhaps in response to this, two out of three new urology posts in Victoria were allocated to women in 1995, an increase of from nought to five over five years.

The British are worried about demographic factors, the danger that there will not be enough surgeons in a decade's time and the need to draw on the whole available pool. In 1991 the Thatcher Government put one and a half million pounds into the Women in Surgical Training Scheme (WIST) to identify women training in surgical specialties and to provide them with counselling, support and encouragement. The scheme was run collaboratively by the college and the Department of Health with the involvement of Health Authorities, practising consultants and Postgraduate Deans and was designed to accelerate the rate of increase in the numbers of women consultants from 9.7 per cent per annum in 1991 to 15 per cent per annum by 1994.

These moves are undercut by other factors that make it more difficult for women. In the UK, there has been an attempt to shift the bottleneck from senior registrar down to registrar, by reducing the number of training grades from three to two (basic and higher specialist trainees). While this makes the future safer for those already in a training program, it makes entry more difficult, because it puts greater emphasis on qualifications. The trend to sub-specialisation adds to the competition and lengthens the training period. The sacrifices that have to be made, by men or women, to follow a surgical career remain enormous.

At the same time, surgeons are deeply resistant to part-time work, fearing a decline in quality and standards. In Australia, 80.4 per cent of female consultants worked full-time, compared with 58.9 per cent in internal medicine (AIHW, 1996). Long hours and total immersion in the work are central to the surgical aura. Most women surgeons, like the men, adhere rigidly to the belief that the training period cannot be shortened. In their view, this makes part-time training impractical because candidates will not reach consultant status till they are about forty-five. They are suspicious of anything that smacks of positive discrimination and they tend to pour cold water on suggestions for change: job-sharing is fine but what happens if one half of the share gets promoted? If you prepare the patient for the operation and someone else does it, how can you look after them without knowing exactly what happened? And what happens if you are at home, your child is ill and your patient has a complication?

Operating can be difficult work when you are pregnant. Miss H. volunteered that her performance dropped 30 per cent. She said her memory for detail went and that from the twentieth week on she had back problems from bending over the table. Nevertheless she went on until thirty-six weeks. Because they work on short contracts, doctors in training tend to miss out on maternity leave. One Melbourne woman had attempted to renegotiate her contract to include maternity leave only to be told by the hospital that they were negotiating with the AMA to make a group contract and if she did not like that she could resign. In the end she was forced to take leave without pay.

We tend to think that part-time inevitably means half-time when all that is required to make life manageable might be a three and a half or four-day week. A number of male surgeons already work four-day weeks. But most surgeons are in solo practice and the egos in surgery make such things difficult to organise: 'Patients come to see you because you are you, they don't come to see the practice.' Miss K. calculated that she could work part-time by confining her practice to ano-rectal surgery without any major operating, or she could just do colonoscopy and ano-rectal surgery. But if she did, she would be perceived as a lesser variety of surgeon. In any case, she would find it hard to diagnose a cancer and then send her patient elsewhere for an operation. There is no reason why women should not reduce their case load as long as they can provide continuity of care. Miss J., for example, bought into a practice which generated enough extra work for a part-time person. It suits her with a small baby. She works three and a half days a week and does her rounds every day, often taking the baby with her.

In Britain, with little private practice, one might expect these arrangements would be easier. In the past there were a lot of part-time positions. While these were originally designed to enable people to work in two or more hospitals there seems no reason in principle why someone could not choose to work in one position only. It has been demonstrated that the work can be structured in this way when it is in the interests of male surgeons to do so.

The other issue that needs to be resolved is training. Dillner (1991) has argued that part-time training, over twice the length of time, is not the solution for either sex. The answer must be to reorganise it around the development of particular competencies. Training should be geographically secure, the hours should continue to be reduced, and it should be possible to complete it in a defined time. Surgeons resist this because they believe that it is necessary to be permanently on call in order to understand the course of an illness and to see enough variety. They make no distinction between work and teaching. For them training actually involves doing all the work, with minimal formal teaching. But it is hard to see why registrars, carefully guided, could not learn adequately in a standard forty-hour week. It would take a certain amount of will and imagination and, of course, an increase in medical staff and hence hospital funding. But it would, finally, make a career in surgery compatible leading with a 'normal' life.

Along with workplace restructuring, it is important to open up surgery to new meanings and representations. By reinventing surgery as a 'feminine' or 'androgynous' occupation, it becomes possible for the woman surgeon to experience herself as 'a fish in water' and to swim comfortably, even against the tide. With fundamental changes in the content of the work, a different kind of habitus is coming into being, and it is one that women can appropriately occupy.

5

Inside Medicine: The Physician Specialties

Women have established a stronger presence in internal medicine and related fields than they have in the surgical ones. As a result, it is tempting to emphasise the contrast between the two, to assume that the problems lie only with surgery and that the physician specialties have their act together. But the contrast can be overdrawn. Fifteen per cent of specialists (the proportions are very similar in Australia and the UK) is still little more than a foothold and, while there is a much higher proportion of women among paediatricians, dermatologists and pathologists, their numbers in the large and prestigious specialties like cardiology barely exceed those in surgery. While the physician specialties appear more open to women, and physicians now come from more varied social backgrounds than surgeons, this is a highly patrician culture. Given the intellectual hegemony of internal medicine, it is here that the achievements of medical women will ultimately be judged.

In the United States, 'physician' is merely another word for medical practitioner. In Australia and the UK, by contrast, it refers to an elite, for whom intellectual superiority is conflated with upper-class status and privilege. Historically, physicians have seen themselves as a cut above surgeons, the intellectuals as opposed to the technicians of medicine, and contrasted their own gentlemanly status with the trade origins of surgeons. Physician culture has been shaped since medieval times by the Royal College of Physicians, whose charter explicitly excluded women and required that members (unlike members of the Royal College of Surgeons) must be university graduates (Elston, 1980: 102). Family and class connections carry a lot of weight in this hierarchical world, and the old-boy network is as strong here as it is in surgery (Allen, 1988). Unlike the United States, where the separate specialties are managed by autonomous boards, internal medicine remains under control of the RCP and its Australasian counterpart, the RACP (which received its own royal charter in 1938). The colleges articulate the political interests of the profession, patrol its boundaries, establish standards of practice and behaviour, and determine what kind of person will be permitted to enter its fold and on what terms. Many women specialists described them as 'stuffy' organisations which are resistant to change and need to do a lot more to overcome discrimination, through facilitating part-time work and training schemes, and the monitoring of syllabus, examination and interview processes.

To recall Bourdieu's description, a field is a network of relations 'between positions objectively defined, in their existence and in the determinations they impose upon their occupants . . . by their present and potential situation in the structure of the distribution of species of power (or capital) whose possession commands access to the specific profits that are at stake'. It is also a *field of struggles* aimed at preserving or transforming the configuration of these forces' (Wacquant, 1988: 39–40). His account applies well to the field of internal medicine, where, it may be argued, power and prestige are maintained through forms of symbolic violence, 'gentle, invisible . . . unrecognised as such, chosen as much as undergone, that of trust, obligation, personal loyalty, hospitality, gifts, debts, piety . . .' (Bourdieu, 1990: 127).

Power operates subtly here: through the unspoken gradation of teaching hospitals and positions within them, in the linking of training positions with patronage, in the acknowledgment or denial that takes place in classrooms and on ward rounds, and in the idiosyncrasies of the examination process. Those who already 'have' the habitus do not need consciously to aim for mastery, for they will spontaneously reproduce the structures of domination. In so far as habitus involves the incorporation of a shared history, the practices it generates are mutually intelligible and produce a common sense world 'whose immediate self-evidence is accompanied by the objectivity provided by the consensus on the meaning of practices and the world' (Bourdieu, 1990: 58). Those from privileged backgrounds have only to 'let their habitus follow its natural bent in order to comply with the immanent necessity of the field and satisfy the demands contained within it'. On the other hand, those 'least endowed with capital, who are often also the newcomers and hence the youngest, are inclined towards subversion strategies, the strategies of heresy' (Bourdieu, 1993a: 73–6). They will have a greater need to interrupt the flows of power and redirect them towards a redefinition of the meanings of medical work and the ways in which it is organised.

Given Bourdieu's emphasis on embodied cultural capital as 'long-lasting dispositions of mind and body', and on the lasting importance of early social and family experiences in constituting the habitus, it is curious that he overlooks gender as a crucial element in the constitution of capital. In her 1992 essay in *Theory and Society* Lesley McCall extends Bourdieu's reading to suggest that, put another way, certain types of disposition are themselves forms of capital (McCall, 1992: 843). Women, she argues, 'carry with them the trait of femaleness by the existence of the perceived female biological body'. Gender identity is a deeply rooted and bodily anchored dimension of the habitus which affects the individual in the most 'natural' parts of his or her identity. When a woman works in a masculine setting she is quickly alerted to the 'non-complicity of her disposition with her environment' and 'her self consciousness arises from the internalization of the masculine/feminine opposition: both sides reflect the reality of her experience' (McCall, 1992: 850). She may take up a position as an exception or work to shift the prevailing gender associations.

McCall describes the dilemmas of woman physicians and scientists, who rarely make a single choice, 'but rather a succession of choices, involving a whole series of practical decisions, consciously or unconsciously made'. In this process, they 'internalize the cultural contradictions of gender in a constant, ongoing process of mediating opposing cultural demands' (McCall, 1992: 849, quoting Elizabeth Free). Women physicians do not simply lack the habitus but encounter, in varying degrees, a sense of misfit between their habitus and their working environment. Not only must they resolve conflicts between the demands of work and family, but they also have to make adjustments to their sense of self as women to feel comfortable in both environments.

Where the habitus of the surgeon expresses the toughness and physical resilience of the male body, demonstrating its supremacy through bravado and rugby playing, the habitus of the physician is more cerebral: possession of traditional masculine prowess is less critical to success in a field which celebrates intellectual mastery and ranks its specialty areas according to their perceived degree of difficulty. The most prestigious specialties, like neurology and cardiology are regarded as the most difficult and habitually draw people from upper middle class, and especially medical, backgrounds. New areas, such as geriatrics and rehabilitation medicine, are not only regarded as 'easier' but contain higher proportions both of women and people from working-class backgrounds. There is a different articulation of masculinity here which, since it is detached from the body, does not draw attention directly to its gender. It expresses itself, for example, in its preoccupation with 'excellence', and extraction of a level of vocational commitment which backgrounds personal life. While women are not excluded from this field, their enactment of 'excellence' requires that they act as if they share the same social location as men. Since women typically have different social obligations, they work at developing knowledges and strategies that will enable them to deal with the contradictions of their situation.

Agnes Miles has identified three factors that affect women's specialist career choices in internal medicine (1991: 144–8). These are:

1 women's greater acceptance in specialties which appear to value aptitudes stereotyped as natural attributes of women such as interpersonal skills, sensitivity and patience;
2 the attraction of specialties in which the conflict between family commitment and work responsibilities can be minimised;
3 lesser competition in specialties which carry lower pay and prestige and hence where the chances of entry seem better.

The 'factor' approach provides a useful starting point for understanding why women are spread so unevenly across the specialties. But by itself it offers a rationalisation for why women are where they are rather than an explanation of how they got there. It is both mechanistic and static. It leaves little place for individual agency, improvisation or tactical manoeuvring and does not get near the lines of force, the tensions and points of collision that Foucault (1980) describes so vividly in the hospital context. It is important to highlight the dynamic dimension of the field in order to pinpoint the ways in which specialties may be reshaped or their working conditions modified and the speed with which status may change, or a labour shortage be turned into a situation of oversupply. The diversity of internal medicine has also enabled women to occupy and shape new spaces.

Individuals are never merely the bearers of structures but strategists who act in a way that is structured but not fully determined by the level of cultural capital they can muster, by their own personal trajectories and their ability to play the game of social interaction. The outcome for any individual is the result of an interplay between their habitus and their place in a field of positions as defined by the distribution of particular forms of capital. Since the field 'presupposes, and generates by its very functioning, the belief in the value of the stakes it offers' (Wacquant, 1988: 39), women are never motivated purely by convenience, or by the need to reconcile work and family life. Unaware of all possibilities that may be open to them they, like the men, nonetheless seek to maximise their cultural capital given their relational position within the field. The habitus that they bring, which is 'structuring' as well as 'structured' may, over time, transform the field.

This chapter, therefore, is concerned with the strategies that women have taken up as relative newcomers in a world where class, race and gender privilege hide behind everyday commonsense. It is based on a sample of forty-three registrars and consultants, and includes thirteen paediatricians (reflecting the high proportion of women specialists in this area), fourteen 'adult' physicians, ten public health specialists, four dermatologists and four pathologists. They ranged in age from mid-thirties to early sixties and their experience spanned the whole period of expansion since World War Two. The issue of how to combine work with family dominated these interviews to a greater extent than the interviews with any other group. Twenty-nine of the women had children, one was pregnant for the first time, and several others were married or planning marriage. But their career strategies are both more complex and less deliberate than 'balancing career and family' might suggest. Drawing on life history interviews the chapter explores not only the resistances that women have faced in internal medicine but the pockets of opportunity they have opened up, and the part that women themselves have played in reshaping the public images of these specialties, as well as their practices and priorities.

Marking out the field

In the early part of this century, Osler defined internal medicine as 'the wide field of medical practice which remains after the separation of surgery, midwifery and gynaecology' (Benson, 1988: 1). Until fifty years ago it remained possible for a generalist to practise right across the field. Haematology, pathology, neurology and psychiatry had established themselves as separate specialties in the nineteenth century, while venereology and dermatology split off from general medicine in the early twentieth. Paediatrics and cardiology were built up in the inter-war years and the latter went on to develop a reputation as the most esoteric of the high-tech specialties. But the general physician reigned supreme and the numbers of 'super' specialists remained small. In 1950, for example, only a handful of physicians practised neurology exclusively though a number combined it with psychiatry. Physicians were a small group compared with general practitioners, and it was not unusual for men to commence specialist training after years in general practice. The growth of scientific knowledge improved their diagnostic powers but provided no more treatments beyond what was available from GPs. There were no drugs to control high blood pressure and patients with hypertension were put in darkened rooms and given rice and water. Before diuretics became available cardiac patients were very difficult to treat and older physicians can remember physically removing fluid from the thoracic cavity. Anti-biotics were in their infancy and one day's treatment of penicillin cost ten times the weekly basic wage.

Internal medicine has changed beyond recognition. General physicians are a disappearing species (although they still have a stronghold in parts of Britain and in some Australian regional cities, such as Brisbane). Where the medical field was once divided between the physicians and the surgeons there is now a large number of separate specialties. The specialties have their own organisations and some, like the pathologists, dermatologists, psychiatrists and anaesthetists established their own colleges and training programs. The RCP and RACP still act as umbrella organisations for the specialties, insisting on the importance of a broad general knowledge as the basis for specialist practice.

There are currently about twenty specialties within internal medicine, of which general medicine is but one. All are further divided into sub-specialties. Paediatrics, while remaining closely associated with adult medicine, contains a further four specialties and is rapidly developing others. The specialties have largely formed around particular organs, technologies and diseases (Rosen, 1944). Cardiology was built on electro-cardiograms and later angiograms and ultrasound. Gastroenterology was made possible by the development of gastroscopes and colonoscopes. Haematology, in its modern form, is associated with blood transfusions, marrow aspiration and treatments for leukaemia. The development of chemical and biological methods of measuring hormones and then the discovery and application of radio-immunoassay, transformed endocrin-ology. Renal medicine grew out of the key diagnostic tools of renal biopsy and the therapeutic potential of renal dialysis. Thoracic medicine became a specialty when the bronchoscope enabled doctors to put tubes into the lungs and, using endoscopic techniques, take out small pieces of tissue for culturing in the laboratory. Intensive care, pain management and palliative care have developed out of advances in anaesthesia. Neur-ology was transformed by CAT scanning, nuclear magnetic resonance and nerve conduction velocity studies.

Not all the specialties are organised in this way. Oncologists claim to deal with the whole patient and use a variety of methods including chemotherapy, local radiotherapy and implants. Geriatrics and rehabili-tation medicine came into existence more because of changes in public policy than the arrival of specific technologies. Geriatrics is concerned not only with the process of ageing but with the special organisation necessary to care for the complex of disabilities arising. As Dr Marjorie Warren demonstrated in the 1940s unnecessary dependency can be avoided by applying relatively simple techniques of rehabilitation. In Britain, regionally based geriatric services evolved with the NHS while, in Australia, geriatric medicine had to wait until 1976 to be included in the list of specialties.

The status and financial rewards associated with particular specialties can fluctuate quite markedly, as can the availability of jobs. Neurology, traditionally the most difficult and prestigious branch of medicine, has suffered some decline, because the new diagnostic techniques were not matched by effective treatments. Despite the range of anticonvulsant drugs available, epilepsy remains a problem, and there is little to be done for dementias or strokes (although this is changing with the development of anticoagulants). Dermatology and psychiatry, which were quiet backwaters, grew in prestige when new treatments developed. Dermatology, once the Cinderella of the specialties, was transformed by the discovery of cortisone-based creams which effectively treated eczema, psoriasis, dermatitis and skin rashes, and by Roaccutane which provides a magic bullet for acne. Rheumatology has grown very fast because there is an ageing population, and strong patient demand for referrals. It now has diagnostic tests for rheumatoid arthritis and lupus, but the effective treatments have so far been in joint replacement, which is in the hands of the surgeons. The physician can offer little more than a GP but this could easily change. Geriatrics and rehabilitation medicine, both female strongholds, may grow in status as their public importance receives greater acknowledgment with an ageing population. (Or if growth hormones, currently being trialled, actually take off as a treatment for the problems associated with ageing.)

Medicine should be seen as a 'magnetic' field whose elements are constantly rearranging themselves as new specialties emerge and old ones are realigned. Existing specialties may well disappear if the technologies on which they are based become outdated. Chemotherapy, for example, would disappear overnight if alternative treatments for cancer became available. The numbers of women consultants in internal medicine and related fields in Australia and England and Wales are shown in Tables 5.1 and 5.2 overleaf.

Women in internal medicine

While internal medicine has become highly specialised, it represents itself, in contrast to surgery, as holistic. For example, much time is spent in long consultations with patients who often have a number of problems simultaneously. If this might be said to privilege supposedly feminine qualities, women are spread unevenly across the specialties in a way that could suggest that they have been systematically allocated to the ones with lower status. In reality, the situation is more complex than this, and I will argue that the existence of diversity has not merely locked women into more marginal positions but created choices and opportunities. Ironically, it was as medicine became *less* holistic and more specialised that women were able to colonise at least some parts of it.

Dermatology has a higher proportion of women than any other specialty. It is also the only one in which all three of Miles' factors

Table 5.1 Proportion of women consultants in
internal medicine and related fields: Australia

	%
Cardiology	7.4
Clinical haematology	18.1
Clinical immunology	11.3
Clinical pharmacology	12.5
Endocrinology	16.8
Gastroenterology	5.9
General medicine	10.7
Geriatrics	19.6
Infectious diseases	18.4
Medical oncology	14.6
Neurology	9.1
Nuclear medicine	8.5
Paediatric medicine	18.6
Renal medicine	17.3
Rheumatology	18.9
Thoracic medicine	10.2
Pathólogy	22.3
Anaesthesia	18.3
Dermatology	29.9
Psychiatry	25.1
Public health medicine	18.5
Rehabilitation medicine	17.5

Source: AIHW (1996). *Medical Labour Force Survey
1994* Canberra: AIHW National Health Labour
Force series no. 6. These figures do not include
South Australia or Western Australia.

operate. It can be represented as 'feminine' through its association with
cosmetics and appearance (although this is to play down its surgical
dimensions); it involves very little after hours or crisis work; and it was for
a long time a backwater. While it overlaps substantially with physicians'
training, in both countries it has its own college, and places less emphasis
on acquiring a broad-based knowledge before specialist training begins.
It is still possible to complete the training program in a shorter space of
time than most other specialties. It makes sense as a career choice for
women with domestic responsibilities, but it is not a large employer.
Though the volume of work is increasing rapidly as the incidence of skin
cancer rises (especially in Australia), no city has more than half a dozen
training positions at any one time and competition from men is
increasing. There are only about 300 consultants in the whole of the UK
and forty approved training positions.

Table 5.2 Proportion of women consultants in
internal medicine and related fields: England
and Wales

	%
Cardiology	4.5
Clinical pharmacology	4.7
Clinical immunology	20.0
Endocrinology	5.2
General medicine	11.9
Genito-urinary	21.7
Geriatric	13.7
Medical oncology	14.6
Nephrology	3.9
Neurology	3.5
Nuclear medicine	28.6
Paediatrics	29.3
Palliative	21.1
Rheumatology	14.7
Thoracic	8.1
Anaesthetics	21.5
Dermatology	22.4
Histopathology	26.5
Rehabilitation medicine	19.0
Psychiatry (mental illess)	24.2
Child and adolescent psychiatry	40.1

Source: Wilson and Allen (1994). Medical and
dental staffing prospects in the NHS in England
and Wales 1993. *Health Trends*, 26(3): 75.

In geriatrics, palliative and rehabilitation medicine, women have had a
strong presence from the start and a hand in shaping their images and
ways of working. These are areas in which hierarchy has always been less
rigid, where a high value is placed on working in teams with other health
professionals. They are also low status specialties with labour shortages
and, because they are concerned with chronic conditions rather than
crises, they have predictable working hours. A geriatrician recalled that
in the 1950s the NHS was 'trying to invent the specialty. It didn't have a
name then.' With a small child, and having been rejected for several
other specialties, she went to see the man in charge of a particular hospital that they were trying to convert into a geriatric hospital. When she
said 'I'm jobless. Have you got anything going?' he immediately replied,
'Yes, come and start tonight. Please come.'

While paediatrics is consistently the most popular choice with female
undergraduates, this is harder to explain in terms of Miles' factors.

Certainly nothing could be deemed more gender appropriate than caring for sick children, but it is a highly competitive specialty, with long and rigorous training, and is intrusive on family life.

Does this mean that the perceived femininity of an occupation is more important in attracting women than its working hours or ease of entry? If this were so, it would be hard to account for the move into pathology, which has not been popular with students of either sex. Most dislike doing post mortems and want at least some contact with patients. Recalling the shock with which Inspector Morse greeted the first appearance of a new female pathologist at the scene of a crime, it is evident that there is nothing conventionally feminine about pathology. Her media appearance may indicate that the image of pathology is changing *because* so many women have entered it rather than the other way round. The novels of Patricia Cornwell have also done much to make the female pathologist a familiar figure in the 1990s.

In real life, most pathologists do not spend their time attending murder cases, or even conducting autopsies. The bulk of their work takes place analysing samples in the laboratory. Women moved in because the regular hours appealed to them and there was limited competition for jobs. Having done so, they began to recast pathology in more 'feminine' terms. For example, a woman who works on liver and renal biopsies described the dialogues that take place between herself and the physician about what to do when a patient is rejecting a graft. She says, 'We talk as a team and make the decision as a team. Therefore I feel as though I am managing the patient although I don't see them.' Women paediatricians were faced with less of an image problem, but most have much more stressful working conditions than the pathologists. Their concern has been not so much to change the image of the specialty as to create more flexible working conditions.

Women in the male-dominated specialties often articulate distinctive ways of working. Neurologists, for example, are often represented as intellectuals who are happiest when they have just completed an esoteric diagnosis, such as identifying a rare muscle disorder. By contrast, a female neurologist spoke of the importance of chronic palliative care, of counselling and support. For her 'the psychotherapy, the listening to people, travelling the journeys with them, just being there, is very much part of the work'. Claims to a distinctive approach enable women to attract a particular clientele who prefer their services; as the number of women specialists increases this has potential to shift the image of the specialty more drastically and challenge men, too, to modify their practice.

Cardiology is by far the largest specialty and has taken up much of the space once occupied by the general physician. This, along with its procedural emphasis, suggests why it has seemed such a daunting choice for women. Gastroenterology and cardiology have the lowest proportion of women specialists and the smallest proportion of women in advanced training. Both specialties discourage part-time training even in the final years and, while job shares are technically possible, it is difficult to find a partner, since men rarely want to work part-time and the number of women trainees is small. Both are regarded as 'macho' specialties with rigorous training regimes. Cardiology has been described as the surgical specialty of internal medicine, while the work of gastroenterologists overlaps substantially with that of urologists. A woman consultant agrees that you have to be 'a fairly strong, tough sort of person to spend your time looking up patients' colons', but represents the specialty in ways that depart from the stereotype. She jokes about the status of endoscopes and colonoscopes as 'phallic symbols' and suggests that, while her male colleagues might 'get off on doing procedures', gastroenterology is 'really a people-based specialty that has been changed by the fancy instruments we use to make our diagnoses'. Having originally intended to become a psychiatrist she is keenly aware of the psychological aspects of illness.

While most of the women found it easy to claim that they had reinterpreted the way the specialty was practised, they had more difficulty coming to terms with the changes that part-time work and training would bring. Like the men, they celebrate excellence and mastery. For them too, working part-time may imply not taking their career seriously, and placing a burden on their colleagues. One said, 'to be honest, I do think it is important to be there all the time. You cannot have the personal care of the patient unless you are there. If you come on in the morning and the patient has her heart attack in the middle of the night . . . even if you talk to them it is not the same as having seen them in the pain.'

Like the surgeons, most believed that part-time training must take double the time or standards would be compromised. The view that a lot of duplication takes place in the span of part-time training, or that part-timers spend just as much time attending necessary meetings and keeping up with the literature, carried no weight. Consequently few would choose part-time training, especially in the first three years. It had more appeal in the final three years, especially if it could be done on a job-sharing basis, the only method of training that was regarded as consistent with maintaining standards. They were not prepared to compromise their medical values, even though it had created personal difficulties. Some even said that long overnight shifts associated with full-time work were preferable in that at least, on other nights, they could be at home with their children. It would be far worse, they felt, to be working till midnight five nights a week.

Despite frequent reference to the help of mentors, few had received any formal assistance with career planning in the course of their training and had been left to work it out for themselves. All knew that if they had children before their training was complete they could have been forced to drop out, so it was often easier not to think about it. Postponement or denial were used as quite deliberate strategies. One woman said that during university, 'you certainly had the boyfriends but not the concept of being married . . . I wanted emotional support, but I didn't want to get married and I certainly didn't want children. I just didn't want them. They weren't important to me. Not until I was in my thirties.' Another said 'I never imagined myself getting married. So it was a great surprise to find that marriage would form a part of my life and that kids would be important.' Some waited to complete their training only to find that 'Mr Right' had not eventuated, while others experienced unforeseen difficulties in late pregnancies. A senior registrar reflected that she had stayed on because 'there has been nothing drawing me out of the hospital system, like a husband or a family'. But another had specialised *because* it fitted in better with her personal plans than general practice would have done:

> My husband had decided he wanted to go overseas and I thought, Christ, I can't commit to general practice. What can I hang around doing? You couldn't just hang around and be a resident for a third year in a row. So I applied for a job as a medical registrar to do the physicians' exam . . . the chairman of medicine was fairly perceptive and didn't think I was bright enough and didn't give me the job! But the rehab registrar position was vacant and they were looking for someone. And I'd never heard of rehab!

This woman was the daughter of a truck driver, who had struggled all her life with the idea that she was 'not bright enough' to do well in medicine. In fact, she continued her training overseas, took her membership exams and went on to manage a spinal injuries unit. For her, 'rehab' had appealed not because it was in any way feminine but because a position was available for which previous terms in psychiatry, haematology and neurosurgery fitted her very well. She had always been drawn towards the surgical end of the roster and managed to discover an opportunity of combining medicine and surgery that had not previously occurred to her.

Those with children all had stories to tell about how they had managed, and strategies to offer to newcomers. Some did it while they were still very young and depended on friends or relatives for help. One had actually hidden her baby in her hospital flat: 'I taught him to have five meals at night, because I was still breast feeding at the time, and to stay asleep during the day. I made him into a nocturnal animal!' Others opted to wait until they were senior registrars doing full-time research; a third group waited until their training was complete and a few were dealing with the problems that had arisen out of having delayed so long. In their own lives they had shown a degree of creativity in countering rigidity. They had not in any simple sense combined 'work' and 'family'.

Subjectivities

Physicians may be more gentlemanly than their surgical colleagues, but they inhabit a particular and hegemonic masculine subjectivity. Men who do not fit the conventions of white, heterosexual, middle-class masculinity also have difficulty in stepping into this world but their sense of themselves as men is not threatened. They have not had to give much attention to the processes of subject formation and can maintain the empowering illusion of the unified and autonomous self.

Women, on the other hand, have to think carefully about their subjectivity. As McCall observes, women who venture into male-dominated fields such as medicine, acquire a certain kind of self-consciousness in which the 'ontological complicity between habitus and field breaks down: *fit* no longer explains the relationship between positions and dispositions' (1992: 850). Often they think of themselves as split subjects, struggling to reconcile parts of themselves that seem to be in conflict. In the past, women specialists often split themselves quite literally, keeping their single names at work and making it appear that they were spinsters, while in their private lives they were 'Mrs'. This allowed them to keep their femininity out of the workplace but created a certain discomfort in moving between worlds. Increasingly women have sought to achieve more integration and to restructure the habitus rather than merely being structured by it.

For British women who trained in the 1950s and 1960s, the endocrinologist, Una Leddingham, became something of a symbolic figure, who showed how the female body of the physician could be incorporated into the habitus. Leddingham worked full-time as a senior consultant but had a dashing husband and two children. She was an androgynous figure, highly feminine in appearance but also tough and professional. One woman remembered:

> You'd ring her in the night when a diabetic came in, and out of two thousand patients she'd say, 'Why has that happened, she has never been in a coma before?' She knew her patients and she focused on her patients as individual people . . . Nobody talked about holistic medicine in those days but her approach I now see was holistic and truly working. It was there in the way she talked to students too. She had Grand Rounds one afternoon a week and it

was a big occasion. She would arrive, wonderfully elegant, beautifully shod and clothed, with opals flashing on her fingers. She would stand at the head of the bed and hold the patient's wrist while delicately taking their pulse. She and the patient together would teach the students. It wasn't the patient being taught on, the patient was working with her. It was done in a very graceful, non-heavy sort of way and it was very impressive. All the wards used to watch and wait for her to come – it was a big deal.

She had a shop that knew her size and the kind of clothes she liked and they would send things round to her in a taxi. She always looked elegant and would say to the students, 'You will miss lunch rather than arrive at my outpatient clinics without tights or stockings on. You will look professional. I don't care if you are hungry, that is how you will look.'

Another woman recalled that she wore large diamond earrings at a time when jewellery in the workplace was generally frowned upon. For them the earrings were an important symbol, and Leddingham provided a model of both elegance and strength.

Success at the highest levels of internal medicine has been fraught with gender identity conflicts. For a number of women in the sample, medicine had represented a desire to follow in their fathers' footsteps and the dispositions of the father were important in forming their habitus. They may have been the substitute son or, as the greatly loved daughter, become locked into oedipal relationships which intensified through their shared intellectual life. Often the mother was entirely absent from the interview, a shadowy figure who may have resented both the daughter's success and her closeness to her father, as well as her own exclusion from their world. As the following three case studies demonstrate, these women have struggled to make choices that balance the perceived 'masculine' and 'feminine' aspects of their selves and to come to terms with the mother that they had earlier rejected.

Dr A. started medicine in 1963 as one of eight women in an intake of 140. She specialised in paediatrics, moved into community medicine and then into academia. She recognises something of herself in the image of women doctors as eccentric, honorary men out of touch with their 'womanhood' who often behave appallingly as a result of their own anger and frustration. She decided on medicine after her father had refused to let her 'swan around' and study music, her first choice, and feels that women who went into medicine at that time had to have a strong masculine identification in order to bring their disposition into alignment with their working environment. In her case she had grown up with brothers, and in the masculine context of a boys' boarding school, where her father was headmaster. Her parents were conservative people who believed 'that men run the world and women have their place'.

Like many others, she postponed thinking about children or long-term relationships during the long grind of medical training and thereafter became entirely absorbed in anti-racist politics. She married late and found herself, at forty, pregnant for the first time. This plunged her into such a crisis that she began therapy with a Jungian analyst and arrived at the interpretation that her own identity was still entangled with that of the mother who had resented her existence and put her down. She now sees her life in terms of a conflict between the 'nurturing woman' and the 'male bit that runs the show at the price of blocked creativity', and has been attempting to free her gentler, 'feminine' side and to find her own authority.

Dr A.'s concerns about inequality may well have derived from the misfit between her gender and the medical world in which she found herself. As a young woman she was unable to recognise this disjuncture. Denying that gender was relevant, she threw herself into a masculine style of politics concerned with class and race. Though she believes that the 'nurturing' side took her into medicine in the first place, she has not engaged with feminism beyond paying lip-service to equal opportunity. She cares passionately about things like the appalling hours that junior doctors are made to work, but has not directly pursued the issues around gender and medicine. Instead she reflects that 'If I went into it now I might go in and be a very high powered nurse'. At this point in her life she manages the cultural contradictions of gender by disengaging from the aggressively masculine styles of medicine, of politics and of her own earlier self and embracing those activities that are consistent with a model of 'nurturing womanhood'.

Dr H. is a consultant oncologist, educated at Oxford and the London Hospital Medical School. Her father, a prominent scientist, was, she says, ambivalent about whether he wanted sons or daughters. As it turned out, he got two daughters and both did medicine, probably to please him. No further mention was made of her older sister, who might have been a role model, and her mother was entirely absent from the interview. By contrast, her father, a 'classically difficult and demanding' man, had been an emotional centre of her life. She had been closer to him than her sister or either of his two wives and had let go of an important relationship in order to nurse him through his final illness. Seeking to emulate her father, she chose medicine over science in the belief that it would minimise any gender conflict: medicine was scientific but at the same time 'feminine, soft science, a caring profession and all that stuff!' Having not married or had children her career has actually followed a 'masculine' full-time path but her subjectivity is constructed around a secure sense of heterosexual attractiveness.

A gracious woman in her mid-forties, Dr H. lives alone in an elegant and well proportioned 'cottage' in the Midlands. There were two pianos and an open fire in the large, comfortable and slightly chaotic living

room where I interviewed her one evening after work. A third piano sat
in the adjoining room waiting, she said, for a good home to be found for
it. She poured a gin and tonic and sat opposite me on the sofa with three
small puppies bounding around her. They, like the pianos, were waiting
for homes and, like the piano, she suspected they would stay on. The
phone rang several times with male callers making social arrangements
for the weekend. She likes to think of herself as flirtatious, appreciates
male company and has a rich network of social relationships outside the
medical world.

Dr H. deals with the gender contradictions of medicine more comfortably than Dr A. Femininity is not something she has recently discovered
but something she has actively enjoyed. She also shares the composure
of many of her male counterparts which often takes the form of
conversational banter, telling stories against themselves, making light of
their talents and understating their achievements. Since the habitus of
the physician is meant to exist naturally, it is important to convey a sense
of easy accomplishment: 'I can speed read things and absorb what I need
to and reject the rest'. This is woven further into a particular form of
upper-class femininity that was characteristic of many consultants. Dr H.
insisted that her career decisions had been entirely based on her social
life and says 'I was considered very odd in my year, to complain about the
extraordinary hours and to make a fuss. It seemed very poor.' As a
houseman she decided that she did not have the stamina to be a GP and
claimed that she chose oncology because cancer patients rarely have a
major crisis in the middle of the night. There was a kind of black humour
in the refrain that a job dealing with the ever-presence of death could be
done on a 9 to 6 basis and may be more manageable than that of a GP.

Despite her claims to have organised her career around her social life,
Dr H. is highly committed to her work and comes home each night
exhausted. She sees 700 new patients a year, all of whom have serious
malignancy, and her work is clearly stressful. A third of her patients die
quite soon and another third need palliative care. She prides herself on
her skill and judgment:

> Really one should be so good at the drugs and the radiation that you don't
> think twice about that. It is like driving a car ... They are just tools of the trade
> but they are magical in the sense that the drugs won't work on everybody and
> you begin to develop a funny sense of what will help for each person ... A
> person's way of life and way of death, what they want and what they fear, is
> what you should be looking at.

Dr H. does not think medicine often works as a part-time job and is
critical of the women who 'drift in and feel they're owed a living ... They

are strictly clock watchers and they often feel they should be made consultants because they've got their exam and done their quota of clinics . . . but really they are not giving it their fair whack.' She cannot imagine where anyone would find the energy to deal with husband and children as well and effectively made a judgment that she could not do both. Confronted with this choice ten years earlier, she had an abortion and ultimately allowed the relationship to end rather than attempt to combine work and motherhood. Now she restricts herself to relationships that are less demanding and probably provide relatively limited emotional support. Dr A., in her current Jungian mode, would dismiss such a choice as 'adolescent', but Dr H. finds enough in friendships to sustain her sense of herself as a social and sexual being. She reflects with some humour on how she copes with ageing and the loss of sexual attractiveness in the absence of a central relationship:

> I have lots of very old friendships that are important and a lot of my old boyfriends are great friends. Now that I'm getting into middle age, an old bag, it is easier because their wives don't care any more. But it has been a painful transition and I am much more solitary now. I enjoy that and no longer crave company or companionship or partnership. I really don't. I think it truly is a very pleasant state.

Dr H. has undoubtedly made sacrifices for her career and taken difficult decisions in her personal life. The contradictions of gender are evident in the way she talks about herself but she avoided the kind of overt conflict between masculine and feminine parts of the self that has troubled Dr A. Her sexual assurance and the social ease that came from her class background, have allowed her to create a less conventional resolution of the conflicts in the same relaxed and understated way in which she approaches medicine itself.

For Dr C., by contrast, sexuality and social life were placed on the backburner for much of her medical career. She came from an academic background and graduated from an Australian university in the late 1960s. She had tossed up whether to study history or medicine and the historical interest is still strongly present in the way she talks about the changes she has seen in the organisation of medicine. Having opted for medicine, Dr C. took it for granted she would become a specialist though she was afraid that if she was too successful her mother would reject her. As a child with a love of detective stories, she had imagined she might be a forensic pathologist. At one point she thought seriously about plastic surgery, but a humiliation at the hands of a general surgeon ensured that she never wanted to go back there. Paediatrics appealed to her because it had been well taught. They were treated like human beings and actually given clinical experience while still students. But she graduated with 'middling' results and did not immediately make a place on the training program. She took her membership exam in England and, after a period in North America came back to Australia and worked in neurology.

As a student, Dr C. rarely went out with men and had very little social life. She was aware then that by not putting time into relationships she was making a de facto choice between marriage and medicine and setting herself on a path towards being a spinster career woman. But this was in no way straightforward. She recalls that when someone said to her, 'oh your job is a substitute for children and a family', she 'nearly threw a brick at him because I did not think it was true'. She had been caught between pleasing a father who wanted her to do well and a mother who did not, and believes that she allowed herself 'middling' success in the hope of keeping both options open. Her career decisions were linked in complex ways to her parents' preoccupations and her own family history as well as to her love of medicine. Eventually she sought analysis in order to work through the self doubts and the compromises and to reconsider the choices she had made. In her early forties she married and had a child.

Dr C. works three days a week at the Children's Hospital where she assesses children with developmental disabilities and organises services and resources for them. This involves working with teams of psychologists, speech and occupational therapists and physiotherapists. She does not work part-time by choice, or because she has a family. For her, the problem now is lack of work rather than too much of it. There is a lot of competition for the available hospital sessions and private work in her area is limited. Nearing fifty she is contemplating retraining in child psychiatry which is, de facto, part of her practice anyway. At present there is more demand for child psychiatrists than there is for paediatricians. Because of her part-time status she has trouble asserting her authority and readily admits that in a hierarchical unit she does not work well unless she is the boss.

Dr C. concedes that she is less single-minded about her work than she was in the days when she was on call twenty-four hours a day and running a much more difficult clinic. But her husband is unemployed and she has come to be the main breadwinner, which is forcing her to be more instrumental again, hence the thoughts about psychiatry. At times she resents the financial obligations but is also angry that her colleagues assume that because she has a husband she has no claim on any extra sessions. Dr C. does not have much truck with contemporary feminism but is passionate about the need for hospital crèches, for permanent part-time conditions for sessional staff, and the proper valuing of the kinds of work that women do in rehabilitation and the long-term chronic areas.

What these case studies illustrate is a complex interleaving of medical careers with issues of sexuality, gender identity and parental residues. All could be classified in terms of whether career or family had been prioritised but to do so would miss the central issues in their lives. These three women also belong to a distinctive time and set of anxieties around medical careers for women which might be passing away. They stand in contrast to the women under forty who voiced few of the same concerns about contradictory identities.

Culture and class

A senior registrar described the 'Golden Circuit', the four or five most prestigious SHO jobs in the London teaching hospitals. These included the 'renal job' at Guys, the 'nerve job' at the National Hospital Queens Square, the 'heart job' at the London Chest Hospital or at the Brompton, and the 'chest job' at the Brompton. A young resident who managed to get one of these would be likely to 'springboard off' into one or more of the others and then very quickly climb their way up the hierarchy. Only a minority of aspiring physicians are in a position to gain a detailed knowledge of the status of some jobs over others, or of the career paths that may open up as a result of specific SHO appointments.

Those from privileged backgrounds are better placed to make sensible and informed choices about their careers. They will aim, not necessarily for the most difficult or prestigious area but one in which they can achieve a comfortable mastery. As one consultant put it, 'if you are from a working-class background you want to get to the very top, to prove you are as good as the next chap . . . (whereas) if you are a sensible, middle-class rich chappie, you know there is more to life'. To pursue a career course that requires an over-expenditure of energy actually undercuts the goal of being able to function with ease and grace. This woman dreamed of becoming a neurologist, but found herself in a cardiac on-call team, doing a one in two roster for the entire hospital, with no time at all to prepare for the exams. Realising that women had little choice of jobs, and that she would have to move all around the country and probably take the exam many times before she passed, she switched to pathology which was then a shortage specialty. Wanting a job in London to be with her husband, 'I just wrote to three teaching hospitals and got offered three lectureships. It was as easy as that.'

While this woman enjoys pathology, she might well have become a physician if she had understood the culture more fully. Dr M. demonstrated how it is done. Coming from a distinguished medical family she was aware that it was 'politically sensible to get to know the consultants very early on as a student' since they 'prefer the devil they know'. She got involved in the social life of the hospital, acting in residents' plays, organising fund-raising activities and editing the hospital magazine. This involved asking consultants to review books and interviewing them about the activities of their department. In the course of these interactions she would say 'oh, you know, you taught my parents . . . or, you were in the same year as my parents'. She conceded, 'yes, that does help. It helps a lot.' It had enabled her to 'land the renal job' followed by the neurology one and place herself on the fast track to a consultant's position.

In order to complete the training program candidates have to find appropriate rotations every six or twelve months. Medical selection committees are notorious for the ways in which they ignore equal opportunity procedures and choose candidates whom they know and trust. The interview often does little more than confirm a decision already taken. Dr M. was appointed to a position over other candidates who had already passed their membership exams. Because she was not expecting to get the job she went into the interview completely relaxed and described what took place:

> One of the consultants, a woman, was very interested in opera. And I happen to know quite a bit about opera and we had this heated discussion about Verdi and his political life which took up about twenty minutes of the interview. We were having this great time and the men were sitting there looking at us. I am sure that had a fair bit to do with me getting the job. It was quite extraordinary.

It is unlikely that Dr M. was appointed purely on her knowledge of Verdi, but the example demonstrates that, in this world, questions of merit are inseparable from social and personal factors. It was a common complaint by women that they were grilled at interviews about whether they were going to have children. One woman reported that the chair of the committee had chastised the questioner and then gone on to say: '"But I need to know, otherwise we are wasting our time." . . . They are usually more subtle about it.'

Isabel Allen has stressed that the patronage system is problematic for women and clearly it favours those who are socially at ease with their teachers and able to acquire an inside knowledge of how the system works. But some felt that women tend to present better than men at interviews and are more articulate. The 'old boys' network is increasingly situated in a broader web of medical relationships that includes women. As the number of women candidates increases it becomes harder to treat them as a unified group, defined primarily by their gender, and it is not always helpful to think of men and women doctors as hostile blocs. A high proportion of women doctors marry doctors, while large numbers have parents and other relatives who are doctors. The men may have complex and ambivalent feelings, both supportive of their partners' careers while longing for domestic stability. Otherwise conservative men may be intensely proud of the achievements of their own wives, daughters or protégés and keen to further their careers.

If the habitus of the consultant physician combines intellectual brilliance with a certain kind of social authority, a small number of women have always made the grade. One woman in my sample had graduated from Cambridge during World War Two and been appointed house physician to the professor of medicine before joining the army as a medical officer. She left with letters of recommendation from the General as well as the professor and went on to an outstanding career. She was able to do this partly because she was at ease with managing domestic staff. It was not the ideology of motherhood, she felt, that caused women doctors to assume direct responsibility for child care and household work, but inexperience in handling staff and awkwardness about their live-in presence. By contrast she 'came from a background, and married a husband from a background, where we were completely comfortable with and had been brought up with live-in help'. Having three children did not interfere with her work because they were cared for by a nanny and a full-time housekeeper. While the children were small she could afford to restrict her private practice and work as an honorary, while completing an MD. She recalls:

> I used to come in in the afternoons . . . and go into my bedroom which overlooked a garden such as this and my housekeeper would bring me a tray and a cup of tea. From then until the children came home from school I would have time to read the journals and prepare lectures and things like that. I didn't have to get the evening meal.

The same kind of upper-class femininity that characterised women surgeons was present among many of the physicians. Dr M., for example, insisted that she 'was never terribly bright' and had been 'quite lucky' in her personal connections. This element of humorous self-deprecation is also characteristic of successful men but they never go this far. They would have taken the same level of mentoring for granted without it occurring to them that they had been 'lucky'. Dr M.'s achievements had also been built on intellectual strength and hard work, yet she felt it necessary to play this down.

A number of times it was suggested that, to be accepted, women have to be 'compliant'. This means that intellectual capacity has to be balanced by a 'feminine' dimension. One woman described the ideal trainee as 'someone who never cries, doesn't flounce around and get upset about things, is cool, always presents well, is feminine in their outlook but tough, passes exams, and usually has an uneasy relationship with the nurses, some of whom think she is wonderful while others think she is a bitch'. Women who are too 'masculine' in appearance cause anxiety, as do those who are too explicitly 'sexy'. A resident described the 'hyper-femininity and high heels' which might work as a short-term strategy but was unlikely to be well received at consultant level. While some male specialists are reluctant to nurture junior female doctors, others clearly take advantage of the situation. Even when the sexual politics is not so transparent, women find that they are more likely to be welcomed if they accept a feminine positioning that does not challenge the basic hierarchies.

'That wretched exam'

To become a consultant physician takes three years of basic training after which the membership exam is taken (in Australia the distinction between membership and fellowship has been abolished and it is known as the fellowship exam). This is followed by three years of advanced training. Two more years and an MD may be required to become established in a sub-specialty or to gain a position in a teaching hospital. Each of the specialties is under the supervision of a specialist advisory committee. Paediatricians generally sit their exams a little later since they are required to have a stronger generalist background. In the faculty of public health the basic training involves a Master of Public Health, and the faculty of rehabilitation medicine accepts basic training either as a physician or a surgeon.

The physicians' exam consists of two parts, a series of multiple choice papers followed by a clinical exam. Where surgeons take the Part Two as an exit examination, physicians take the two parts closer together and relatively early in their training. In their memories the two are rolled into one as 'that wretched exam'. One woman spoke of 'this stupid thing that has dominated my life for so many years. There is no opportunity for spare time. You are either at work or you are studying.' Physicians regard their Part One as 'harder than that of the surgeons'. Passing it is a mark of intellectual achievement and so endows substantial cultural capital. Now that the pass rate for first timers has gone up to about 80 per cent, those who keep failing tend to get counselled out of the program but 95 per cent of those who complete the exam go on to finish their training.

Some made light of the multiple choice exam, dismissing it as 'a motivation test'. Others stressed its difficulty: 'It is like learning the phone book *and* using it like a chess game'. But it was the clinical exam that they found more difficult. One argued that clinical examinations are oriented towards things that men regard as important, and that accurate diagnoses of clinical signs are given much more weight than other aspects of managing the patient that women might regard as more important, such as coming to terms with death or disability. They also described how, at a point when they were barely half-way through their training, they had to display the qualities of the consultant:

> You are expected to talk and act and think like a physician and demonstrate that. You have to be part of their culture yet you have never been given a chance to actually be in that culture. You may have watched it from the outside but you have to give a good imitation. A lot of the exam is about performance. I don't see that as a bad thing. People have expectations about how physicians should behave and it is reasonable to act in a fashion that at least gives confidence.

This woman passed first time, but it may present particular difficulties for women who, whatever their competence, have been used to deferring to others. The truck driver's daughter failed several times, not because she did not know her stuff but because she did not present herself confidently enough:

> I felt I had done so much in rehab that there would not be anything I couldn't answer. And I did know the answers in terms of what I was asked but I was still being a senior registrar. I was experienced and knew what I had to do but I was still assuming I would hand it over. I wasn't thinking through a plan of what I would do if this were my patient.

Even Dr M., with her medical connections, failed the exam twice. She commented that:

> If a consultant doesn't think you are worth passing, they won't pass you. You used to get so uptight about the things you would forget that you actually knew, and you felt they didn't make allowance for it . . . but they are not necessarily looking for the fine details but for confidence and authority.

A consultant must be able to see the wood from the trees, and to take responsibility for exactly how the patient is treated. To demonstrate this, a candidate must be able to present themselves as relaxed under tense conditions. Dr M. was asked:

'Why are you examining the abdomen with two hands?' And I said, 'I don't know. I have always done it.' He said, 'What does your left hand do?' And I said, 'It's just checking what the right hand is doing.' The whole thing was much more flippant I mean, it was a stupid thing to ask, since everyone has their own way of examining.

Most acknowledged the personal cost of preparing for the exam. Dr O. commented:

I see a lot of my friends, particularly my female friends, being so absolutely overtaken by that whole process of studying for physicians' training . . . It is really, really demanding. It changes people's personalities. It makes them incredibly irritable; they get terribly distressed; and they lead even less of a normal life than if they were not doing that exam.

She began physicians' training but left 'because the lifestyle was crazy and I felt the lack of growth of other dimensions of myself'.

While men are confronted with similar difficulties they are more likely to have social supports in the form of wives or girlfriends who are willing to remain in the background during the training period. Many women described the loneliness and isolation, the loss of their youth, their anxieties about whether they would be able to establish relationships or have children. Dr Q., now a senior registrar, and recently engaged, said:

Medicine is one big career of loss. You lose your youth. You lose your vitality. You lose your vibrancy. You lose your frivolity. Peter and I were looking at pictures of me as I was growing up. As a medical student I was a fresh faced flower, as an intern shiny eyed and slim. And then as a resident I was grimacing and had put on about two stone. As the years went on I looked more and more haggard and unpleasant. I just don't know if I want to sacrifice my entire life to this God of medicine.

Confronted with these sacrifices, women are more likely to torture themselves with alternative possibilities:

You get in a real bind sometimes when you are in medicine as a female. Are you doing something because you want to do it? Even if you want to do it, is it because it is ideologically sound to be wanting to do it? Or are you just reinforcing the stereotypes about women in medicine? Should you be doing something that is less accepted by the medical profession as a whole?

On the other hand, once women become serious about studying for the exam, they often have a much stronger sense of commitment while some of the men take it more casually.

A key part of the training program is the ritual of daily ward rounds.

Surgeons also carry out ward rounds but theirs tend to be shorter and less elaborate since the theatre rather than the ward is the centre of their existence. Consultants use ward rounds to monitor the work of their registrars and to ensure that their instructions have been carried out. It is also an opportunity to display their own mastery, to praise or humiliate their junior staff, and to evaluate their progress. The registrar or resident who has admitted the patient may be expected to present the case in front of the assembled group and answer questions about the treatment that has been given. They may have to present a review of the literature of the subject and it is helpful to demonstrate that they are aware of the latest research. It can be an intimidating experience for junior doctors since it involves competition with peers and the ever-present danger of making a fool of themselves.

Apart from their own fear of speaking up, women experienced a number of problems with ward rounds. A thoracic specialist said that when she went on ward rounds, 'patients often call me nurse even though they know I am in charge, and will defer to the junior male medical staff'. Women are regularly overlooked when they wish to ask a question or make a point. By ignoring them or failing to ask them questions, a consultant may deny them the opportunity to demonstrate competence. A few years ago women might have said they 'felt uncomfortable' in those situations; now they are more aware of the symbolic violence perpetrated on them as a euphemised form of control.

The surge into paediatrics

The surge of women into paediatrics may be partially explained with reference to the factors that Miles put forward as important in determining women's career choices. Paediatrics is obviously gender appropriate, but the training is long and the hours erratic. It was only in the late 1960s that separate training programs were established and paediatricians are still required to be members of the RCP or RACP. Once the training is completed, however, it may be more manageable than some other specialties since most patients do not require hospital admission and there are fewer ward rounds. While adult physicians typically admit 75 per cent of their patients, in paediatrics the figure is between 10 and 20 per cent and more time is spent seeing outpatients. Paediatrics is also perceived as less stuffy and hierarchical than adult medicine. Though there is disagreement on this, paediatricians are often said to be gentler, less pushy people who cannot afford to be pompous if they wish to get on with their patients. Traditionally the power base of a hospital has been in adult medicine and surgery and paediatricians have been seen as 'baby doctors' in more ways than one.

Women have played a leading role in constituting the specialty. Margaret Harper, an early graduate of Sydney University developed an international reputation as one of the first to differentiate between coeliac disease and cystic fibrosis. She was an instigator of the Tresillian Mothercraft Homes and in 1926 published a popular book on infant care, *The Parents' Book*, aimed at fathers as well as mothers (Webb, 1984: 231–2). Adelaide graduate Helen Mayo was a foundation member of the RACP; Phyllis Cilento became a national figure as a mothercraft expert as well as having six children of her own; and Elizabeth Turner was the first woman superintendent of the Royal Children's Hospital in Melbourne.

In England there have been opportunities to train part-time. A number of supernumerary positions have been funded centrally and can be taken up in any hospital in the area that is willing to accept them. But these are regarded as a second-best option, 'a scheme for married women who can't cope'. They have not been won in competition with those seeking full-time jobs in the same specialty and are therefore regarded as second rate. Women are wary of them and have shown a preference for job-sharing, where two women take on a 'real' job rather than one that has been specially created. Because of the larger numbers of women in paediatrics it is easier to find a partner at the same level and in the same area. It is most popular at senior registrar level because you can by then be more confident of your partner and you do not have to remember as much detail about test results and so there is less trivial stuff to hand over. But job-sharing cannot be a total solution and only a general reduction in working hours can provide one.

Women will soon make up a third of paediatric consultants, in both England and Australia. But far from being an area that men are willing to vacate it has become highly prestigious. In the UK there is a shortage of high quality applicants for consultant positions because many of the female senior registrars leave. But it is highly competitive at the registrar level. The Australian women were unanimous that the profession is currently overcrowded and that the number of positions for general paediatricians are in sharp decline. It is an area that seems open because more senior people are used to staff hospitals, especially new-born intensive care. As a result there are more registrar positions available and, 'almost every year there are more female paediatric residents employed than male. But they all seem to get pregnant and leave.' From the hospitals' point of view this is fortunate since there is a shortage of consultant or VMO positions.

As competition for jobs becomes more fierce, and sub-specialty training becomes virtually obligatory, it remains to be seen whether the influx of women will continue. In Australia it seems likely that paediatrics will become two-tier. One group will be part of teaching hospitals, while the other will be half-way between general practice and paediatrics. This has already happened in the United States where the majority of paediatricians are seen as interchangeable with 'family physicians'. The suburban general paediatrician now deals mostly with chronic but not particularly sick children who could as well be treated by a general practitioner. Children no longer get the severe organic diseases that they used to. It is rare to see measles or mumps, mastoiditis, pneumonia or rheumatic fever. What is left is a relatively small number of very severe cases of gastroenteritis, leukaemia and nephritis. These are children who need hospitalisation and continuous surveillance.

Dr C. predicted that success as a generalist 'will require a lot of running round, an ability to sell yourself, pushing a lot of patients through'. And she thinks that this 'will mostly be done by the fellas . . . because it's where a lot of money will be'. Under these circumstances the proportion of women in paediatrics will decline unless women take up the new specialties of renal and respiratory medicine, intensive care and neurology. While a number have done so, others feel they have been led up the garden path and are considering their options carefully. One in my sample had moved to the country knowing that her work would be more varied. Another, a senior registrar, was planning a career in hospital administration, while a third had commenced sub-specialty training in rheumatology, having identified that as a growth area.

Flying high, part-time

Given the strength of the view that part-time work is in conflict with medical excellence, the following comments might come as a surprise. The three speakers are Australians, and all are considered by their colleagues to be high fliers:

> As soon as I got back to Australia I had lots of offers of locums. But I had made a decision when I was in England that I wanted time to devote to my children and also satisfying work. When all these guys rang up I said, no, I want permanent part-time work. If you give me that I will cover for you when you go away. I had an offer within a day from a guy who had never thought about it before. It suddenly seemed ideal to him. (Dr T.)

> If I have a patient who needs to go into hospital I tell them one of the men will look after them. I point to the photo of my two little girls and say, I don't do hospital work for that reason. They say, oh yes, entirely appropriate. I know if David said that his patients would think very poorly of him. But there is a strong perception that it is okay for a woman to be a mother and a doctor. Some respect you for that. (Dr Y.)

I have been lucky. I have always been head hunted. I could choose to do anything I wanted . . . Just recently I decided it is better to go part-time for a while because I am not willing to give to the public hospitals at the level of responsibility they need. If they want me back they will have to offer me permanent part-time. They haven't done that in cardiology yet but they have in other departments. (Dr V.)

The first, a gastroenterologist, works the equivalent of three full days a week. She carries out her procedures in a private hospital and refers public patients who need endoscopies or colonoscopies to her male colleagues. Her waiting list is longer than theirs, not only because of her limited hours but because people are prepared to wait to see her. She says that 'women prefer to have a woman looking up their bum rather than some strange man' and, in any case, they are more likely than men to have gastrointestinal illnesses. Even working part-time, as a procedural specialist Dr T. makes a lot of money and, unlike her GP friends, could easily afford a full-time nanny. She prefers to look after her children herself and, should a third child come along, would stop working entirely for six months. She says, 'people throw up their hands in horror but I take the view that since I have established myself once I can do it again'.

The others are both cardiologists. Dr Y. currently works two days a week and rarely sees patients outside the hours of nine to three though she may go to the hospital to look at coronary angiograms. She too has been swamped with offers of part-time work and links this with the idea that men are beginning to recognise that the presence of a woman enhances the broad appeal of their practice. Her male colleague had sent a letter out to GPs when she commenced, indicating that her special interests included women's health. 'He threw that in purely because I have two breasts, for no other reason!' she laughed, but it pushed her to acquire expertise in the area and she has become passionate about the potential of hormone replacement therapy for treating heart disease.

Dr Y., who has two children, discontinued her PhD but makes light of her supervisor's observation that women with children doing part-time PhDs 'never quite work as effectively and their minds are distracted'. On the contrary, her decision was a positive move driven by growing uninterest in the topic, and there are no regrets. She says, 'I sometimes joke about it and call it my lack of ambition', recognising that her career options will probably be limited to an appointment at a small district hospital, but likes to think of herself as different from most of her colleagues who are definitely 'type A' people.

Dr V. explains that she ended up in cardiology because each time she had to make a career choice she chose the hardest option. She readily accepts the 'type A' label, loves the drama of hospital cardiology, and has completed a PhD, but currently restricts her clinical practice to two afternoons a week. A partnership is on offer whenever she chooses to accept it, but Dr V. prefers to remain an associate and keep control over her working hours.

These women completed their training full-time, in this way paying their dues to the standard criteria for 'excellence' before opting for part-time work. But their decision to work part-time still comes as something of a shock to anyone who has internalised medical norms. The shock comes in two waves. There is initial surprise that anyone would go to the trouble of completing the most rigorous and demanding of training programs, and then take 'the marriage track'. A second later it registers that this is *not* 'the marriage track' in the old sense. Women who have spent a minimum of six years in full-time postgraduate training find it laughable that they should be treated as people who are not serious about their careers. While their presence could be dismissed as just a continuation of the old part-time/full-time division in a new form, it is also possible to view them as improvisers, attempting to reshape the medical habitus. Still in their thirties, they are sure of their talent, aware of the demand for their services, and confident about their ability to negotiate positions that will allow them to combine specialist practice with more rounded lives.

The demand has now gone beyond 'part-time jobs for married women' of the type that have been common in the UK. A thoracic physician who manages a training program comments:

> You have to go through rigorous training to do a fairly demanding job. Once you have done that it is important to be a bit more mature about it. You don't lose your skills because you work four days a week instead of five. More people are accepting that it can be done, but how to do it is also a challenge.

She argues that hand-over is a critical issue and suggests that resistance has less to do with concerns for continuity of care than the fear of many doctors that if they arrange themselves in shifts they will be 'just like the nurses'. But if nurses are able to arrange hand-over effectively doctors should be able to do it even better, since they are trained to write up more detailed notes.

In Australia, women are now 40.3 per cent of all advanced trainee physicians (AMWAC, 1996: 78) and similar trends are evident in the UK. Even if a disproportionate number drop out, the proportion of women consultants will increase dramatically over the next decade. This is placing pressure on the colleges to create more flexible working environments. There has been at least a degree of democratisation and, while they are reluctant to 'commit mass policy changes', a number of individuals in the colleges have been sympathetic to women's desire for different career structures and access to part-time work. The election of Priscilla Kincaid-Smith, Professor of Medicine at the University of Melbourne, as president of the RACP in 1987 provided a source of encouragement to younger women. Professor Kincaid-Smith had herself married and had three children after she completed her training.

If flexible working hours remain a sticking point, women's presence is contributing to a shift in the way internal medicine is viewed. While medicine is more cerebral than ever, as new technologies provide more sophisticated diagnostic tools, there is an increased expectation that physicians should be emotionally more rounded and have better communication and understanding skills. Women's presence draws attention to the importance of these skills in procedural areas where they have not previously had any priority. One woman says, 'I have a reputation of being an empathetic female neurologist. I have a long waiting list. It is finally personality, the art of medicine that gives you a long waiting list, not your skills.'

A female geriatrician suggested that her specialty, rather than cardiology, was the true successor to general medicine because it is holistic. She believes that geriatricians are the only physicians who spend a lot of time dealing with problems in a multidisciplinary fashion. Where patients normally wait to see doctors, she accepted that in her area, because her patients often had such difficulty getting to the hospital, she must be prepared to wait for them. Those in rehabilitation, palliative care and paediatrics do a lot of their work in teams. An oncologist said 'One of the nicest things is when my patients say, you don't look like a doctor, though it sometimes creates identity problems in that people think they haven't been seen by a doctor for two weeks when I've seen them every day!' Rehabilitation requires cooperation with ancillary staff since it is the physiotherapists and occupational therapists who decide when a patient can safely be sent home and make arrangements that will enable them to cope.

As these specialties gain a higher profile, and as new meanings become associated with the existing male-dominated specialties, the culture of internal medicine will change. In the process, women's health is also taken more seriously. For example, the presence of more women cardiologists helps to draw attention to the lack of research on women and heart problems. It is thought to be men who are the victims of heart attacks and the main research has been carried out on them, but women have heart attacks later and under difficult circumstances (Broom, 1995). Women neurologists are aware that the headaches they treat are often linked to domestic violence. Women paediatricians find that they are dealing with sexual abuse, since people are generally happier to bring their children to a paediatrician than a psychiatrist.

It remains to be seen how far the specialties will go to adjust to the new female presence. In Britain there has been an increase in the number of staff grade posts as well as part-time consultants' positions (Wilson & Allen, 1994: 70–1). This at least begins to complicate the dichotomy between 'full' and 'part'-time work and may be a stepping stone towards broader solutions. Much will depend on the responses of men, whether they will cling to the old patterns and privileges or embrace the alternatives that women are starting to explore. While few will admit to an interest in working shorter hours, their concern to find reliable locums suggests, at the very least, a desire for some relief from on-call responsibilities. Some men are finally realising that they cannot continue to construct professional identities that assume full-time wives at home.

Intellectual brilliance has allowed growing numbers of women to enter the field of internal medicine. To make it their own, to feel truly at home in it, they have begun to reshape the contours of the field and the habitus it calls forth. It would be foolish to overstate the changes to a field so large and complex, and with so many vested interests. But women have undoubtedly interrupted the flows of power, and turned ideas that would once have been dismissed as heresy into matter for debate and action. As their numbers increase, and the possibilities for collective action become greater, the pressure to restructure medical time and working relations will increase.

6

The Medical Unconscious:
Anaesthesia and Psychiatry

There is no mystery about why women are well represented both in psychiatry and in the 'non-patient-centred' specialties of anaesthesia, radiology and pathology (NPCs). These specialties are seen to be compatible with family and domestic responsibilities, offering regular hours, limited night work, flexible training programs and, in the case of the NPCs, little or no ongoing responsibility for patients. Where jobs are of relatively low status, or not of interest to men, and when there are also staff shortages, new lines of career development may open up for women. Before formal training programs have been rigidly set in place, it is often possible to walk into positions at short notice, to work without formal training, and to have a hand in shaping new occupational identities.

These are specialties that have had to struggle for recognition within mainstream medicine. In the public mind, psychiatrists are regularly confused with psychologists, psychoanalysts and other therapists. Radiologists are confused with radiographers while pathologists are represented as laboratory scientists with a macabre interest in corpses. People often do not remember the name of their anaesthetist and usually rely on the surgeon to decide who it will be. One commented, 'most lay people seem to think we just give the intravenous anaesthetic and walk away'. As service providers, they are also perceived to be at the beck and call of other medical staff. It is not well understood that all are specialist physicians whose medical training is every bit as rigorous as that of the groups described in previous chapters.

This chapter will explore the movement of women into and around two of these fields, anaesthesia and psychiatry. They may seem like an unlikely pair, the one dealing with the unconscious patient, and the other with the patient's unconscious. There is some shared past, since before the successes with chloroform and ether, doctors were beginning to explore whether hypnotism might provide a form of psychological anaesthesia. Hypnosis was, in fact, to become much more significant in the development of psychoanalysis than in surgical anaesthesia (Magner, 1992: 282–4). The Parisian neurologist, Jean Charcot, famous for his studies of hysteria in the late nineteenth century, was also interested in the psychic states that anaesthesia could induce. Showalter (1987: 147–54) records that, along with experimenting with hypnosis, he used ether and chloroform on his hysterical patients.

Anaesthetists have worked with psychiatrists on some of their most notorious treatments, including psycho-surgery and ECT, but they have not been held directly responsible. While anaesthesia and its usage has certainly raised political questions, anaesthetists themselves have not been subject to much political scrutiny and are rarely in the public eye unless at the inquest of a patient who has died on the operating table. Despite their enormous exercise of power on the body of the patient, anaesthetists are essentially backroom people. Psychiatry, by contrast, has been a matter of public controversy since its inception. It is 'backroom' in the different sense that the claims of medicine to any special expertise in dealing with mental problems have long been contested.

Both occupations have their origins in the mid-nineteenth century but achieved full specialty status only after World War Two, in each case with some difficulty. They are of similar size, each constituting about 8 per cent of all specialists, in both England and Australia, and they have the dubious honour of sharing the highest suicide rates. Both have been located on the outfields of medicine and have had to find ways around the barriers of 'repression' in order to gain recognition in medical consciousness. Since women doctors may also be thought to represent 'the repressed', their place in these emerging specialties is interesting. They have had an important, and largely unrecognised, influence on the specialist identities that have been established.

As anaesthesia and psychiatry struggled to establish their specialist credentials, women occupied an ambivalent place. Men often fear that an influx of women will cause a slide in status and renew their efforts to assert both the importance of the field and their own dominance within it. Anaesthetists, seeking to establish autonomy, wanted to avoid any implication that they were the handmaidens to surgeons. Psychiatrists, anxious to secure their boundaries with GPs, social workers and psychologists, and to prove that they are 'real' doctors, have resisted any 'feminising' influences that might derive from the range of therapies that treat mental processes as functionally autonomous.

While it became relatively easy for women to enter, first anaesthesia and then psychiatry, the strategies they had to adopt in order to succeed are far from straightforward. Their presence is a reminder of the 'feminine' underside, which each specialty wants to suppress. In the case of anaesthetists, this is their subordinate relation to surgeons; in the case of psychiatry, the understandings it draws from non-medical fields. Women must be seen to affirm the identity, priorities and values of their specialty; at the same time a subtle usage of these other 'feminine' associations creates opportunities to reshape the field and consolidate their own place within it.

Female anaesthetists, while still barely 20 per cent of the profession, have a way of talking about it as if it is entirely female dominated. The fourteen women in my sample ranged in age from thirty-three to ninety-two and came from a variety of backgrounds. But what was striking was the way in which, collectively, they produced a cohesive account of the history of anaesthetics and their place in it. Their discourse had a strategic quality about it which was for them both empowering and validating. It was not based on any shared politics or feminist commitment but rather on a shared identity as anaesthetists. While they have not, at any stage, been in public confrontation with their male colleagues about the practice or politics of anaesthesia, they have been able to take advantage of the handmaiden image to secure employment and have also contributed to a remaking of the anaesthetist as someone who 'treats the whole person'. In recent years anaesthetists have succeeded in laying claim to surrounding areas, like analgesia, intensive care and resuscitation techniques, where they more clearly function as independent practitioners. Since these involve a shift from the unconscious to the conscious body of the patient and require skilled interaction with the client, they fall well within women's perceived expertise in human relations.

In psychiatry, the stakes are different. It has been the subject of long-running critiques from feminists concerning the relationship between femininity, mental illness and medical dominance. This literally creates a minefield for women practitioners, who may opt to defend the orthodoxies of the profession, or to position themselves with its critics and establish lines of connection that create the possibility of new frameworks and practices. Like women in obstetrics and gynaecology they occupy a 'between' space which makes possible a reassessment of the value of psychiatric knowledge for women.

The subject of anaesthesia

While medical history generally has been turned into a history of medical dominance, the history of anaesthetics remains by and large a straightforward story of progress which we enjoy having related to us. It begins with the discovery of chloroform in 1846, famously legitimated by

Queen Victoria's use for the birth of her eighth child in 1853, tracks the gradual improvements in techniques over the next century, the development of gas machines, the use of spinal and local as well as general anaesthetics, and the introduction of intravenous drugs such as pentothal. It reaches its high point with the discovery of curare pioneered by the Canadian Harold Griffith in 1942.

Curare is a relaxant drug, originally used by the indigenous peoples in South America to poison the tips of their arrows, inducing paralysis. It was quickly developed by the British Army in India during World War Two, because it enabled small mobile teams to perform life-saving abdominal operations close to the front line. A single injection makes possible a deep muscle relaxation which previously could only be achieved by very high levels of anaesthetics which made the patient unconscious for much longer than was necessary and often extremely sick during the time it took for the drugs to pass through the liver. It was also difficult to plan theatre times because of uncertainties about how long it would take to get the patient ready and then to bring them round. With curare it was possible to use a light anaesthesia. Perfect relaxation was achieved within a few minutes and the patient was awake and talking soon after the end of an operation.

Curare is not very discriminating in its action on different muscles. It was not possible, for example, to relax the abdominal muscles without also depressing the breathing muscles. Previously the patients breathed a mixture of gases but used their own natural respiration. With relaxants they stopped breathing and the anaesthetist had to assume total control of all breathing apparatus. Respirators were eventually developed to ventilate the lungs artificially but at first no one knew what sort of pressures were safe to use on the lungs, or the effects on the heart if you reverse the normal pressure relationship. Research into respiratory physiology took off and the 1950s and 1960s were a time of a very steep learning curve. The next step was to find ways of preventing people from losing body heat which was a major problem during long operations. There were dramatic improvements in monitoring devices. Instead of relying on ECGs and blood pressure readings, there is now a pulse octameter which measures oxygen levels from just a probe on the finger. It measures the level of oxygen in the blood and as soon as it starts dropping an alarm goes off. Prior to pulse octameters there was no sure way of knowing if a ventilator disconnected (until the patient turned blue) and otherwise healthy patients sometimes died during routine surgery. The introduction of curare thus changed the practice of anaesthesia from a craft into a science and paved the way for the development of a new specialty.

Included in this story of progress is the idea that women have always been accepted as equals in anaesthesia. They were present from the beginning and, when the first Society of Anaesthetists was set up in London in 1893, it had four women members at a time when there was no more than a handful of women graduates.

In the inter-war years there were a number of women working as GP anaesthetists. Winnie Wall, my oldest interviewee in Australia, completed her intern year in 1921 and worked with her GP husband who did a lot of surgery. By the 1950s she was working as a hospital anaesthetist in the days before special training was necessary. Gwen Wilson (1995), in her history of anaesthesia in Australia, claims that Australian anaesthetists were unique in accepting women as equal colleagues. Mary Burnell, a founding member of the Australian Society of Anaesthetists in 1934, went on to become the first woman president, the first woman dean, and a key player in the establishment of the faculty of anaesthetists within the RACS. In the 1950s, when there were only eight trained anaesthetists in the whole of Queensland, a succession of women ran the anaesthetic services at the Royal Brisbane Hospital and one of them, Tess Cramond eventually became dean of the faculty and then Professor of Anaesthetics at the University of Queensland (Best, 1988: 153–8).

But here the story becomes more complex. The real heroes of the story of anaesthesia were not the anaesthetists themselves but the surgeons, empowered to do ever more daring and complex operations. After centuries in which two groups had controlled the entire medical field, the physicians and surgeons viewed the multiplication of specialties at this time with considerable alarm and were not prepared to accept any of them on equal terms. When, in 1948, British hospitals were taken over by the government it was the physicians and surgeons with whom it initially negotiated. The surgeons fought to prevent anaesthetists gaining consultant rank arguing that they should be employed as senior hospital medical officers. Though a diploma in anaesthetics had been available in the UK since 1934, there had been very few specialist anaesthetist positions before the war. Most anaesthetics were given by GPs or residents and sometimes by surgeons themselves. Surgeons employed the GPs and paid them privately, deliberately refusing them the right to send the patient an account. Believing that 'anyone' could give anaesthetics, they were reluctant to acknowledge the new levels of skill or to concede autonomy. General practitioners also wanted to continue to perform the anaesthetics for the patients they had referred.

Dr A. recalled arriving to take up her first position as resident anaesthetist at a London hospital at about five o'clock one afternoon in 1947. She was greeted by the head porter who said, 'Oh yes. You are the new anaesthetist. Would you go up to the theatre and relieve Dr W. – he wants to go and do his evening surgery.' She laughed and continued, 'GP anaesthetists you see. He was giving anaesthetics but he had to clear off to do a six o'clock surgery – that is the way things worked.'

By 1960, the GP anaesthetist had virtually disappeared and the work had been taken over by a new breed of specialists. A core group set up a separate faculty within the College of Surgeons in 1948 (with Australia following in 1952) and managed to convince both governments that they needed a training that was rigorous enough to warrant consultant status. Dedicated hospital positions had been created. But, despite its technical excitement, anaesthesia retained an image problem. While it was acceptable for men to give anaesthetics as part of a wider medical role, the presence of a category of doctor who did nothing *but* give anaesthetics was a more difficult adjustment for the medical profession. Dr B. recalled a male colleague saying to her in the 1950s, 'You know, it is not a thing for a man. The surgeons wait about and expect you to fit in with them and to be sycophantic and I don't like that. It is more suitable for a woman to do that.' Anaesthetists have not been able entirely to shake the view that, as a service specialty, they were essentially subordinate to surgery.

Even in the 1990s, Dr M. could say: 'I certainly wouldn't do it if I were a chap. A woman like me who can work for half the week is a very different kettle of fish from a man who has to be out until 9.30 or 10 o'clock at night, always at someone else's beck and call.' She described how, as a student, a decade earlier,

> I went to see the professor of radiology a month before I decided to do my anaesthetic term because radiology seemed quite intellectually interesting. He said, 'Have you got any paranoid tendencies at all?' I said, 'Oh yes, quite a lot.' And he said, 'Well don't do it because everyone treats you like dirt. I'm the professor and some little intern came in this morning and said, "Hey you! Where are Mrs Jones' films? I need them."' And he said, 'Would you speak to your surgical consultants like that?' And apparently this little child said, 'No,' and he said, 'Well don't speak to me like that!' Here's the most senior radiologist being treated like an absolute nobody because he's the X-ray doctor. So he said, 'Don't do it, Okay?' And then when I got my anaesthesia appointment, I saw him in the cafeteria and he said, 'I just heard that you've been appointed anaesthetic registrar,' and I said, 'Yes, that's right.' And he said, 'That's worse!'

Where men shied away from anaesthetics because of these connotations, women were often drawn to it as a gender-appropriate space in an otherwise hostile medical environment. The evolving specialty was acknowledged to be 'a good job for a woman' while at the same time its perceived 'femininity' had to be repressed. While women had a stronger presence there in the 1950s than in most other specialties, they were also contained and marginalised in ways very similar to those experienced by women working in other parts of medicine. The minority with formal qualifications often fared the worst and were passed over for consultant positions while being given jobs as assistants. If surgeons felt more comfortable with GPs than with colleagues of equal standing, male anaesthetists feared that the presence of too many women would make it harder for them to press their claims to autonomy.

Dr G., for example, had gained wide experience in spinal and local anaesthesia in Australia during the war. But she was refused entry to the new DA (Diploma of Anaesthesia) course by the head of the Post-graduate Committee, ostensibly because she was married and had a child: 'He said, go home and play with your baby and don't waste your time. But he didn't know me. That only made me the more determined.' She got the DA, one of the first to qualify. It was, she said, a fairly harrowing exam which involved a practical with an anaesthetist from a teaching hospital who 'asked me to do what I thought were a few very odd things. I argued with him and he got very cross with me. He told me that this was his clinic and it would be run his way.' She did not know whether he was testing her to see if she would say the wrong thing or whether it was an attempt to shut out women. Even with the diploma her path was not easy. Finally, a surgeon offered her his private practice cases on condition that she bought her own gas machine, since private hospitals still did not have them. When, three years later, this man 'dropped dead on the third tee of a golf course', she was back to square one. For some time she continued to be offered assistant rather than full hospital positions.

The 1950s was a period of flux while specialist training programs were put into place. Many reached consultant status without formally acquiring either the DA offered by the universities or the new FFA (Fellow of the Faculty of Anaesthetics) which became the standard qualification, requiring four years of specialised training. Hospitals, faced with difficulties in establishing the new registrar positions, could be extremely cavalier about staffing and training procedures. Dr B.'s first anaesthetic post in the late 1950s was as a locum in the East End of London at a hospital that had difficulty attracting junior doctors.

> I worked there for two weeks, never having done any anaesthetics before. I was a rather cautious individual. I used to shanghai other members of the junior staff who at least had some experience in anaesthetics because I only had what I had learnt in medical school. It was terrifying.

Ironically, women without formal qualifications often found it easier to get work. Before World War Two, there were already a number of female GP anaesthetists, often in partnership with husbands who were GP surgeons. Winnie Wall had become skilled in the use of endotracheal tubes and during the war, when her husband was away, took on sessions at the hospital. After the war she gave up general practice and took on anaesthesia full-time, carting her own gas machines to private hospitals and dentists all over town. She experienced no shortage of work even though she was not trained in the new techniques.

When my first interviewee, Dr P., told me that she had worked for her father, husband and son I was astounded. If I had been deliberately looking for an exemplar of the handmaiden role I would not have expected to find one so literally. As it turned out five out of my sample were married to surgeons or gynaecologists. One had met her future husband over the operating table while another currently worked with her husband about 80 per cent of the time.

Graduating at the end of the 1940s Dr P. commenced her medical career right at the beginnings of specialist anaesthesia but, because she had three small children, never sat the fellowship exams. Her father, a busy general surgeon, was keen for her to do his anaesthetics and persuaded her it was both an exciting new area and one that could be combined with family. After only four months as a resident, she was given a registrar's job when a vacancy came up and was allowed to use relaxants for the first time. After leaving to have her first child, she was able to return to the same hospital, having established a reputation for punctuality and efficiency, and because there was a shortage of anaesthetists. The surgeon with whom she worked in the public hospital gave her his private lists and she built a successful career. Twelve years later he retired and, when the Whitlam government replaced honoraries with visiting medical officers, she was sacked. Ostensibly this was because she did not have the FFA but she claims the men were jealous of her lists and felt that, as a married woman, she had no right to them. Probably because of her family connections she was able to survive for longer without formal qualifications than most others, retiring only in the late 1980s. But she reduced her working hours as the competition from young men became more intense. Anaesthetists froze her out by putting pressure on surgeons not to employ her.

Women who acquired professional qualifications in anaesthetics were able to get work relatively easily because this was an expanding specialty and it was not the first choice for very many men at a time when training positions were expanding in surgery, medicine and gynaecology. In Australia, anaesthetists have organised themselves in groups, combining independent practice with assistance in covering rosters and some collective power in negotiating with surgeons. In the past, women were excluded from the more successful groups and had to organise separately. In Brisbane, for example, there was a group of about a dozen men (called 'the octopus' because it had so many arms) which only invited in as associates those who would 'bring us surgeons'. Since they did not think women could add to their 'stable' of surgeons, they were never included. An all-women group (known as 'the girls') was established, most of whose members were unmarried and worked full-time and, during a period when anaesthetists were in short supply, they were very successful.

'A good job for a woman'

Most of the women recalled from their training days the refrain, 'it's a good job for a woman'. Dr B. thought at the time this was quite absurd because she was doing alternate nights on-call. And Dr K. dismissed the idea as 'a furphy'. 'It is,' she said, 'a very physical specialty. You have to be able to use your hands. It is not something you can do every ten days, because you lose your skills.'

Operations have become more involved, and surgeons now operate on patients with conditions that would not previously have been considered. Both the drugs and the equipment have become increasingly complex. As a result, it is harder to leave registrars to work unsupervised and consultants spend more of their 'on-call' time at the hospital than they might have in the past. Because anaesthetists still have generalised on-call rosters, these may be particularly stressful. Someone who has done little work with neurosurgeons will not be happy to be called at one in the morning to administer anaesthesia at such an operation. The need to fit in with the surgeons also creates some difficulty in predicting their working hours. The Australians said that, particularly when they were starting out, they dared not refuse a surgeon's request for fear of being labelled unreliable. Where a surgeon could choose to postpone an operation, an anaesthetist could not. Dr G. drew attention to the early starts: the anaesthetist has to be at hospitals ahead of the surgeon to get things ready.

They did acknowledge that it was in some ways easier than other specialties. Though the training has recently increased from four to five years, it is still possible to complete it earlier than in many other specialties. It also requires very little initial financial outlay since anaesthetists do not need consulting rooms unless they are also working in pain management. Because of the limited after-care responsibilities, it also encroaches less on home life:

> If you're a surgeon you have to cut somebody up. And then you realise they've got cancer. You've got to talk to the relations, tell them it's all unpleasant, it's

cancer. And then, if you've dissected their bowel, it's difficult because they can get very sick from that and in those days sometimes they died from the join not working. Or they can get a deep vein thrombosis and die from a pulmonary embolus and that's another thing for which the surgeon is responsible and it is not my problem. So there is a continuing responsibility with being a surgeon until that patient is totally recovered . . . If I saw my patients ahead of time, assessed their physical state, wrote it on my notes, gave a nice anaesthetic, woke the patient up – that's the end of my responsibility. The minute I leave that hospital with regard to that particular case I have no responsibility at all. (Dr P.)

Legally, anaesthetists have a responsibility for what happens to a patient in the first 24 hours after an operation, but they rarely have to make the primary decisions about the patient's treatment.

You are told to go and see someone and decide on an anaesthetic technique for them but you haven't decided or told them that they should have the operation and it is not very often really that you would actually say, look I don't think you should have this operation, the risk is too high. You would usually just have a bit of a chat to them about the risks and benefits. So I guess in some ways it is a bit of an easy option if you don't like making difficult decisions about patient care. (Dr K.)

The women agreed that 'as a surgeon either you're full-time or you don't exist'. They thought the training for surgery was harder and took longer to complete. During training, anaesthetists had typically been on a one-in-four-type roster while surgeons were on a one-in-two. And, though the anaesthetist might have to arrive earlier at the theatre, the surgeons and registrars would probably already have done several hospital rounds.

While it can be done part-time, even short breaks from work can be dangerous. Given the need for mental alertness and quick reaction time, the issue of the minimum hours a week needed to maintain skills is a live one. One woman recalled:

I did probably only about three lists a week. I have always worked. Six months was the longest I ever stopped for. It is one of the things about anaesthetics, you cannot stop because you do kill people if you stop for too long. You get completely out of touch. You lose your confidence. Even after the kids were born, and I went back six months after my son was born, I felt really no confidence at all. It took me quite a while to build that up again and feel secure. Because it is so technical and you are doing practical things all the time, you have to keep good at things, like putting drips in and finding a vein quickly. You never really forget but it is the mental thing as much as anything. I even find when I am on holidays after I go back I am not on autopilot for a day or two.

In this woman's case, a compromise was negotiated. She and the hospital were persuaded that it was possible to work half-time perfectly safely, although anything less than that was considered dangerous.

Working less than full-time involves sacrifices. Dr R. said that, though a half day is three and a half hours, a session invariably takes longer than that and it was always assumed that part-timers will give more. They are also likely to get the sessions that no one else wants to do, such as Friday afternoons, or the mentally handicapped lists. Dr R. works half-time in the NHS and has a half a day a week in private practice (where she earns more than her NHS salary). Like Dr P., she experiences hostility from her male colleagues who still believe that married women, by taking private work, are stealing their bread and butter. And, while anaesthetics might be easier than some other specialties to combine with family responsibilities, that is not to say it is smooth sailing. The difficulty of finding appropriate work put unbearable strains on Dr R.'s marriage and her husband finally walked out, leaving her with three small children. Although he eventually came back, there is:

> quite a delicate balance between his job and my job and the children. It takes all I've got to give each of those things what they need. There is no doubt that I have to be the organiser. He is very committed to his job and there is a lot of tension when he is dealing with children with cancer. I feel that I am the one who has to be reasonable. He has to sacrifice quite a lot to let me work. I go off at 7 o'clock in the morning and he has to get the kids up, and that is a big deal for him.

Recasting occupational identities is sometimes easier than changing domestic relationships.

Occupational identities

While many surgeons may perceive the anaesthetist as a handmaiden, anaesthetists certainly do not see themselves in this way. The women were as adamant in their rejection of this role as any of the men. Dr J. said:

> I would be furious at that and very insulted. Lay people might see it as that, definitely, but we would see it as the reverse. If surgeons tried to treat you as a handmaiden they would be out on their ear very fast. There are six men too in this practice and there is no way they would see themselves as handmaidens. The surgeon doesn't start until you say so and the surgeon will have to abandon everything if you say so. I don't want to have any victim status as a woman. I think it is very important to be seen on equal terms with the men.

Dr T. was at pains to distinguish between a handmaiden relationship and a marriage, which could involve feelings of both love and hate. Her preferred analogy was that the surgeon was captain of the ship but that 'he would be a bloody fool if he didn't listen to the pilot'. All the women stressed the importance of good working relations with surgeons and though they agreed the relationship can be delicate, their criticisms were restricted to good humoured quips about intellectuals versus manual workers. The partition between the sterile and unsterile areas of the operating theatre, they suggested, could be seen as the blood/brain barrier. But they declined to take such remarks any further and were quick to defend the skills of the surgeon and affirm the professional nature of the relationship. Rather than being in a relation of tension with the surgeons, they often found themselves in a mediating role between surgeons and others in the theatre. If a surgeon barked at the nurses or registrars, it was often the anaesthetist who found ways of defusing the tension.

Surgeons are also aware of the importance of the anaesthetist. One observed that an anaesthetist had the power to make or break a young surgeon by delaying operations or disrupting theatre schedules. It was clear they felt a lot in common with surgeons as well and that most had established good working relations with them.

Nevertheless, anaesthetists do have long stretches of boredom in their work. While this at least signifies that the patient is doing well, it contrasts with the hyper-activity of the surgeon:

I think when you're sitting on a chair as the surgeon goes on for five hours doing an operation, you tend to sort of peer over the drapes and make a droll comment. Ask, 'Has the wound healed yet?' Check the calendar rather than the clock and things like that. I mean that's only to get your own back a bit because you're frustrated sitting on a chair. I don't mind. (Dr D.)

To me, I'm paid good money to be bored out of my brain making sure the patient is safe. And that's fine by me. I think other people find that very hard and I suppose particularly fellas because you're sitting there while the surgeon's doing what he needs to do and the handmaiden role chafes. (Dr F.)

I've got a facelift this afternoon and basically I'll have to sit on a chair for four hours while the surgeon is having fun and doing artistry and there's no way I'm doing anything clever or scientific. I mean I'm just making sure everything's safe and I'm paid good money to just make sure it's safe and that's fine. But there are other times like yesterday, when there were some really crumbly oldies and the anaesthetics were tricky and the surgeon just goes and sits in the tea room and you call him in when you're ready. And you do feel much more responsible. (Dr J.)

There are times when the anaesthetist has to be more decisive than the surgeon: 'whereas the surgeon has time to think and plan, we have to react almost instantaneously. Three minutes is a long time in anaesthesia.' While Dr T. used the metaphor of the harbour pilot, others compared themselves with airline pilots. Both airline pilots and anaesthetists are faced with complex sets of dials that have to be continuously monitored, and both occupations are described as 90 per cent boredom and 10 per cent sheer panic, with take-off and landing the key points of difficulty. It is the level of concentration and the constant double-checking of alarm systems that are relevant here. Dr R. used the metaphor to describe the power she felt in her work:

> . . . there's an incredible feeling of power. It sounds pretty awful but when I first started driving these machines it felt like driving an aeroplane. Okay you only have one person in the passenger seat but it was a similar feeling, that any error could potentially be fatal and that, despite the fact that you have other people around you, you are the only person who chooses which drugs to give and you have almost a life and death control of this person. It is quite a heady sort of feeling, tempered by the fact that however skilful you are every now and then you will come across a sudden crisis that is life threatening.

This association with airline pilots adds a certain glamour to the occupation and shifts the focus away from relations with surgeons to relations with high powered technology.

Many anaesthetists work closely with physicians, especially as the latter spend more of their time on procedures. Because their areas of expertise overlap, there is more space here for boundary disputes. While anaesthetists pioneered the area of intensive care, for example, physicians have contested their expertise. Dr T. recalled a medical superintendent saying, 'Surely you can't have an anaesthetist in charge of intensive care. The physicians won't come and work there if an anaesthetist is in charge.' But, she said proudly, 'we are their equal in knowledge and superior in technicalities'. In Dr T.'s view, physicians are 'an arrogant lot . . . who seem to have the idea that they *own* the patient. A lot of them think we're not quite as bright because we don't have as many drugs to deal with and we work with other people.'

Working in teams has become a source of pride for many anaesthetists who now work in pain clinics and recovery wards, doing procedures on conscious and highly stressed patients. This requires an additional range of skills, for example in treating people who have very bad circulation to their legs. Resuscitation is another important area of work where they need to be highly adaptable. There is also an increasing emphasis on relations with patients. Dr J. recalled that in her training years she barely related to patients at all. The night before an operation whoever was on duty went and saw all the patients for all the lists. It was a matter of technicalities: the drug dose, how to put up drips, and how to put in local blocks successfully. 'So in fact your patient was dished up to you and you hadn't related to them before you put them off to sleep.' By contrast, 'now, it is regarded as important to see a patient and to talk to them and establish their confidence. We take the whole patient into our care on our pre-op. visit and see them right through it.' While these pre- and post-operative visits are usually rather token, they do signal a shift away from the purely technician role.

If women have contributed to the changing occupational identities of anaesthetists, they have also done much to shift the public image of them as misanthropes. Personality profiles suggest that anaesthetists are self-sufficient, self-reliant people who like to control their own affairs without being directed from outside. Dr R. says it appeals to people who like quick results but who are also obsessional and finicky in their approach to life. I had expected them to be loners, rather withdrawn from the world. Instead I met an unusually gregarious and sociable group of women who enjoyed talking and in some cases responded collectively to me and to my project. They are often the ones to fine-tune theatre schedules and ensure a smooth progression from one operation to the next. If arrangements need to be made during an operation they are the ones to leave the theatre. While their interactions with patients may be limited, their interactions with hospital staff can be intense. All stressed their enjoyment of team work:

> The camaraderie of theatre is really good. You roll up and everyone says, 'Hi!' and it's a team you're expecting to see. You tend to see the same team. They rotate all the time. But you've got your team and you get to know them and you chat about how life is. I find a team is a really nice work environment. And what else did I like about anaesthetics? You have a set day's work. As opposed to being, say, a physician where you, I don't know, these poor people wander in and you review their dreadful state and at the end of the day, have you achieved anything? Whereas it's a little bit like making furniture. You've got these five people to anaesthetise and at the end of the morning you've done it and you feel good.

Male anaesthetists were described by the women as generally intro-spective and quiet people, and they may need to be in order to negotiate their relations with surgeons. Women choose anaesthetics for different reasons, and in any case can fall back on the familiar scripts of gender relations in dealing with the egos of male surgeons. The ones in my sample covered a wide spectrum of personalities but they tended towards the extroverted end. In personality they seemed closer to the surgeons than to their male colleagues. Several said they would have liked to be surgeons themselves, suggesting a complex set of identifications and loyalties.

Despite the claims that anaesthetics is friendly to women they have yet to be accepted on equal terms. A 1993 survey of 199 Australian women anaesthetists still found significant levels of dissatisfaction (Khursandi, 1994: 14–15). There were a lot of complaints about 'sought after' lists being allotted to males, and about the 'old school tie' and the 'old-boy' network, while 79 per cent said that training schemes needed to be more flexible. More than half had at some stage worked part-time, and said that part-timers were regarded as less capable, less committed to their careers, and less available (even when fully available). At the same time, women anaesthetists eschew a victim status. They have indeed played an active role in anaesthetics throughout its history and have contributed beyond their numbers to its changing public identity.

The unconscious of medicine

Psychiatry is the unconscious of medicine in rather different ways from anaesthetics. First, it is centrally concerned with the ways in which subjectivity is constituted and the splits between the 'rational' self and its irrational and unconscious dimensions. Second, it has itself been a divided field, split between those who insist on the organic basis of all mental illness and those who want it to break its strong associations with medicine and explore the psychological and/or social dimensions of mental illness. And third, despite its status as a medical specialty, psychiatry evokes the pre-scientific past from which medicine has sought to escape and it makes other specialists uneasy. Littlewood and Lipsedge quote a professor of surgery who described British psychiatry in 1980 as a haven for 'misfits and incompetents'. They suggest that medicine may be described as a 'scientific parvenu, anxious to discard those mystical elements which remind it of its own disreputable past' and that 'to be interested in the insane is still regarded as faintly suspect' (1982: 21).

Busfield claims that psychiatry has provided 'few opportunities for the heroic, technologically sophisticated, scientific medicine that is so esteemed by the medical profession itself' (1986: 30). Psychiatry is not considered properly scientific by many in the medical profession. Where medicine is concerned with cure, and is in its element with acute cases, psychiatry is more likely to deal with chronic illnesses, with only limited prospects of cure. Where patients normally seek medical attention voluntarily, psychiatry has developed around the work of the professionals employed to deal with those compulsorily detained on grounds of insanity and has shared the stigma attached to mental illness. Though many mental hospitals have been shut down, or integrated with general hospitals, public psychiatry is still seen as isolated from general medicine, dealing mostly with the poor and the underprivileged. Psychiatrists have not entirely shed their custodial image.

Critics of psychiatry have often set up an opposition between a 'repressive medicalised sector' and 'a life-enhancing psychotherapeutic alternative' (Miller & Rose, 1986: 3). They contrast the 'hard' end of medical and institutional psychiatry with 'softer' ideals of 'community' drawing on various forms of psychotherapy. This distinction is misleading. As Miller and Rose argue, it is not helpful to view the power of psychiatry as 'some kind of monolithic and malign presence', a mechanism of social control which we 'must strive to abolish' and it may be far more useful to reflect on how that power opens up new ways of thinking about and solving problems (1986: 2). At the same time, Miller and Rose completely understate the power struggles within psychiatry that have appealed to ideas about its 'hard' and 'soft' sides, and they pay no attention to the ways in which representations of psychiatry construct gendered places for those working within it. In practice most psychiatric work contains both 'hard' and 'soft' elements, and women are not obviously concentrated in the latter, but they are nevertheless associated with the 'soft' underside of psychiatry, its concern with social factors, with caring, and with 'talking cures', including psychotherapy. The position of women in psychiatry cannot be understood without some attention to these divisions.

Several of my informants described the tension within psychiatry between its caring dimension and the collective inferiority of the profession in relation to other medical specialties. They felt that this had resulted in a *more* macho culture in academic circles and around the college than is present in other specialties that are more secure about their knowledge base. An academic commented that while the women in her department were strongly compassionate, 'they often have to do battle with the power bases of the more masculine models. Their external facade has to be more the other way and sometimes they may be converted.'

While medical psychiatry does acknowledge the importance of social and psychological factors, it is not prepared to allow them an autonomous existence. In relation to psychiatry, the 'social' and the 'psychological' take on a set of feminine meanings which are subordinate to the organic dimensions through which the progress of the specialty is measured. If women in psychiatry show a weakness for these feminine meanings, they are disciplined. When Sydney psychiatrist, Carolyn Quadrio, observed in a letter to the college journal that delegates to the Royal Australian and New Zealand College of Psychiatrists (RANZCP) congress had shown little interest in exploring social issues, and that virtually no female speakers had been invited, she found herself on the receiving end of an extraordinary barrage of hostility and sarcasm from senior men in the college (Quadrio, 1989). The editor, Robert

Finlay-Jones, pronounced in a footnote that 'leading psychiatrists, of whom the majority are women' would be invited to the next congress, while Phillip Hamilton suggested that Quadrio should have applied to present a paper entitled 'Reflections of a Paranoid Anti-Narco-therapeutic Feminist on Popular Socialist Themes' (*SMH*, 10 May 1990).

Many women in psychiatry agree privately with the feminist criticisms of the profession put forward by Quadrio (1991, 1992) but detach from what they see as her 'anger' and her understanding of women as victims. This enables them to avoid the substance of her criticisms. They agreed that the specialty had taken on a 'macho' identity but generally concluded that the safest strategy was to avoid head-on collisions with the men. Psychiatry has fled from any feminine image and women who want to succeed in conventional terms have to act tough. An ex-college president recalled: 'They used to say, you can't send a woman to Canberra to negotiate, she won't be taken seriously. There is a fear that if you let women be in charge of it, it will reinforce the wimpish side and the sense of inferiority. Men regard it as important to be in control of the academic agenda.' This implies that women have a less 'comfortable' presence in psychiatry than in anaesthetics but they also constitute more of a threat. They have the potential to transform the specialty; but they are also under greater pressure to conform than in perhaps any other area of medicine.

This pressure derives from the long history of warfare between psychiatry and feminism which has accused it, for more than a century, of crimes against women. Psychiatrists have regarded women not only as physically and intellectually inferior but as by nature prone to mental instability. Henry Maudsley, the founding father of specialist psychiatry, after whom London's leading mental hospital is named, considered that menstruation, pregnancy, childbirth and menopause were in themselves causes of mental derangement (Russell, 1995: 20). The decades between 1870 and World War One saw a running battle between psychiatrists and feminists over the nature of womanhood.

Charlotte Perkins Gilman identified clearly the sexism at the centre of psychiatry and her book *The Yellow Wall-Paper* was a spirited protest against psychiatrists, and the rest cures they imposed on women like herself who tried to fulfil their creative potential and be something more than wives. From hysteria in the nineteenth century to schizophrenia in the twentieth, the dominant images of psychiatric patients have been of women. The attributes of femininity which appeared to qualify them so well to be its patients seems to work against their presence as practitioners. Feminists have not called for more women in psychiatry but for alternatives to it.

At the 1970 annual meeting of the American Psychological Association women members asked for a million dollars in reparations for the damage done to women by psychiatry. They wanted the money to get women out of mental hospitals and develop other types of therapy (Castel et al., 1982: 231). Feminists established that lobotomy was more frequently practised on women and drew attention to a widely used British text published in 1972 which recommended psycho-surgery for a depressed woman 'who may owe her illness to a psychopathic husband who cannot change and will not accept treatment' (Showalter, 1987: 209–10).

Women's autobiographies, novels and poetry documented the atrocities that women had experienced at the hands of psychiatrists. Sylvia Plath's *The Bell Jar* and Janet Frame's *Faces in the Water* became feminist classics. In *Women and Madness* Phyllis Chesler detailed the abuses of women by psychiatry. She argued that psychiatry treated femininity itself as a form of mental illness and punished women both for conforming to it and resisting it. 'What we consider "madness,"' she said, 'whether it appears in women or in men, is either the acting out of the devalued female role or the total or partial rejection of one's sex-role stereotype' (1972: 56).

Since the 1970s there has been considerable debate about feminist therapy and mental illness. Foucault's seminal work on *Madness and Civilization* created a different kind of space from which to think about women in psychiatry. Feminist therapy had till then assumed a fairly direct correspondence between social circumstances and psychical states. If women's problems were mostly social in origin, women could most effectively help each other through support and consciousness-raising groups. Women could thereby challenge both the psychoanalytic and the medical categories of traditional psychiatry and develop alternative forms of psychotherapy and of political activism (Showalter, 1987: 250). Rather than calling for more women psychiatrists, the feminist therapy movement wanted to deprofessionalise mental health. They argued that therapy should be democratised and made fully accessible to anyone who wants to learn, and that 'expert' knowledge is merely mystification. This left little space for a specialised knowledge which requires a long training period

But mental illness is less straightforward than this approach suggests. Mental processes do not mirror 'reality' in any simple sense, and the links are not always quite so obvious. Organic theories were rejected out of hand because they appeared to be the basis of medical power. To dismiss a body of knowledge that claims to understand mental processes, in the name of some alternative 'truth', is to do little more than counterpoise one set of truth claims with another. Adlam and Rose (1981) suggest, following Foucault, that, rather than relying on any single theory of mental distress, treatments should be assessed in terms of their conditions of application, the risks and side effects involved, and evidence as to their therapeutic success. Even for ECT, there was evidence that it was effective in the treatment of depression and it was used in good faith. As one psychiatrist pointed out in its defence, 'We shall probably, in the future regard chemotherapy with the same horror we now have for ECT; for the moment, it is the best we have'.

In their preoccupation with psychoanalytic therapy, feminists have tended to ignore the senile, the mad, the disorganised, the deluded, the impoverished and the inarticulate and cut them off from any form of help (Allen, 1986). The extreme resistance to non-social factors meant that they could have little to say about areas like senile dementia where social and psychodynamic explanations hold little sway. Senile dementia is an irreversible degenerative condition and women are grossly over-represented among those who are hospitalised as a result of it. In their preoccupation with new forms of therapy for women, feminists were in danger of by-passing most of what psychiatry was about: 'modern psychiatry simply does not exist as [Chesler] depicts it' (Allen, 1986: 105).

The social control argument has also been subjected to criticism, since any society has norms of behaviour and social processes for their regulation. All medicine involves the application of some kind of norms concerning definitions of sickness and levels of health and there are competing conceptions of diagnosis and treatment both in psychiatry and general medicine. Feminists have begun to reassess their arguments about social control theory and the medical model, while psychiatrists regularly affirm their commitment to social explanations. In the environment of 'eclecticism' that has existed since the 1970s new spaces have opened up for a practice of feminist psychiatry.

Origins

Professional psychiatry began in the mid-nineteenth century when it was thought that by separating the mentally ill from the poor, the criminal and the vagrant, it would be possible to work with the patient's 'moral capacities' to restore health and the capacity to work. Attention soon shifted from environmental factors to the organic and hereditary bases of medical illness. Doctors established control of mental illness through a complex process in which they were able to define a terrain in which practitioners, relatives and the mad themselves operated and which entered into the construction of those very behaviours and emotions designated as mad (Adlam & Rose, 1981). This involved the development of classificatory systems and treatment regimens based on drugs and physical techniques. Patients were alternately purged and sedated, given hot and cold baths, subjected to electrotherapy and, where necessary, placed in strait-jackets. There was little expectation of cure and the asylums became large scale, regimented institutions, and places of last resort for the unwanted and chronically dependent (Busfield, 1986: 256–7). The early decades of the twentieth century saw declining rates of discharge and an increasing use of restraint (Garton, 1988: 172).

Lunatic asylums were not thought appropriate places for women to work in, either as doctors or nurses, since they required a lot of physical strength and personal safety could not be guaranteed. Despite difficulties in filling hospital positions, very few women applied. In 1927, when the first two women were appointed to London hospitals, there were only about forty women practising psychiatry in England (Showalter, 1987: 196). When Flynn and Gardner (1969) surveyed all women who had graduated from the Royal Free between 1945 and 1965 they found that only twenty, or 1.9 per cent had completed the DPM (Diploma of Psychological Medicine).

During World War One, the problem of shell-shock presented a challenge to the prevailing organic theories. Neurosis began to be accepted as a functional mental problem which could be legitimately treated with psychotherapy. To understand the nature of neuroses such as shell-shock, it was necessary to posit unconscious mental processes. This in turn meant that madness stopped being seen as some form of 'fundamental otherness and unreason' and could be located on a continuum (Rose, 1986: 47–52). Psychiatrists emphasised the need for early and preventative treatment and attempted to break down the stigma that still surrounded lunacy. The Maudsley Hospital was set up to treat early and acute cases, while outpatient clinics were attached to London and St Thomas's Hospitals and the Tavistock Clinic was established as a centre for psychotherapy.

In Australia, Broughton Hall was the first clinic to open, working closely with Royal Prince Alfred Hospital, a teaching hospital of Sydney University. While the large mental hospitals were still the main game, the way was open for the development of private and clinical psychiatry. With the new interest in psychotherapy, psychiatry gradually became more open to women's participation, and to new thinking about female psychology. In contrast to the United States, however, private psychiatry was slow to develop in either Britain or Australia and what was done was carried out mostly by GPs. Australia took its lead from Britain and, until the 1970s was dominated by British-trained psychiatrists.

Through the 1930s and 1940s, mental health gradually became more integrated with health services cases as a whole. Considerable excitement was generated around new physical treatments. Malaria therapy provided the first effective treatment for general paralysis of the insane (GPI) while drugs like insulin and cardiazol were claimed to be useful with chronic depression and schizophrenia. Psycho-surgery was introduced to relieve severe depression and reduce aggressive behaviour while electro-convulsive therapy (ECT) was widely practised and sometimes led to dramatic recoveries. These treatments, with their unpleasant side effects, did little to make psychiatry more popular but they did galvanise medical staff and allow them to think of themselves as something more than warders. The development of the NHS brought a structural integration and broadened the range of services provided by the state. The superintendents were being displaced by a new kind of physician who sought the integration of psychiatry into the general hospital and valued the range of new treatments becoming available, both physical and psychological. The growth of the apparatuses of the welfare state also saw the expansion of clinical psychology and the growth of psychiatric social work. Increasingly psychiatrists were working in teams with other health professionals (Rose, 1986: 60–5).

By the 1960s, psychiatry had emerged from being the Cinderella specialty to place itself at the forefront of medical discovery. The advent of psychotropic drugs had allowed for the treatment of chronic patients in the community or in hospital outpatient departments. Psychiatrists like to think of this period as the end of the 'dark ages' when psychiatry 'came of age'. It was finally possible to take away the fences, open the doors, run activity programs and use psychotherapy to explore their difficulties. At long last psychiatry was seen as able to solve problems, and it became important in the training of GPs. The new pharmacological technologies, whether they worked or not, 'provided the conditions for conceiving of the management of the severely deranged or psychi-atrically disabled upon the new psychiatric terrain' (Rose, 1986: 65–6).

At the point when, to most psychiatrists, an end to the 'dark ages' seemed in sight, the anti-psychiatry movement appeared as if from nowhere to proclaim a new dark age. Led by R. D. Laing and David Cooper in England, and Thomas Szasz in the United States, they rejected organic psychiatry and treated mental illness as entirely a social con-struction. For them, the central object of psychiatric knowledge, mental illness, had no objective existence. While accepting its subjective reality, this was not an appropriate area for medical intervention. While psych-iatrists claimed that new drug treatments could do wonders for schizo-phrenia, the anti-psychiatrists argued that it was not an organic disease at all, but a social process that could only be understood through analysing family interactions. Mental illness had to be placed in its social context, including the emotional dynamics of the family and the drive to power of psychiatry itself. They accused doctors of inventing spurious organic theories in order to convince people that madness was real, and that only doctors could treat it. Tranquillisers and antipsychotic drugs, they argued, merely replaced one kind of medical control with another – ensuring social conformity at the price of turning people into vegetables. Hospital walls had been replaced by chemical walls, which were hardly an advance on the savagery of ECT.

These ideas were relatively short lived, but their legacy lingers on, and contributes to the general wariness of psychiatry expressed in Denise Russell's book *Women, Madness and Medicine* (1995). Rather than repressing these ideas, mainstream psychiatry has attempted to absorb them under the banner of eclecticism. Criticisms of psychiatry as a repressive and custodial project for social control probably did assist the shift away from the segregation of the mentally distressed and the greater emphasis on therapy. In the 1970s, universities expanded their psychiatry departments and the new colleges began to coordinate training programs and define the political interests of the specialty. Training programs were increased to five years, with an exam at the end of first year, three years of supervised training on the main rotations, and an elective year devoted to specialty training.

Contemporary psychiatry stakes its professional reputation not on medical expertise alone but on the diversity of its knowledge base. As George Lipton put it in an address to the RANZCP Council:

> I follow Maddison and Ellard who always maintained that the essence and strength of psychiatry is its breadth and depth, and its fundamental basis in the biological, psychological and sociological sciences. The psychiatrist is an integrator and through his or her integrative capacity can find insights which are often unavailable to other professionals . . . The College must ensure . . . that it does not become embroiled in the dichotomous struggle between nature and nurture, between constitution and experience and between ideologies . . . The corpus of psychiatry must never become identified by one philosophy. (1993: 10)

Psychiatry's claim to leadership of the mental health field is its unique capacity to synthesise a range of knowledges. Since other practitioners have access to parts of the knowledge, psychiatrists fear that health services, anxious to reduce costs, will cut corners and downgrade them. They worry that social workers too easily claim a professionalism they do not have, because they do not understand the physical bases of illness and are not trained to diagnose it. They also claim to be broader than psychologists 'who are often very focused on psychological models rather than broader socio-cultural models'. Women have had to counter any implication that they are the 'weak link' in this chain and to affirm the expertise of the profession.

Women in psychiatry

Psychiatry has not been a popular specialty with either male or female medical graduates. Dr L. who trained in England in the 1970s said 'I think my parents felt I had gone down-market when I said I was going to be a psychiatrist rather than a GP!' The period saw a dramatic increase in the numbers of psychiatrists, and women participated in the general expansion. As employment opportunities expanded, it was a relatively easy choice for the larger numbers of women who were graduating. At that stage, the membership exam was not necessary for official registration and it was possible to get by with the three-year diploma in psychological medicine, which was offered by a number of university departments.

Iona Fett found that by 1974 psychiatry was the most preferred specialty among Australian female graduates whereas it was the fifth most preferred among men. The proportion of Australian women choosing it (16.9 per cent) was higher than American women (11.8 per cent) and well ahead of UK women doctors (4 per cent) where it lay in sixth place, after paediatrics, anaesthetics, internal medicine, obstetrics and gynaecology and public health. However, seven years after graduation the British women were ranking psychiatry as second behind general practice (Rhodes, 1989: 130). By 1990, they had caught up and passed the Australians and, in both countries, more than 25 per cent of psychiatrists are now women – a higher proportion than in any other large specialty (Joint Working Party, 1991: 22; AMWAC and AIHW, 1996: 9).

The movement of women into psychiatry coincided with the brief ascendancy of the anti-psychiatry movement and the existence of a feminist movement which put a lot of energy into its attack on psychiatry. While some women who went into psychiatry were touched by these campaigns, most remained detached. Their primary allegiance was to the specialty and they fully accepted both the centrality of organic theory and the need for mental illness to be treated by professionals. They did not enter psychiatry in a moment of feminist zeal, seeking to reform the profession or overthrow its deeply patriarchal biases, but for far more practical reasons. Their own problems with sexism in psychiatry were of a different order. Over time, they have taken up many of the issues raised by feminists and attempted to translate them into the language of psychiatry. Politically they are a diverse group and, while not prepared to go out on a limb for feminism, they certainly claimed to be responding to the contemporary articulations of women's needs. Issues of sexual abuse and domestic violence were a large part of their practices, whether hospital based or clinical. Drawing on the concept of 'eclecticism' they had been able to carve out pockets of practice that are consistent with feminist goals as these are currently being formulated.

Psychiatry has undoubtedly provided a home for some who experience themselves as 'radicals' within medicine. The critiques of psychiatry became part of the consciousness of the specialty. Studies indicate that psychiatrists are more likely to identify as atheists or agnostics than other doctors and that a high proportion actively support the Labour Party (Littlewood & Lipsedge, 1982: 23). Several of the women I interviewed had been attracted by the ambiguity of psychiatry's place within medicine. Dr S. recalled an almost conspiratorial atmosphere in the 1960s among undergraduates who were interested in psychiatry. They were careful not to show their interest, except to others who were going to be psychiatrists, because to do so would signify that they were not serious about medicine. She admits 'I couldn't have been less interested in physiology or anatomy . . . but I had planned to be bored out of my mind during that period.' Dr M. recalled that as a student in the 1970s 'medicine was a terrible disappointment to me at first – until I found psychiatry. I realised straightaway that a conventional medical career wasn't to my taste.' A contemporary, Dr P. had rejoiced in the fact that psychiatrists did not need to behave as 'real' doctors: 'You didn't have to wear white coats. You didn't have to dress like a doctor. If you were a bloke you could have a pony-tail. You could wear what you liked. People expected psychiatrists to be a bit eccentric and different.'

Psychiatry also attracts many people who have confronted their own issues around mental health or sexual identity. A high proportion of psychiatrists are said to be gay or lesbian – several of my British respondents estimated it to be as high as 20–25 per cent. This indicates a broad range of people within psychiatry who do not conform to the 'medical model' as defined by feminists and who are reluctant to see themselves as agents of social control.

Women were and are attracted to psychiatry for a number of reasons. In the first place, jobs were available. Those trying to staff busy wards often begged women to apply. One woman accepted a psychiatry registrar position in the 1970s when she was separated with a one-year-old baby. She says, 'I hadn't any intention of doing psychiatry. I really wanted to be a neurologist but once I had the child, I didn't know what I was going to do. I was walking around in a mess. So I did it.' Another recalled:

Frankly, there weren't many people who wanted to go into psychiatry. It was regarded as a backwater. I just rang up the teaching hospital in Birmingham and said, I want to be a psychiatrist, any openings? And a very famous man rang me back and said, can you start on Monday as an SHO?

In England, there are fewer SR posts than consultants' posts vacant so, in contrast to many other specialties, someone at a SR level is virtually guaranteed a job. In Australia, psychiatric staff leave the public sector in droves, so jobs there are relatively easy to get.

As psychiatry shed its custodial image and became integrated into the public health system, the work came to be regarded as gender-appropriate. Many women who had started out as GPs said that what brought them in was a realisation of their capacity for personal interaction. For some, it is less demanding of personal life than general practice and it was, in the 1970s, possible to move across relatively late from general practice. While consultants still have a 24-hour responsibility for their patients, those in private practice have considerable flexibility in their working hours and it is rare to be called out at night. While many work from home, psychiatric patients may pose particular risks and the cover provided by the hospital can be useful.

It is possible to see in their stories why psychiatry came to be taken up as a women's specialty. One had commenced training in obstetrics and gynaecology only to be told by the men that she was wasting her time because women only want to be examined by males. For reasons she now has some difficulty reconstructing, she believed them. She switched to psychiatry and began to build a new women's health specialty spanning psychiatry and gynaecology. Another said she was tempted by obstetrics but put off by the hours. A third said her career was 'derailed by her reproductive cycle'. After having three children and working part-time as a GP for several years, she decided on psychiatric training. A fourth had started working for the Part One in surgery but dropped out because of the pressure. During GP training she discovered that she enjoyed psychiatry. 'It was a small unit, no one was very disturbed, most were mildly depressed. So I went into psychiatry training and had my membership in two years.'

Dr W. had trained in paediatrics and moved across into psychiatry in her forties:

> I think it has the highest proportion of women consultants because there were so many of us who were stuck at about the age of forty and switched over and a lot went into child psychiatry.

While her husband's career 'went bombing along', she found herself sinking into depression as she juggled part-time registrar positions and babies. Depression was a common theme in the stories of many women who felt that, in overcoming their own problems they had discovered the capacity to help others.

While it happened more out of necessity than a concern for equity, psychiatry claims to be the trend-setter in providing part-time training programs. While many women have benefited, others were less fortunate. Dr S., unable to find a part-time position while her children were young, did a psychology degree instead and was then 'given a cleaner's contract' to apply for a training post. She was given credit for her first-class honours degree in psychology but her child-rearing experience counted for nothing. Carolyn Quadrio notes the paradox that while the profession places more and more importance on early childhood, and postgraduates even attend infant observation groups, yet when students work part-time in order to spend time with their own infants they are perceived to be taking time off from training (1991: 99). Despite the high profile given to the existence of part-time training opportunities in psychiatry they are not readily available (Quadrio, 1991). In Australia in 1994 only 17.2 per cent of women trainees were part-time (AIHW, 1996). As training positions in psychiatry become more competitive, there is a danger that part-time training opportunities will be reduced, or restricted to the high shortage areas.

The expectation that women might be concentrated in psychotherapy and, in the Australian context at least, in private practice is not borne out. More men than women work in private practice (69.9 per cent compared with 63.1 per cent, AIHW, 1996) and, while it is possible that the women spend more of their time on psychotherapy, most practices are very mixed. It is common for salaried psychiatrists to establish lucrative private practices from the wards of public mental hospitals of long-term mentally ill needing comprehensive ongoing care. Most UK psychiatrists are attached to hospitals where the opportunities to practise psychotherapy are probably much less. Whether in public or private practice, most psychiatrists deal with a broad range of patients. Alongside schizophrenia and manic depression, they treat depressive neurosis, anxiety states and psychosocial problems. None of these women would be recognisable in the feminist anti-psychiatry discourse.

When not seeing patients privately, psychiatrists are likely to be working in teams with psychologists, nurses and social workers. The amount of time spent with patients is very variable with fifteen minutes about the average for a hospital psychiatrist. A general psychiatrist seeing a twenty-year chronic attender to adjust their medicine might take only five minutes while a family therapy session would take more like an hour and a half. Dr K. sees a full spectrum of psychiatric disorders in the DSM III sense and makes all her appointments for fifty minutes but does not see all her clients weekly. None of the women interviewed saw any contradiction between drugs and psychotherapy. While they accept that there is an organic base to schizophrenia, they also pointed out that sexual abuse is an important cause. They were emphatic that schizophrenics are just as entitled to psychotherapy as anyone else. But as far as they are concerned, drugs are what make any kind of communication possible.

Challenges

As in other branches of medicine, psychiatry has divided into a number of sub-specialties. Women are heavily represented in child and adolescent psychiatry, in mental handicap and geriatrics. The last two, being regarded as low status and unchallenging, were largely staffed by married women working as clinical assistants. In the 1980s a new breed of doctor began to move in. Dr E., for example, became fascinated by the area of geriatrics and determined to raise its profile:

> I knew that if one was really going to do it seriously I would have to get proper academic qualifications. I looked around for a prestige research job . . . and I went to work with a very distinguished sociologist to get an MD doing research in the community. The circumstances of old people with dementia at home living in appalling squalor, apparently unsupported, with nobody organising services and families utterly desperate, was a very shocking experience . . . the other aspect was that people were suffering from untreated depressions in old age who clearly could be helped.

After becoming a consultant Dr E. moved into an innovative research and policy position, and like many of her female contemporaries in psychiatry took up a senior administrative position.

In the 1980s, women psychiatrists were confronted with a tidal wave of women clients who had, as children and adults, been victims of sexual abuse and domestic violence. There was not one who did not mention this as an important part of her practice. Male psychiatrists have had to respond to these shifts too, but it is fair to say that access to women psychiatrists has made it possible for larger numbers of women to seek help and that the issues raised constitute a major challenge to psychiatry and its understandings of mental illness, including schizophrenia. The presence of women has also drawn attention to sexual exploitation in the therapist–patient relationship, especially of female patients by male therapists (Quadrio, 1992).

Psychiatrists now work closely with other specialists to treat the psychiatric dimensions of a range of diseases. Consultation liaison psychiatry is an important area, where the psychiatrist must try to assess the extent to which a range of health problems are psychically based. Back and abdominal pain, for example, often have psychogenic dimensions. Women psychiatrists have worked closely with women going through gynaecological surgery and breast cancer and made important contributions to a number of areas of women's health including postnatal depression, menopause and sexual problems. They are also likely to work in the community arranging psychiatric services for shock, trauma and natural disasters.

With five presidents of the college in Australia and New Zealand, and one in England in recent years, women are taking an important role in defining the field. The names of women like Anne Dally and Jean Lennane, in the area of drug and alcohol addiction, have become very well known. Both women took a drubbing from the medical establishment, in England and Australia respectively, for their outspokenness. Quadrio (1991) has documented the under-representation of women in senior academic positions, their absence from examination processes, and from all public forums organised by the college.

The main challenge may come, not from psychology or social work but from general practice and particularly the work of women GPs. As Rose (1986) has indicated, the power of psychiatry extends beyond the specialty itself and is linked to a process whereby the concepts of psychiatry have taken over society as a whole and we have become accustomed to thinking of our personal fulfilment in relationship to mental health. While psychiatrists are careful to preserve the division between psychiatry and general practice, the boundary is artificial and women are the ones who cross it most regularly.

7

The Subalterns of General Practice

It is 3 p.m. on Saturday and I have just sat down to lunch
after a typical Saturday morning surgery.

In the course of the morning, I have seen depression,
phobia, drug dependence, chest infections, infertility, and
abdominal pain with bowel symptoms (which turned out
after more than an hour of close questioning and careful
physical examination to be acute pelvic inflammatory
disease).

In short, I have been a paediatrician, a gynaecologist, a
gastroenterologist, a respiratory physician and a psychiatrist
all in one morning.

Now to my delight I find I am to be 'immediately trained
to take over minor surgery'.

[quoting *SMH*, 22 October 1994]

Apart from the general patients I see every day, like most
practitioners, I have areas of special interest . . . Unusual?
Any GP could tell a similar story.

Professor Baume could not be further from the truth
when he says that the last 50 years have seen a systematic,
long-term deskilling of the GP. We are highly trained
professionals whose skills lie in diagnosing from the specific
to the general and the general to the specific.

We may have fewer procedural skills than our
predecessors, but as the information revolution gathers
pace, we know more than they ever did.

(Dr Carole Hungerford, *SMH*, 26 October 1994)

This is a fighting statement which proclaims the skills, diversity and spirit
of general practitioners and celebrates a heroic tradition of which the
speaker is proud to be part. But the story of general practice is a story of
exclusion from advanced medical practice and a struggle to remain part

of the medical field at all. The past heroes, who functioned as physicians, surgeons, obstetricians and anaesthetists, working solo, on-call twenty-four hours a day, seven days a week, dealing with every kind of emergency, are no more. Most GPs work in group practices, and even those who do not, use locums at evenings and weekends and maintain a physical separation between their home and their practice. GPs now spend the bulk of their time treating hypertension, upper respiratory tract infection, asthma, arthritis, bronchitis, anxiety and depression, sprains and strains, dermatitis and diabetes (Walsh & Willcox, 1992). It is a common view that they have been deskilled. Medical students, who commence their studies with all the accolades of having been the best and brightest of their year, with the highest matriculation scores and a shining future in front of them, move into a different reality when they take up general practice. Having graduated with the title of 'Doctor', a title bestowing considerable prestige and cultural authority, they find themselves in a subordinate position, excluded from the hospitals, patronised by medical specialists and struggling to carve out a distinctive role for themselves.

GPs are the subalterns of medicine, who partake of its authority but from a place to the side. They are admitted to the field, they know its rules and stakes, but their authority is qualified by their subaltern status. If the metaphor is military, unlike sub-lieutenants, most have little hope of advancing to full officer status. Cut off from the hospital elite, they are nonetheless bearers of cultural capital, at least in relation to their own constituencies, expecting and receiving respect as 'doctors', from patients, other health workers, and the local communities in which they live and work. While some may attempt to move closer to the centre of the field, the majority are content to consolidate their place in the outfield. Often they will deny the subordinate status of general practice, pointing out that they too are specialists who have to complete three years of postgraduate training in order to be accredited. A significant number have additional diplomas in areas such as obstetrics or paediatrics, while many more claim areas of special interest, even encroaching on the non-medicalised area of alternative therapies such as acupuncture and homeopathy. General practice is in this way a highly differentiated area. The positioning of GPs on the boundaries is also not without strategic possibilities. Since they are the ones who come into most regular contact with the general public, they contribute a great deal to the reputation of the medical field as a whole. And, since the task of defending the boundaries of the field also falls to them, they have choices about when to repel invaders and when to cooperate with them in ways that might reconfigure the whole field.

If GPs are the subalterns of medicine, it may be argued that women are the subalterns of general practice. Jonathan Gathorne-Hardy's historical account of general practitioners in London (which, though published in the 1980s scarcely mentions women) quotes an old-timer as saying that it was necessary to have an abundance of doctors struggling to be consultants so that the best came to the top through competition. In the past, he said, the surplus had either gone into general practice or out to the colonies. Since those options were no longer possible, he believed the new solution was to produce lots of women doctors who would be unable to become consultants because of child care responsibilities. They would give the men a run for their money and then retreat into general practice where, since most would be working part-time, there would be plenty of room for them (Gathorne-Hardy, 1984: 258). Gathorne-Hardy reproduces this without comment but it has a certain currency. It is ludicrous to argue that the 'best' can rise to the top if half the field are forced to withdraw. But it rings true as the way in which many male doctors have been able to position women. Many think of women as a part-time subsidiary force, helpful in dealing with psychological problems, but not real doctors.

Women doctors are placed in a difficult boundary situation. Medical men may regard them as the weak link, vulnerable to a reverse take-over from the social and psychological arenas. Enough women doctors have spoken out against their profession to fuel these fears. At the same time women doctors have to negotiate all kinds of expectations that they will practise differently as the 'human' face of medicine. They are seen not only as 'women doctors' but 'women's doctors'. Most women doctors attempt to resist these discourses by insisting on their own individuality. Some emphasise their medical credentials while others strive for more open relationships with other health workers. Many attempt to do both. Perhaps the one thing they have in common is that they are situated in that turbulent area in which the 'medical model' meets the domain of the 'social'. They resolve this differently and usually with all kinds of contradictions. So they may embrace feminist principles at one moment and rage against midwives the next, or complain about being relegated to Pap smears while insisting that nursing staff are not qualified to do them. Whether they like it or not, women GPs occupy the territory in which the restructuring of general practice will take place. Their physical presence mediates the tensions between the medical profession and its critics.

Despite the inroads they have made, women GPs have been written about as the proletariat of the medical world (Annandale, 1989), who have not only failed to become consultants, but been relegated to the lowest ranks of general practice (Allen, 1988; Newman, 1991). A high proportion work part-time, in salaried or casual positions rather than in partnerships, earning less for the hours that they work, dealing predominantly with gynaecological and paediatric problems, and suffering all kinds of exploitation at the hands of employers. The woman GP is frequently a second-class citizen among the doctors in the practice. She may be exploited financially and her domestic commitments may be used to exclude her from decision-making (Eisner & Wright, 1986). A Melbourne University study indicated that while doctors are twice as likely to commit suicide as the general population, women doctors are six times more likely to do so. They are also more prone to depression and drug addiction than male doctors. It is now claimed that medicine is 'a health hazard for female GPs' (*SMH*, 5 November 1990).

While women GPs may be 'failures' against masculine benchmarks of success, and live with a great deal of stress, the stories told to me were animated, and had a heroic quality about them, whatever the career outcomes. These were narratives of struggle, with the profession, with husbands, and with forces deep within themselves, all fought to resolve what seemed like overwhelming contradictions in their lives. The tales of difficulty and harassment, of exploitation and sheer exhaustion, were more than balanced in the elements of pleasure and satisfaction in their work and personal lives. There were regrets about the specialist paths started and dropped but little lasting bitterness. They had adjusted to their current lives, and often saw themselves as trailblazers, creating new ways of practising medicine. While to a lot of people the life of a GP is harrowing to contemplate, many said they had chosen it because it offered more flexibility than other professional and managerial occupations.

At the 1991 Australian census, 62.7 per cent of female GPs said they were married (compared with 58.2 per cent for other female professionals) and 22.2 per cent of employed female GPs had children under five, compared with 13.8 per cent of other female professionals. In December 1994, only 34.5 per cent of female primary care practitioners were working full-time, compared with 76.8 per cent of their male counterparts (AIHW, 1996). These figures indicate that, despite, or perhaps because of, discrimination in the medical field there is, nevertheless, a greater flexibility of work schedules than are available in many other occupations. Women have gone into general practice at least partly because it enables them to balance their work and personal lives, and their understandings of 'success' do not necessarily require that priority be given to maximising *cultural* capital within medicine. As they increase in numbers they are collectively building up *symbolic* capital, the power to reshape the field of general practice and their place in it.

Certainly they are, as a group, more approachable than most specialists. I found myself more quickly on first name terms, being treated as someone who had equal or equivalent knowledge, in what felt more like a dialogue than an interview with 'an important person'. While, in earlier chapters, I have addressed my subjects formally, here I use names and titles fairly interchangeably, in much the same way that they were used at the time of the interview. (The real names have of course been changed.)

The habitus of the GP

As a subaltern figure, the GP is expected to share the habitus of the specialist but is also seen as lacking the intellectual mastery, social prestige or skill base that are manifested in the consultant physician or surgeon. Historically GPs were small businessmen who, in the nineteenth century, rose on the coat-tails of the surgeons and physicians. Though they managed to claim the common title 'doctor', their status depended very much on that of their clientele (Hart, 1988). In the 1950s the problem was not a decline in social status but the potential severing of the established links with consultants, which threatened to redraw the boundaries and exclude them from the medical field entirely.

In order to survive, GPs needed a body of knowledge that was quite distinct from that of the hospital specialists. In England, Michael Balint, the psychoanalyst and refugee from Hungary, contributed much to this in his attempt to apply psychotherapy to general practice. One of my informants, who worked in a weekly group with him in the late 1950s, recalled how he encouraged them to think about treating the whole person, recognising how his or her psychological state could influence the illness and the ways in which illness might be a solution to the present situation. Armstrong (1976) has described this as the 'biographic' approach to medicine as it is concerned with interpreting signs and symptoms in the context of the patient's biography. It was taken up by a small but influential group around the college and aspects of it became widely incorporated into practice.

GPs now say with pride that they 'treat the whole patient', although this may be difficult, given the pressure to whiz through as many people as possible with six-minute appointments. General practice is likely to be experienced as a quick fix supermarket. Nevertheless, I was repeatedly told that GPs care about the patient, whereas specialists care only about the disease. GPs mark themselves out from other health workers both by their diagnostic skills and the 'personal' skills of managing, explaining and coordinating what is going on for the patient. Because they have had prior contact with the patient, they claim to be uniquely able to differentiate psychological problems, to educate and to screen, and are best equipped for continuing care and liaison work with other community-based helping professions (Mansfield, 1991: 31).

The emphasis on holistic medicine has served general practice well in its struggle to differentiate itself from the specialists but it has problematised its place in the medical field. In Bryan Turner's analysis, the shifting place of the GP is accompanied by a change in the definition of illness:

> To some extent stress has replaced the germ as the major explanation of modern illness; the concept of cure will be increasingly replaced by concepts of rehabilitation and care. The result is that the general practitioner will come to depend more and more on sociological skills as their education in the physiological, chemical and biological aspects of disease and illness becomes increasingly less relevant in the treatment and management of patients. The age of heroic medicine has been replaced by the mundane medical management of chronic as opposed to acute illness. (Turner, 1987: 8)

The change is summed up by a young woman doctor as follows:

> In the medical model we are taught that in treatment a disease gets better, it goes away, and in general practice that doesn't happen. The more you get to know someone the more you realise what their home circumstances are like, what their beliefs are, that they are trapped. You can't help their headaches, you can't help their irritable bowel, you can only be nice to them and go over and over the same stuff. And some of them progress and some of them don't.

One of the difficulties here, as Hart remarks (1988: 97–9) is that since the new territory lay outside of organic physical disease, the traditional core of clinical practice was left to the specialists. Many GPs felt they were being turned into glorified social workers, seeing this as a diminution of their skills. Their professional aspirations were still modelled closely on hospital practice, with demands to be let back into the hospitals and to carry out procedures that had been handed over unnecessarily to specialists (Calnan & Gabe, 1991: 145–7). Dr Frank Mansfield has interpreted the changes as 'castrating', as depriving 'men' of their self-esteem:

> while it was the mid-19th Century that saw the establishment of the GP role as we understand it today, it was the mid-20th Century that saw its decline, with the massive growth of technology which naturally focused medical resources on the hospitals and their attendant specialists. The GP began to lose his role and his glamour, and also I believe his self-esteem. (1991: 30)

Many older male GPs attest to this feeling of emasculation brought on by the loss of status and authority to which they feel entitled. For them, 'the feminine' is somehow implicated, whether it refers to a 'softening' of general practice or the actual incursion of large numbers of women.

Faced with this reality, two distinctly different schools of thought have emerged, one stressing a social orientation, including health promotion, and the other reclaiming the more traditional clinical approach, including the right to do minor surgery. To some extent this is a gender division, with women more likely to locate themselves on the social and psychological side and men on the clinical. Of course not all women GPs want to do counselling or feel they have any particular expertise in it – and not all patients want to be counselled. Practices often contain a mix of people with procedural and counselling skills, with different gender patterns clearly discernible.

Women move in

In September 1990 a spokesman for the BMA predicted to me that by the early 21st century women would make up 80 per cent of general practitioners. A conservative British Government had recently announced a 'Patient's Charter' which included the right of everyone to have access to a woman GP. Surveys were indicating that a majority of women believed that women doctors had a better understanding of their problems, that women took more time, were gentler and more caring than men, more willing to listen and to explain things (Williams et al., 1991: 27–9). The promise could not easily be fulfilled. As was soon pointed out, 'only' 50 per cent of practices had a woman and, since many of these worked part-time, there were still nowhere near enough to go around (Gilbert, 1993: 67). But twenty years earlier, such a promise and such a complaint would have received a bemused response. In 1970 women doctors may not have faced quite the problems they had earlier in the century, but they were by no means universally accepted. The idea that large sections of the public, men as well as women, would come to *prefer* them, or that women would eventually account for the vast majority of GPs, would have been treated as fanciful, despite the experience of the socialist countries.

By 1990 women were 23.5 per cent of GP principals in the UK, 47.2 per cent of trainees and 59 per cent of assistants (Women in Medicine, 1992a). In Australia, by 1994 female clinicians made up 30.9 per cent of the primary care workforce (AMWAC, 1996) and more women than men were entering the Family Medicine Program (McBride, 1993).

Far from constituting a liability to a practice, women doctors are now in high demand. Instead of being perceived as unusual or anomalous, they are often idealised as combining the best features of doctors and nurses, and as 'family' women who understand everyday problems. Whether there are actual differences in the practice of male and female doctors is not at issue here. Recent evidence confirms that there are

(Britt et al., 1996). And the widespread belief that women GPs are 'better', at least for some ailments, places women in a strong bargaining position. In Australia the National Women's Health Policy statement of 1989 identified significant consumer preference for female service providers. By that time, most group practices in Australia and the UK had recognised that they needed to include at least one woman.

This shift got under way in the 1960s and escalated in the early 1970s when women suddenly made up 35 per cent of medical school enrolments in both countries. Many in the medical establishment tried to turn the tide. As they could no longer get away with questioning women's capacity, or the appropriateness of their doing medicine, they developed a new argument about women's low productivity and the wastefulness of training them (Elston, 1977; Lawrence, 1987).

In Australia, where entry to medical school was unrestricted (numbers were controlled by a very high failure rate in early undergraduate years), pressure was placed on the universities to use quotas to limit the numbers of women. Expensive medical training, it was claimed, was wasted on women who would only marry and have children, leaving the medical profession seriously understaffed, while 'well-motivated males' were being redirected to other professions (*Australian*, 10 October 1971). There was a sense of panic in the profession about the shift in public opinion in favour of women doctors. A 1980 Australian study found that, while 60 per cent of respondents still preferred a male doctor, younger people of both sexes had no strong preference (Bretos, 1984: 18–19). Seven years later, a group of women, selected randomly from the Melbourne phone directory, were asked their preferences. Only 16 per cent said they preferred a man, while 26 per cent preferred a woman and 58 per cent had no preference (Schlicht & Dunt, 1987).

A Manchester study found that women were choosing to consult women about a range of sex-related conditions, and drew attention to the growing numbers who, for cultural and religious reasons, would refuse to see a male doctor (Cooke & Ronalds, 1985). Graffy (1990) found that 40 per cent of women in a London surgery actively sought appointments with a woman doctor.

The increasing numbers of women, with different patterns and expectations of work, have important implications for future workforce planning, as both the British and Australian governments have realised. The British government sought, through the 1990 contract, to encourage more doctors into genuine full-time practice but has been slow to consider how to make conditions more attractive for part-timers. Extraordinarily, the Australian authors of an issues paper on 'The Future of General Practice' (Walsh & Willcox, 1992) did not mention gender at all, as if they believed it was 'sexist' to do so. While they did not reproduce stereotypes of women doctors as uncommitted part-timers, they failed to take up crucial questions about the relation between women's employment patterns and the future organisation of general practice. The omission was rectified when, in 1995 AMWAC (the Australian Medical Workforce Advisory Committee) set up a working party to explore the implications of the increasing numbers of women doctors. Of particular concern has been the question of how to attract more female GPs to rural areas.

Britain and Australia

Before going on to consider how women are positioned in general practice, I shall pause briefly to outline the place of GPs in Britain and Australia. Contrary to many popular beliefs, British GPs are not salaried but remain independent contractors working for Family Practitioner Committees. GP leaders fought the creation of the NHS fearing they would lose their independence and be put on salaries set by local councils. This did not happen but they were forced to rely heavily on capitation fees and were cut out of the big-spending hospital sector. The poor working conditions of the 1950s led to serious morale problems. The gap between GPs and specialists continued to grow as the specialists, who had previously worked in hospitals for no direct payment, and supported themselves by private consultations, drew salaries with Merit Awards to compensate them for any private income they forfeited. There was a major exodus of doctors from Britain during this period, with North America and Australasia the favoured destinations. General practice stayed in the doldrums. Assistants were taken on and exploited, often promised a partnership which never eventuated. This created a lasting bitterness. It was not a context in which women throve although, conversely, there was plenty of low-paid casual work available. One informant said she became:

> an expert in part-time jobs. In those days you could do a lot of welfare clinics and ante-natal stuff without any qualifications . . . I also worked for the blood transfusion service . . . then I started doing general practice two evenings a week.

During this period there were struggles to reinvent general practice and to lift its morale. The establishment of the Royal College of General Practitioners in 1953 – against the opposition of the three existing colleges – was an important milestone (Hart, 1988: 85–90, Calnan & Gabe, 1991: 144–5). By the mid-1960s, as a shortage of GPs developed (a result both of the brain drain and the cuts in the medical school intake during and after World War Two) something had to be done. A new contract was established in 1966 which immediately lifted incomes, status and morale. Pay was increased to make the base rates equivalent to those of specialists. Cheap loans were provided for buildings and equipment, while each partner could claim reimbursement of 70 per cent of the wages for two full-time support staff. Suddenly it became desirable for small practices to take on an extra partner to take advantage of the new grants, and that person was likely to be a woman. Dr Rose recalls:

> I came across someone who had known my husband in the past who was a local GP. I started doing one weekend in four for his practice and then they asked me if I would join them as a partner. That was in 1967 – the year when those GPs who were two became very anxious to take in a third partner. You then got a group practice allowance. By the time they got the basic allowance for the third principal and the group practice allowance, and given that they no longer had to pay locums, they could almost employ a third partner for nothing, assuming that partner didn't have parity. So I worked as a salaried partner for five years and became a very popular doctor in the practice. As the practice numbers went up I did more work but got no more remuneration.

Solo practice, which had already fallen to 23 per cent by 1968 dwindled further under the impact of the new contract. Nurses, health visitors, social workers and midwives were increasingly attached to practices, as part of 'primary health' teams, and vocational training schemes were expanded though not yet made compulsory (Hart, 1988: 92–4). By the mid-1970s in England 'general practitioners had gained control over their working conditions and created a distinct environment in which a profession could flourish' (Calnan & Gabe, 1991: 145). So women moved in at a time when the status of general practice was rising, as it found new meanings for itself and attracted stronger government subsidy. If anything, the presence of women contributed to the new status and more optimistic mood among general practitioners.

The Thatcher Government came to power in 1979 determined to curb spending on health and to limit professional power. It set up the Griffiths Inquiry into the management of the NHS and quickly implemented its recommendations, establishing 'general managers' whose task was to make the NHS internally more competitive and accountable (Cox, 1991; Elston, 1991: 68–9). GPs were not initially affected but eventually they too were brought within the ambit of a more competitive health care system. In the first place, they were made more financially responsible for their clinical decisions. In 1990 the government introduced a fund holding scheme which allows practices with over 11,000 patients direct control over the money spent on secondary care for their patients. Rather than simply admitting patients to the closest appropriate hospital, GP fund holders now choose the hospitals on the basis of cost and quality. General practices are becoming major business organisations with substantial power over hospital spending (Ellis, 1991: 333–5; Calnan & Gabe, 1991: 153–4). These reforms have been interpreted as an assault, in the name of managerial efficiency and accountability, on the medical profession's autonomy in the workplace (Elston, 1993).

The government also imposed a new GP contract which, for the first time brought GPs under detailed surveillance, with their activities monitored by the Family Practitioner Committees. It increased the allowance for full-time practitioners by increasing the proportion of income derived from capitation grants. While the government argued that the new contract would make more women doctors available, by creating inducements for doctors to work full-time, critics predicted it would have the opposite effect. Before 1990 many full-time GPs had arranged their surgeries over four days of the week, using the fifth for other activities. This was no longer acceptable. Basic practice hours were increased from twenty to twenty-six hours a week and it was specified that these must be worked over five days. This made it difficult for women who had used the extra day for domestic tasks: 'I had always had my Thursdays off and I had to start working every Thursday'. Though it was possible to be a principal and to work half or three-quarter time, in practice it became more difficult (Newman, 1991). Since the financial penalties for small list sizes and limited hours increased, it was less likely that a practice would want to take on partners who wanted a less than full load. Those women who were in partnerships had to make hard decisions whether to fulfil the conditions and stay on, or to work only as assistants.

College surveys had already indicated that young women had difficulty obtaining suitable partnerships, especially if they had to move from one part of the country to another. In reports that echo the 1960s, many complained that they were being expected to work three-quarters of the week for half a salary, or that older male partners thought they should restrict themselves to 'ladies' complaints' (McBride, 1993). It seemed likely that practices would stop appointing new principals and appoint assistants instead. Since assistants do not have to be vocationally trained, they can step in straight from hospital jobs. While women were present in general practice in growing numbers, they were in great danger of getting trapped as GP assistants.

In Australia, the Chifley Labor Government of 1945–49, like the British, wanted to establish a national health service staffed by salaried doctors (Sax, 1989: 109; Daniel, 1990: 21). It was thwarted by High Court challenges and the relentless opposition of the doctors. From the 1950s the Menzies Liberal Government gave money to the States to provide public ward hospital accommodation and medical treatment free of charge to pensioners and the very poor. For the rest of the population, voluntary health insurance was encouraged by subsidies to hospitals for insured patients and supplements to medical benefits entitlements. Since doctors were subsidised on a fee-for-service basis their incomes sky-rocketed. Concerned about escalating medical costs the government passed a *National Health Act* in 1970 which introduced differential benefits for GPs and specialists and brought medical incomes under limited state control, by defining the 'most common' fees on which rebates would be based. GPs saw this as relegating them to the rank of second-class doctors, but it did confirm them as gatekeepers, whose referrals were necessary before patients could claim rebates on special-ists' fees. Although Australia has more closely followed the American system in some aspects of medicine, with regard to GPs Australia's practitioners retain the same generalist function they have in the UK. Since 1989 in Britain, and 1995 in Australia, three years of specialist training, administered by the colleges, is required for vocational regis-tration. Both programs specify two years of relevant hospital experience beyond the intern year, as well as a year of supervised GP training.

While British GP incomes are based on capitation fees, and Australian incomes on fee-for-service, the distinction has become blurred. British doctors are paid bonuses for vaccinations, Pap smears and family planning consultations. Under the 1990 contract 15 per cent of their incomes is made up from fees, 60 per cent from capitation and 25 per cent from salary in the form of practice grants (Walsh & Willcox, 1992). By 1992, three-quarters of Australian GP services were bulk billed (Ragg, 1994: 30) and the Medicare schedule of benefits exerts federal control over the activity and remuneration of doctors, irrespective of whether or not they bulk bill. The differences between the two countries are more subtle than the differences between 'public' and 'private' medicine would suggest and, for the purposes of this book, the similarities are more important.

Subaltern stories

In both Britain and Australia the subaltern position of women GPs is abundantly clear. The question is, how do they live out this positioning and how, if at all, do they modify it? What became clear from my interviews is that they have very different criteria of 'success' from the conventional ones of medicine. While these criteria necessarily confirm their subordinate position, it can be argued that they also have their effects in changing how medicine is publicly perceived. GPs are, after all, the first port of call and the public face of medicine for most people. How they behave with their clients is likely to change the expectations that people also have of specialists.

Maria Markus (1987) has reflected on these issues in relation to a study of the experience of women engineers. Three-quarters of the women in her sample formulated 'success' in private terms, to refer to satisfaction with specific aspects of their lives. This could mean regaining self-confidence after time out of the workforce, or gaining some professional credentials within specifically difficult circumstances, or coping with multiple roles. The overcoming of obstacles and difficulties was almost an intrinsic part of the meaning of 'success' to them with relatively little concern for external recognition, usually taken to be an important marker. Rather than 'failing' to plan their careers properly, women are unwilling to concentrate exclusively on careers, to the detriment of other interests, attachments and loyalties. Satisfaction came from the character of interpersonal contacts, and from the ability to be 'useful' or helpful, and they brought these qualities even to jobs that had not previously required them. Markus suggests that the 'privatisation' of women's standards of success is an ambiguous phenomenon. On the one hand it contains a promise of a new model of career orientation; on the other, it expresses and maintains the inequity of their current situations. She believes that men and women must work together to restructure the conditions of work and domestic life, and to democratise the meanings of success.

These ideas strike many chords with the experience of women doctors. The meanings of 'success' produced in the following case studies may confirm them in a subordinate position within medicine but they also have the potential to challenge both medical organisation and domestic hierarchy.

On her own terms

Robyn Edwards recently celebrated her fortieth birthday. One of four partners in a Sydney inner-city practice, she works 'part-time' which currently means thirty-five consulting hours a week and a lot of paperwork to take home. With a small daughter she joined the practice on condition that she would work school hours and take school holidays. Robyn graduated with honours but received no encouragement to specialise and realised as an intern that she would never be part of 'the club'. Whether this was to do with her gender or her lower-middle-class background she was unable to say. She left the hospital system after two years and, uncertain about her future, did what many Australians still do and went off to England for two years, and worked in a variety of short-term hospital jobs. The English experience was positive because she was given a lot of responsibility and gained self-confidence. Returning to Australia, Robyn worked in community health centres and developed an interest in paediatrics and child psychiatry. This could have taken her into the school health service but instead she joined the family medicine program, then in its early days. Having by then been through marriage and divorce and with a two-year-old to look after, she moved to the country and was quickly offered a salaried position with flexible working hours, by a man she describes as an entrepreneurial type, 'a specialist in the five-minute consultation and the handing out of scripts for Valium', who made a lot of money out of radiology and in-house pathology. Although she was unhappy with the way the practice was run, as an employee there was little that she could do about it. When Tania reached school age she returned to the city and eventually settled into her current position.

Robyn epitomises the new kind of 'women's health' practitioner. Most of her clients are women and children and her time is spent on counselling, paediatrics and gynaecological matters. This is not to be dismissed as 'paediatrics and Pap smears'. Robyn has built a solid reputation for treating fertility problems and menopause, and she is a skilled counsellor. She gets many referrals from women's health centres. Like a number of other women's health specialists she has also begun to get HIV patients of both sexes. This allows her to make use of her counselling skills and is intellectually challenging. 'If you are sloppy it makes a big difference', she says, 'whereas you can't go far wrong with coughs and colds.'

Robyn found her way into medicine by being good at science at school. General practice was attractive because it combined science with 'being with people' and removed her from the elitist atmosphere of the training hospitals. Her practice is egalitarian and her concern is to see people taking responsibility for their own health. Rather than placing herself on the treadmill of a training program, she had travelled, worked in a variety of settings, and to a significant degree, organised her work around her personal preferences and domestic needs. She is aware that by doing so women risk exploitation and marginality. Becoming a partner was therefore an important, though scary, step.

Robyn enjoys the flexibility of general practice and continues to find new challenges in it. She is happy to be called a feminist, if this means a commitment to equality of opportunity and the provision of quality health care to women. Whatever personal disappointments she has suffered (and she guards her privacy here) she has balanced her work and personal life without having to make unacceptable compromises. She likes and respects her colleagues, from whom she draws emotional as well as professional support. She became a partner on her own terms and if she returns to full-time work that too will be on her terms. She has continued to develop new skills and to practise these in a supportive environment. She would be appalled by any suggestion that she had failed to fulfil her potential or that, as a part-timer, the quality of her work was inferior.

There are enough women like Robyn around to suggest some major shifts in what general practice represents and in how it is organised. They are aware that they have opportunities to restructure medical practice in ways that are better for both doctors and patients. While they continue to have difficulty getting partnerships, negotiating flexible working hours and leave arrangements, the pressure is on.

A broken career path

The interview with Dr Wade was facilitated by an English colleague of mine, a feminist with a wide professional knowledge of health and medicine, who had reason to be hyper-critical of general practitioners. She had been a patient of Dr Wade and considered her the best GP she had ever consulted. This high recommendation set up in me an expectation that I would find an assertive, career-minded woman with strong feminist views. Dr Wade, who was in her early 60s, had worked all her life, but refused to locate herself in a discourse about career aspirations, insisting that she had never wanted to be a high flier but just to be 'middle of the road' and 'able to do a mixture of things.' While now a senior partner, there were times when she had struggled to stay in the workforce at all.

After graduating in the 1950s, Ellen Wade had three children in barely three years. On the first pregnancy, she worked until a month before the baby was born and returned three months afterwards. Doctors were usually so desperate for locums that they would say, 'bring the baby with you!' So the baby was taken to work in a carry-cot and breastfed between sessions. After the second one, she employed a carer and reduced her sessions to three a week. After the third she worked in family planning clinics and then schools for ten years. Tiring of schools she joined a general practice as the 'nice part-time lady assistant' who deals with family planning and psychosexual problems. Her husband is entirely absent from her narrative of these years and clearly gave little support.

It is a typical story of a woman's restricted career, cut off from specialties or partnerships, working in marginal areas of the health service, poorly paid and exploited. And it gets worse. The marriage broke up, and she developed a drinking problem and had difficulty holding a job down. This period was described without anger or frustration, as if to practise medicine was enough. She simply stressed how much she had enjoyed the children. With few other options left, she set up in solo practice, and was eventually able to take on two full-time partners. She stopped drinking and still regards this as her greatest achievement. A second marriage brought the intimacy the first had lacked. Had I interviewed Dr Wade ten years earlier, I might have been less convinced of her 'success'. Seeing her now, there is little doubt. She has triumphed over personal difficulties, maintained a process of self-education and treats her patients with the kind of empathy that comes from shared experience. This is why my friend found her such a good doctor. Dr Wade expressed no views on feminism except to note that it had a very bad name for itself and that some of her clients became angry when she refused to conform to their notions of what a feminist should be!

Dr Wade's story is echoed in the later ones: struggles to remain in the workforce with small children, the resort to family planning, school health services and locums, the stresses that can lead to marriage breakdowns, addiction and self-destructive behaviours. It is notable how often solo practice provides a way back in because it does not require either building trust or asking for what might be seen as 'favours' by other doctors.

Have I made the big sacrifice?

Maeve O'Leary lives in a sprawling Victorian house on the outskirts of Manchester. Thursday, she said, was her day for indulgences. These included picking me up from the station, taking me home, and later driving me to my next interview, in each case some distance, talking nineteen to the dozen all the way. Aged 38 she was married to another GP, had three small children and, at the time of the interview was pregnant with a fourth. Like Robyn, she came from a lower-middle-class family and had no idea initially what she wanted to do. It was only after she was accepted into nursing that she thought at all about the possibility of medicine. After graduating in Ireland she began paediatrics training, but was quickly brought 'to her knees' by the physical stamina required and mental stress involved. 'I actually used to be sick into the sink before I started because I'd worry about what I'd be faced with. You could be left in the special care baby unit and a baby might go flat and you'd have to intubate . . . which is terrifying to do for the first time.'

Confronted with the power structure of hospitals 'bells started to ring' and she opted for general practice.

There she encountered an older woman in the practice, who was interested in psychotherapy and together they made it central to the way they worked. The two women ran into conflict with their three male colleagues who complained they were not seeing enough patients but, after six months 'we were able to confront them and say, look, you guys. We're mopping up the depressives, the suicides, we're doing a lot more psychiatry than you are and it takes time.' This is a common story.

Women GPs are more likely to have long consultations and patients often come to them with expectations that they will 'take more time' and 'listen' (Lawrence, 1987: 141). But, when the waiting room is full, GPs are under pressure to push people through quickly.

Having learned the value of therapy in her medical practice, Maeve eventually sought help to explore her own family dynamics. She dropped from full-time general practice to working two days a week in a diabetic clinic. This point was reached only after a long struggle with her internal work ethic and, it would seem, the insistence of her therapist. Maeve enjoyed the 'kudos' of being a doctor and had battled to work twenty-six hours a week with three small children and little practical support from her GP husband.

> I used to go into work and sit at that desk and leave the hassles of home and being the dogsbody to the kids . . . I used to get a charge when people came to the door, just being able to deal with things. I liked being able to exercise my brain and solve problems that were mentally taxing . . . Being a GP is a privilege because it is a window on life that few other jobs give you. I think some of the peak moments of my life have been sitting in the surgery. . . It has put the whole of my life into perspective.

Maeve asks herself, 'Have I made the big sacrifice?' and answers, 'I don't feel that I have because I've got so much out of it myself. If I was sitting here thinking everyone else is happy but I would like to be out there being an amazing GP, I would have.' She claims her confidence is better. 'Even though I'm not out there blazing a career trip, I don't have any self-doubts . . . Our quality of life has improved dramatically in the last eighteen months.' She plans to return to full-time practice when the children are older and expects then that she will be able to get a partnership.

Maeve is animated about her current work with the diabetic clinic and her attempts to involve other general practitioners in preventative work. She regards it as perfectly reasonable for women to take time off to look after children. Though her husband too went to therapy there is no question of reorganising his life. Sexual difference is here taken for granted, and backed up by the therapist, with most of the redefinition being left to the woman. It is in the workplace rather than the home that she wants changes.

I might hesitate before interpreting Maeve's career a success. But a nervous breakdown has been averted, a marriage saved and, having brought four children into the world, she retains a passionate commitment to medicine and an unbroken participation in it. Dropping out permanently has never been a serious option. And the insights from her personal life are applied at work in ways that significantly affect her practice and presumably that of the people with whom she works.

General practice is full of women like Maeve, who are often considerably less philosophical about the compromises they have made. For instance, an Australian counterpart, who is married to a surgeon and has two children, restricts her work to two sessions a week. Yet *she* graduated with first-class honours while *he* scraped through on the basis of her lecture notes. He was the one who went on to specialist training and only his career is to be taken seriously.

Senior partner

Jane Butler is an acquaintance of Maeve's, who has similar issues, but has so far remained in the full-time work force. The organising theme of her story was the sudden death of her beloved father, a scientist, when she was seventeen. At thirty-eight she grieves the loss of an adult relationship with him (her mother, who played a conventional wifely role does not appear in the narrative). Married to a businessman and with three small children, she is a partner in the kind of busy practice where they each see a patient every five or six minutes. She would like to give patients more time, but the reality is a full waiting room. As the only woman in the practice she gets more than her share of gynaecological problems and jokes that 'when you have done eight vaginal examinations in a row you do begin to wonder what the world looks like'.

While working full-time Dr Butler has the main responsibility for her household. It is 'her' money that pays the nanny and the housekeeper, and it is up to her to manage them. Her husband is supportive but only capable of doing one thing at a time.

> He's unable to put the washing machine on as well as look after the children. When I went out for the morning I came back to find he hadn't cleared away the breakfast things. He said, 'well, I've been entertaining the children.' Can you believe it! These days I put the washing machine on myself.

Jane is struggling with difficult choices. She would like to take time off without it signifying (to herself or anyone else) that she had fallen short. The assumptions of male doctors that women are second-class because they go off and have babies infuriate her:

> Well, they get their wives to do it for them. And have their heart attacks when they are fifty and take three months off. We don't have heart attacks when we are fifty. We have them when we are sixty or sixty-five and retired, thank you very much. And we don't have hernias. So we have three months off when we have a baby. Big deal!

Part of her would like to take up sewing again, make the children's clothes, get involved in their schools, bake cakes and do all the things Maeve is doing. She feels she has 'lost control of her house' and is missing out on some crucial aspects of her life. Given her husband's large salary, she does not need to work. What keeps her there is a strong sense of vocation (she sees herself as priest and social worker) and a desire to please her dead father. More practically, she knows that as a part-timer she would be paid a lot less for doing much the same volume of work and that grates. But the increasing administrative work may yet tip the balance. She is perilously close to burnout.

Going solo

Though solo practices have become the exception in the UK they still make up nearly a quarter of Australian practices. Before leaping in to interpret group practice as a feminisation, an assault on the macho or heroic style of the solo practitioner it is important to note that women in both countries have taken that path for at least some of their working lives and they have had good reasons for doing so (Lawrence, 1987). It has not been uncommon for two women to take over a solo practice and run it between them as a job-share, sacrificing income for flexibility. Arrangements have to be negotiated within group practices for maternity leave, duty hours and holidays and women are dependent on the good-will of their partners and vulnerable to exploitation.

Dr James started out solo in London in the 1950s to avoid this and Dr Williams did the same thing in Adelaide in the early 1970s. The latter said, 'It was better than knocking on doors and saying, here I am, a female practitioner, do you want me to work with you . . . To have females in your practice wasn't recognised as a good thing in those days.' Dr Williams had started out part-time in a group practice but quickly got herself into trouble with her tongue: 'How have you managed without this equipment . . . We really need to do this . . . I know she's your wife but she is not the best receptionist you know!' After being sacked from that job she bought a practice from a woman who was shifting cities, and hence did not think of it as macho, and enjoyed running the business in her own way. Five years later, sick of working the long hours needed to finance the mortgage and wanting more time for family and literary interests, she moved into a group practice, eventually becoming a full partner.

By contrast, Lydia Zakharov set up a solo practice in a new middle-class suburb on the outskirts of Sydney and has built it up to more than 2000 patients. She is a smartly dressed woman in her late forties with wide-ranging interests in the humanities and a recently completed Master of

Arts. The combative streak in her had clearly been looking forward to an argument about feminism. She denied that she had ever had any problems as a woman in medicine and hated the 'whining' of a lot of women doctors. Proud of her practice, she was not at all unhappy to concede a 'macho' dimension. She is pleased to have risen above the prevailing definitions of 'woman doctor' and avoiding the typical 'female' profile. For her, 'success' means a practice that attracts a mix of patients, male and female, young and old.

Dr Zakharov describes herself as a bright student, who deliberately chose general practice and was made to suffer for it by the hospital specialists. Far from treating it as 'what women did', in her case they dropped her 'like a hot potato' and made it difficult for her to get placements that were appropriate for the family medicine program. For her the growth of vocational training has been important and general practice has its own specialised skill base. She resents the way failed specialists think they can just fall into general practice when they have nothing better to do. Because of her commitment to high standards she finds it difficult to hand over, though at the moment we were talking, a locum was handling the regular Friday afternoon slot. Many patients, however, will wait to see her.

Dr Zakharov is married to an engineer and they have a twelve-year-old daughter. Her husband is supportive and they have no difficulty sharing domestic tasks: 'Whoever gets home first does the cooking and he's an excellent cook'. Parenting, however, appeared to fall primarily into her domain and had structured her life to a substantial degree. She worked until the moment Jenna was born, literally breaking waters at work, and was back a week later with the baby under the desk. A second pregnancy ended in miscarriage which caused pain and disappointment.

The practice originally operated from home, and they had bought their house with this in mind. But working from home was difficult:

> The neighbours ask all sorts of things of you like keeping the key for the electrician in case he calls, or would I mind bringing in the washing if it rains, or, that bird that fell out of their tree – would I mind doing something for its wing? I know that they would never do it to my husband.

As a compromise the surgery shifted to the local shopping centre two minutes up the road – a good move because there was no doctor practising there. A local woman looked after Jenna: 'I'd drop her off on the way to the surgery and pick her up on the way back. I worked my hours around it. Later Jenna went straight from school to this lady and it was great.'

In this case a balance between home and work has been achieved by integrating them closely, with her husband's full support. Lydia does not dwell on the amount of on-call work but, given that she is permanently available, it must be considerable. Presumably her husband or the after school carer are there when she needs to go out in a hurry. Two thousand 'spoilt' patients could make severe inroads on evenings and weekends. Time also has to be found for continuing vocational education and non-medical interests. While she has been in solo practice for fifteen years, there are attractions in taking on a partner. To be too controlling is to risk letting a successful partnership pass her by. If the right person came along she would now consider going into partnership and lightening her workload.

Mature age

Dr Jenny Boyd is in her late 30s and an assistant in a large general practice. She would like to be a partner and more involved in decision-making but it is not financially attractive. Having started out as a social worker, Jenny was already in her mid-twenties and married before deciding on medicine. She had two babies during training, saying to herself at each point, 'if this doesn't suit the family I'll drop out'. Her husband Barry, a teacher, was immensely proud and intelligently supportive. He asked if he could be present for some part of the interview as it would help him to get a new slant on the issues they had struggled with. I was to discover late in the interview that a driving force in their commitment to equality was a shared spiritual life and struggle with Christian concepts.

Jenny felt that having a family had been an advantage during training: she had something to come home to and did not suffer the loneliness that women students often describe. Her relations with the men were easier too, since they were more able to treat her as a friend and colleague when her sexual status was clear. But there had been compromises. Jenny had deliberately given up the time that she knew would have brought her to honours standard in order to be with the family. She watched while the wives of male students did everything for them, while telling her she was 'lucky' that Barry did so much. In other circumstances she would have specialised in obstetrics or paediatrics but with a family the long years of hospital training posed impossible demands. She has put her energy into doing general practice well, even if it is mostly 'a run of throat infections'.

Jenny works 'part-time', which for her means three-and-a-half days (seven sessions) a week. On Friday, her 'day off' she attends practice meetings and sits in on the menopause clinic. She has completed the women's health course at the college and is fast becoming an expert in that area. While not concerned about doctors' pay ('I'd be happy earning the same as tradespeople') she feels there ought to be more acknowledgment of the responsibility doctors carry. After making a number of sacrifices to study medicine, it is not clear at this point what the future holds.

To be or not to be?

Dr Helen Yuen is thirty years old and married to a doctor who is active in politics. Both chose general practice so they would not be separated by having to take consultancies in different parts of the country. Now she is having second thoughts because she believes general practice is 'paranoid' about women having babies, and she would like to start a family soon. She has already experienced discriminatory questioning when she applied for the GP training scheme and had to say that she did not intend to have children:

> It is the key issue because what is going through their minds is how committed you are going to be to your career. You are not seen as such a good doctor if you are a woman. Maybe you are more scatty or more likely to be distracted. You need to be a little bit better to convince them you will contribute equally well.

With that kind of hostility, women feel nervous about the whole business of negotiating pregnancy. She mentions colleagues who had unplanned pregnancies only to find that their trainers would not take them back. In GP posts you are usually not entitled to any maternity leave for the first two years. A friend had been forced to choose between joining a partnership and having children and, having chosen the first, was very unhappy.

Helen had been fully committed to general practice. She completed the vocational scheme and had experience as a locum as well as working in a community health centre. She has done terms in all the relevant fields including obstetrics. The last she says is particularly difficult because GP trainees are given the one in two and one in two-and-a-half rotas. But it is important to get the training because British GPs are again taking on antenatal care and many are doing deliveries. Practices are therefore favouring those who can share the burden. People prefer to go to a GP because hospital care is poor. 'It is like cattle markets. You queue for three hours, have two or three minutes with a doctor who probes your tummy and sends you home . . . So as women get wind of the services offered by general practice they are taking them up.'

Despite the commitment she has made to GP training, Dr Yuen will probably leave and become a specialist in public health. Once regarded as the bottom of the barrel ('if you failed hospital medicine you went into general practice and if you failed that you did public health'), it is now opening up. She will come out in five years with a Master of Science and a consultant's position guaranteed. Meanwhile, she will have access to maternity leave.

GP obstetrician

Dr Beryl Kenny is in partnership with another woman GP and they have a third working with them two days a week in a practice in rural Queensland. The three women share a child minder. Beryl comes from a Catholic, working-class background, is married with four children and looks much older than her forty years – I would have placed her in her early fifties. Running a full-time practice, delivering around one hundred babies a year and caring for her own family has taken its toll. She gets very tired and feels trapped under the pressure of work, although her husband does much of the cooking and household work. It is becoming harder as the children get older and need more emotional and intellectual time.

It was only after completing the Family Medicine Program that Dr Kenny moved into obstetrics and she made it seem almost accidental. An obstetrician's post had been downgraded to a Diploma of Obstetrics post and she was persuaded to give it a try. Following from a strongly holistic philosophy, she is hostile both to specialists and to community health centres which deal with one-off problems and make the coordination of health services difficult. Obstetrics makes sense since her clients are already part of the practice. While she does not have independent access to the operating theatres she regards herself as perfectly competent to do Caesareans and claims it is a myth that newer techniques have made them more difficult. She does not feel in competition with midwives and would like to think that she offers all the benefits of midwife and specialist rolled into one.

In search of the single

Every one of the women discussed so far is or has been married and all but one have children. This was not deliberate choice on my part but it is an indication of how few single women there now are in the ranks of general practitioners except in the older age groups. Single women, and those in lesbian relationships, are more likely to be found among the specialists or in community medicine and public health. There is some reason to believe that single women (and men) may now be disadvantaged in general practice, either on the assumption that they have unstable personal lives or they will not fit the 'family' ethos of general practice. The traditional GP was a 'family man' (Lawrence, 1987: 134–5) and ultimately women have been accepted into general practice as 'family women'. The small number of single women in the sample who were principals represented themselves in strongly maternal terms.

Psychiatry and general practice

A number of women went further than Maeve to argue that for them general practice and psychiatry had become virtually interchangeable. Many had come to this view as a result of working through their own experience of childhood, family, work and career decisions. Dominant fathers often loomed large in these stories. Jill Mason gave a vivid description of an intense relationship with a father who gave her very mixed messages. Because he was proud of her achievements and treated them as an extension of his own, she felt enormously powerful. On the other hand, she had difficulty achieving any separation from him and she was also expected to behave in non-threatening ways. As a result, she learned always to protect men's egos and thinks that intelligent women frequently become simpering idiots in front of their boyfriends. Still in her twenties, she has specialised in adolescent medicine and draws on her own experience to help her patients, and to reflect on the dilemmas of 'success' for women.

Maggie Stephen's father was a consultant physician for whom anything else wasn't 'the real McCoy'. He was a workaholic who believed that 'if you weren't working 80 hours a week, you weren't a consultant, you were just piddling about'. Even paediatrics, in which she initially chose to specialise, was a bit dubious 'because, you know, it was only kids'. She rationalised that he would be pleased with her choice as long as she became a consultant. Forced to drop out of the training program she felt a failure both as a doctor and a daughter. For her, medicine was inextricably mixed with the messages learned in childhood, and it was a struggle to find a separate identity. Slowly she came to realise that it was possible to work part-time, and to concentrate on counselling, and still be a 'real' doctor. Although Maggie does not have children, 'having experienced the joys of part-time work' she has no intention of working full-time again. She cares passionately about incest and domestic violence issues and sees a lot of survivors in her practice. Perhaps this is work that cannot be carried out on a full-time basis without burnout.

'Female practitioners'

An Australian study has established beyond doubt that there are significant differences in the work patterns and patient mix of male and female GPs even when what statisticians like to refer to as 'confounders' (in this case salient characteristics of both doctor and patient that may not be linked to gender), are taken out. Britt et al. (1996), used a database of more than a hundred thousand doctor–patient encounters, to confirm previous more limited findings.

Women work less hours on average and are more likely to be working part-time than their male counterparts and they have twice as many long consultations. They deal with a younger group of patients, and they attract proportionally more female patients than do male GPs. There is a 'considerable selectivity' in the problems patients bring to male and female GPs. The women are presented with more female specific and psychosocial problems, along with those of the endocrine, metabolic and nutritional systems. Male GPs spend more of their time on musculoskeletal, respiratory and male genital problems. Britt et al. (1996) worry that as more women move into general practice these differences will become even more pronounced and may reach a point where individual practitioners have too little experience in the treatment of a group of problems and will choose to refer. It could lead to the development of two distinct sub-specialties of women's and men's primary care. This seems a huge exaggeration which translates statistical differences into absolute ones and ignores the continuing commonalities of male and female practice.

It may be suggested that the differences are linked not to any inherent difference or to women's greater capacity for empathy, but to the subaltern status that women GPs have long had. 'Female practitioner' is a nineteenth-century term dating from a time when it was assumed that women doctors would 'naturally' develop a distinctive kind of practice, with an emphasis on gynaecological issues, and combining elements of the midwife, nurse and male GP. In the discourse of Elizabeth Blackwell, the dominant female figure of nineteenth-century medicine, the woman doctor would be a moral and maternal force, countering masculine scientific pretensions with caring and intuition (Morantz-Sanchez, 1985).

Women doctors are ambivalent about such a role. They can see market advantages in being located in the discourse of 'caring', but they are also anxious to preserve their medical prestige. While proud of their counselling role, they resent any assumption that their time is less valuable than men's or that they cannot deal with the full range of problems. Several complained that men will often see a woman when they have something they want to talk about, like a marriage break-up, but go to a 'real doctor' for their organic problems. They are also ambivalent about their obligations in relation to women's health, simultaneously insisting, for example, that they, rather than nurses, should do Pap smears because only they can do adequate internal examinations, and deeply resentful when their male colleagues expect them to do them all. Clare Leabeater complains that the Australian government has eroded their treatment repertoire by funding the collection of Pap smears by pathology sisters rather than doctors and a cervical smear attracts no rebate (Leabeater, 1992: 6–7).

If 'the limits of the field are situated where the effects of the field cease' (Bourdieu in Wacquant, 1988: 39), then Pap smears present a boundary dispute. At stake is the question of which group of women dominates the women's health agenda. Women GPs tend to be hostile to nurse practitioners and extremely threatened by women's health centres. One GP commented:

> Nurse practitioners do not want to be doctors but a lot have been trained to the point where they might as well be. I'm sure that a demarcation dispute is brewing out there in western Sydney because if you train these nurses to such degree what you will have is barefoot doctors essentially. Then why bother with doctors? The local general practitioners got their knickers in a knot because patients with suspect Pap smears are being sent straight from nurses on to specialists, circumventing the need for a GP. Nobody has explained to the patient really what's going on. The next time she's due for a Pap smear, nobody has a clue about the history.

While there is a national database for Pap smears, she claims the authority of medicine to argue that, whereas GPs diagnose, monitor and educate, nurses are trained 'like robots and are basically technicians'.

The spread of part-time general practice has caused a great deal of concern to the medical establishment. By 1994 a majority even of the RACGP trainees were working part-time (54.2 per cent). Given the old view that 'real' doctors make a full-time commitment to medicine, the fact that two-thirds of women GPs work part-time confirms their fears about loss of status, declining standards and the disappearance of a vocational ethic that set medicine apart from other occupations. Some of the criticism amounts to a moral panic. It is argued that doctors do not build up enough experience, particularly in emergency work, and lose skills and confidence if they are not doing things regularly. Dr Peter Arnold from the AMA (1992) claims that medical mothers have, by accepting low rates of pay been responsible for a general downgrading of the worth of general practice in Australia. The twenty-four hour clinics are destroying the livelihoods of smaller practices and give poor quality care. As a result:

> . . . patients who once attended a constant, usually male, doctor – day or night, weekday or weekend – now often attend whichever female doctor is on duty at the time at the nearest clinic. There is no need to describe the adverse

impact of this trend on the 'doctor–patient relationship', of which we have long been so proud.

He suggests, with tongue only partly in cheek, that the most efficient solution would be for women to take the specialties, most of which can be done part-time, and for men to retain general practice, which requires continuity of care.

As subalterns, some women GPs voice the same fears about part-time workers. Dr Kenny, the GP obstetrician, is aware of the strain it places on full-timers. Reflecting on the part-timer in her practice she commented:

> Mary is a very good doctor but she has got two kids and a husband and works about two days a week. Actually she does another day somewhere else giving intravenous anaesthesia for gastroscopies but that's very low tension work compared to face-to-face consulting. It is a common pattern – which keeps women in the medical work force but doesn't provide a full service.

Mary, on the other hand, is less aware of the after hours question and more concerned with the quality of what she does:

> I get angry that the men often will hire a woman for two afternoons a week so she can do the Pap smears. They see it as inferior work. And I also get angry whenever I go to conferences and people say, you only work part-time, you haven't seen enough. I realise the limitations of what I am doing but being part-time if anything I am more careful not to miss things. And I go home and worry about people. Whereas if I worked longer hours I would reach a point where I couldn't worry about people and I'd miss things more often. I just think you burn out.

Jenny Boyd, who works part-time, is troubled about the lack of continuity. She gives an example: an elderly woman comes into the surgery with a pain which is likely to develop into shingles. Since there is no sign of a rash nothing is done. A few days later, on Friday, the woman phones to say she has blisters but declines to see anyone else and waits to see Jenny on Monday. But the relevant tablets are only effective if they are given in the first seventy-two hours. Though this situation could presumably have been avoided with adequate anticipation or telephone contact, Jenny articulates the usual medical concerns.

Yet general practice can be expected to become more diverse. Practice sizes vary enormously and GPs develop particular areas of interest and expertise. In many situations continuity of care is unimportant and the community seems satisfied with a more casual relationship with the GP than they had in the past. A declining percentage now have or want a 'family doctor' although most still go to a single practice for diagnosis and treatment. In Australia people may find it cheaper or more convenient to go elsewhere to deal with what they regard as trivial ailments. In an environment where people self-diagnose and shop around, GPs have to convince the public that they have something to offer.

The basic existence of general practice is not in danger, as it was fifty years ago. It retains its central place because it provides a cost-effective way of dealing with minor medical problems and some control over specialist and hospital costs. As a subaltern, general practice is firmly placed in the overall medical field. It both retains its deference to the medical specialties and takes pride in their shared identity as 'doctors'. In other ways it has shown distinct signs of subordination, the main one being the reorganisation entailed by its part-time workforce. This is starting to have repercussions in the specialties, where women are making similar demands. On the boundaries, relations with nurse practitioners and other health workers are in a highly fluid state. Given that so many of these workers are women, medical identities, especially those of women GPs, are on the line. In some situations, women GPs respond to this by heavily marking out the boundary. In others they are more willing to accept a fluid boundary and to work in partnership with other health professionals. If the latter tendency continues it marks an important step in the democratisation, not only of general practice but the entire medical field.

8

Nursing a Grievance: Doctor–Nurse Relations

Nurse: Nurses nowadays don't go around looking for
               doctors as husbands. It is something your
               mother says, 'Ooh, you might marry a doctor
               dear'.
Interviewer: Do nurses give women doctors a hard time?
Nurse: I can't believe that you asked that question!

Relations between nurses and women doctors appear only as a very small footnote in the larger literature on doctor–nurse relations (Walby & Greenwell, 1994: 70–4). There is some evidence that nurses feel they are better treated by women doctors (Wright, 1985) but this is undercut by suggestions that it might be a matter of wishful thinking rather than any behavioural difference (Mackay, 1989). Some nurses have claimed that women doctors, having taken on the same medical ethos as the men, behave no differently towards them (Savage, 1986). The one detailed study, by Carolyn Stegman (1987) in the United States, indicated significant differences in the ways in which male and female doctors relate to nurses. The nurses that she interviewed acknowledged that female doctors go out of their way to be nice to them but they also require that female doctors understand that there is a cost of deviating from this expectation (p. 181). The nurses well knew that their higher expectations of female doctors could create feelings of hostility (p. 220). For this reason, while teaching–learning transactions between nurses and women doctors were generally more positive, they contained an undercurrent of manipulation on both sides. A British study similarly found that nurses scrutinise the credentials of women doctors more carefully and that this subjects the doctors to extra stress (Firth-Cozens, 1990: 91).

More than 80 per cent of the female doctors in my sample felt that at some time in their careers they had been given a harder time by nurses than male doctors received. The nurses, both men and women, were considerably more positive about women doctors. But the two versions mesh: nurses prefer working with women because the latter are less demanding and have a more consultative style; doctors, on the other hand, often resent what they see as the preferential treatment given to their male colleagues.

Women doctors have the added problem that they have frequently been mistaken for nurses, both by patients and by male doctors. They are struggling not only to get on with nurses but to differentiate themselves from them. There is a sense in which women doctors occupy a middle ground between male doctors and nurses. They have successfully appropriated many of the caring demeanours previously attributed to nurses and so taken over some of the territory that nurses once securely occupied. But there is always the possibility that nurses will take back the territory. For this reason women doctors often feel that they have much to fear from the advance of midwives and nurse practitioners. If relations between nurses and women doctors are more egalitarian, they are also marked by a degree of uncertainty about the shifting boundaries between medicine and nursing.

All the women doctors interviewed were asked about their relations with nursing staff. Did they find the relationship a difficult one? Did they develop conscious strategies for managing it? Were relations better at some times and places than others, in different specialty areas or at different ages? What were the main areas of tension? Did they experience sexual rivalry between themselves and nurses and did they have nurses among their friends? In addition, twelve focus groups of registered nurses were brought together specifically to discuss their experiences of working with women doctors. The groups, each consisting of three to five people, were arranged in London and Sydney through the Royal College of Nursing and through nursing contacts at a number of hospitals and community health centres. Each group was organised around a common theme. In some cases this was a particular kind of workplace (general and psychiatric wards, children's hospitals, intensive care units, theatres, nurse practitioners, family planning), in others it was linked with seniority (groups of graduate students were included) or gender and sexuality (lesbians and both gay and straight men). A further six individual interviews were conducted with nurses who were unwilling or unable to participate in groups. Finally, six interviews were carried out with senior nurse educators and policy makers who were asked not only for their own experiences but their reflections on the general subject area.

Given the diversity in the social backgrounds and work experiences of both doctors and nurses, generalisations are difficult to interpret. People often make sweeping statements on the basis of one or two cases and both the doctors and nurses acknowledged that women doctors might be particularly likely to be praised or blamed as the result of a response to one individual. Therefore respondents were asked to recall specific experiences. The sample is undoubtedly weighted towards the higher status end and is predominantly Anglo–Celtic in background. Nevertheless they are a diverse group with interesting responses on the subject of women doctors.

When the doctors said that nurses 'gave them a hard time' they were in the first instance asserting their medical superiority:

> You have the feeling with some of the college trained nurses, . . . that they have this set body of knowledge and they will not veer from it. They don't see a dynamic process of learning or interacting with you . . . and they come in with this established concept that you're going to treat them badly. They think, what are we going to fight with the doctors about today!

Further, they claimed that nurses would not do a lot of the things that they did for the men, such as getting equipment ready, fetching and carrying, cleaning dirty trolleys or writing up files. A gynaecologist commented:

> The theatre staff are more likely to say, oh well, Miss D. won't mind if you haven't got her sutures. Women consultants are more easy going and much less authoritative with the theatre staff. I have felt I have been manipulated because they think I'm not going to complain about something that isn't quite right. All the little things that make the difference. Like it is easier not to take the bottom off the table – it is a heavy thing to do. But if you are sitting doing vaginal surgery, particularly if you are small, unless you take the bottom off the table you can't sit comfortably. You can't get your knees underneath and you can't get access. You think well, shall I ask them to take this off? It makes me a bit nervous – I have asked three times already. With the male consultant it would just be done.

A theatre nurse confirmed that:

> . . . when a new surgeon is coming the place up-ends and the nurse unit manager will make sure she is getting precise feedback about his needs. If it is a woman they feel less pressure.
> When the guys come in you always feel, oh my god, have I got this out for him. He might pick up an instrument and start complaining it is not sharp enough or the wrong company sent it in. The women will say, never mind, this will do today, but next time I want something done. They won't go off at you because there is no need to, because we're there to help each other.

Some women doctors also spoke of times when the nurses would not carry out their instructions, even in life-threatening situations. A paediatrician recalled:

I have a friend who had a child die from asthma . . . because she was having a fight with the nurses on night duty. They refused to help her . . . and the child died. The hospital covered it all up. They blamed her inexperience. And that was half the problem; but the other half was that this stupid feud was going on. The nurses were angry at her and they had decided to punish her for being snooty by putting her in Coventry. This boy had been in hospital for an hour and a half and he died without a drip in him. She said, what could I do, the nurses were having their break and they wouldn't help me . . . He'd started . . . to get so little oxygen to his brain that he was struggling . . . so she was physically trying to hold him down. She couldn't put a drip in or give him any drugs – she was the only one by his side and you can't do everything at once. The nurses were very shocked when he died.

In addition, the women doctors felt that female nurses were cool to them while flirting with the male doctors. They were acutely aware of their positioning as outsiders to the conventions of doctor–nurse games in which male doctors use their authority as men and their sexual desirability to ensure that the nurses not only obey their instructions but run around trying to please. Some women doctors hugely resented the more favoured treatment received by the men while others criticised the ways in which male colleagues treated the nurses. A minority denied they had ever had any problem with nurses, representing themselves as so confident of their authority that they were rarely challenged. Most of the women doctors had thought long and hard about how to improve the relationship and had been prepared to make compromises

Where the doctors stressed difficulties in the relationship, the nurses denied behaving any differently with them. The nurses said that in so far as they felt any hostility to women doctors it was because they had much higher expectations of them and were angered and disappointed when they were let down. In general, the nurses were more positive about women doctors than vice versa. Very few thought they were more demanding than the men, and while they had cherished stories about dragons and tyrants, these were, by definition, the exceptions. The gay male nurses in particular welcomed the presence of women doctors as signifying a crack in the hierarchy and a challenge to the mystique of medicine. They felt they shared with them a transgressive relation to the gender order. All groups of nurses decisively rejected the sexual meanings attached to doctor–nurse relations and many individuals expressed appreciation of women doctors' more collaborative and 'against the grain' ways of working. Even if they were saying what they thought I wanted to hear, this was significantly different from the doctors' stories. Nurses do assume that women doctors will be less demanding and more cooperative which some women doctors experience as taking liberties. Not surprisingly nurses also have a weaker investment than doctors in the gender dynamic which has situated them as handmaidens.

Both nurses and women doctors agreed that relations were generally better in some areas than others. They mentioned intensive care units and paediatric wards as having informal and cooperative relationships and generally preferred acute over long-stay wards (but physicians over surgeons). As Mackay points out, doctors may be little seen on psychiatric or geriatric wards or with the mentally handicapped who have a greater demand on nursing skills than medical skills. As a result, doctors have a less interventionist role and nurses may gain greater confidence in their own abilities and behave less deferentially to doctors (1989: 41). It was the women psychiatrists in my sample who spoke out most strongly about what they perceived as aggression and hostility directed at them by the nurses.

Gender and class identities

The Nightingale reforms which created 'modern' nursing in the late nineteenth century are generally thought to have established nurses as handmaidens to doctors. Yet the actual power relations were more complex (Gamarnikov, 1991). In the first place, while nurses were expected to obey doctors' orders, an element of interpretation and translation had crept in and there were tensions around issues such as drug dosages, wound healing and palliative care. As nurses were the ever-present carers and doctors were for the most part absent the latter were forced to rely on conditional rather than direct orders. In the second place, there was a significant shift in class relations. Modern nursing was removed from its historical antecedents in domestic service and established as a respectable occupation for middle- and upper-class women (Abel-Smith, 1960). Nightingale and other nursing leaders came from elite backgrounds and some, like Mrs Ethel Fenwick, sought to restrict nursing to 'ladies' by erecting educational and financial barriers to entry (Hart, 1994: 28). Upper-class women, having trained as nurses, were able to secure key hospital positions by cultivating powerful friends on hospital committees and in government. An elite cadre of matrons and sisters controlled nursing (Chua & Clegg, 1990: 140–4). A centralised nursing hierarchy with a matron at the top acquired a powerful position within the organisational structure of the hospital. Sisters ceased being directly answerable to doctors in matters relating to patient care and became the matron's subordinates.

Nursing has continued to draw on women from a variety of class backgrounds but the dominant images have been middle and upper-class ones. The creation of the College of Nursing in 1916 and establishment of a register in 1919 meant that nursing was defined more broadly than Mrs Fenwick would have liked but nevertheless it was a career for educated women (Chua & Clegg, 1990: 147–8). Over time this has been confirmed by the growing emphasis on educational qualifications and eventually the movement of nurse training into the universities. One of the implications is that registered nurses and doctors have frequently come from similar class backgrounds and it was not uncommon for the girls in a family to do nursing while the boys did medicine. Given these similarities in social background, the subordination of nurses to doctors could not be a simple matter of class domination.

In the late nineteenth century, 'medical dominance' still had only a precarious existence and the future organisation of health care and health care workers was an open question. The 'woman healer' could often cross the emerging categories of doctor, midwife and nurse. Women medical practitioners were seen as very different from men, but were not sharply differentiated in the public eye from nurses or mid-wives. Women doctors and nurses were both located in relation to a set of ideas and practices concerning spirituality, self-sacrifice, philanthropy and vocation rather than ideas about science or professional careers (Bashford, 1994: 68–91). The possibility lay open for a category of person who combined these elements rather than choosing one of them.

As nursing and medicine each took on their 'modern' forms, gender was used quite deliberately to reconstruct threatened power relations within medical care (Gamarnikov, 1991: 123–6). Medical men wanted to limit nurses' knowledge but at the same time to take advantage of their expertise. Alison Bashford (1994) has traced the way they mobilised femininities in order to defuse the challenging implications of creating scientific women. Nursing texts mixed scientific knowledge with detailed instruction on appropriate ways of behaving. Doctors constituted their subject positions as medical men by deliberately positioning nursing as feminine. In the process, a bond was established between male doctors and female nurses. In this landscape female doctors were something of an embarrassment. They did not share a common class position with male doctors as against nurses and they were on the 'wrong' side of the gender divide. Although the possibility was held out of the 'female medical practitioner' as an ideal blend of nurse, midwife and doctor, by the early twentieth century it was the new mass occupation of nurses rather than doctors, who laid claim to the role of female healers (Bashford, 1994). Male nurses and wardsmen were also relegated to the background, their presence acknowledged only in the mental health area where they were likened to prison warders rather than 'real' nurses.

Women doctors thus existed in a context where women's 'natural' place in health care was perceived to be as a nurse, and where relation-ships were organised around what came to be identified as the 'doctor–nurse game'. This was the subject of a famous paper by the American psychiatrist Leonard Stein (1967) who commented on the ways in which both medical and masculine authority were confirmed in the simultaneous acknowledgment and denial of nursing expertise. Medical omnipotence was not simply imposed but required the active cooperation of the nurses. Nurses learned to play the game very much earlier than doctors and had to play it competently if the relationship was to work. Since doctors could not know everything, they had to learn how to request advice without appearing to do so. For their part, nurses had to make recommendations in a way that made them look as if they had been initiated by the physician. The cardinal rule was to avoid open disagreement. Those doctors who were unskilled in picking up messages were regarded by the nurses as fools; those who interpreted the messages as insolence, and failed to appreciate what was being done, were given a rocky road. In return for being prepared to behave as handmaidens nurses could expect gratitude and protection, the approval and recognition of powerful men.

Returning to the game twenty-three years later, Stein et al. (1990) noted some changes. The absolute authority of medicine has been challenged, the women's movement has brought a redefinition of women's roles, and a changed historical and cultural milieu has provided the space in which it was possible for nurses to develop new subjectivities which are more assertive than those usually presented in the sociological literature. A game based on medical omniscience now seems archaic. In any case, nurses had unilaterally decided to stop playing. Where they have had support from their nursing administration they have been able to see themselves not as handmaidens to doctors but as professionals working with them as part of a team. The shift of nurse training to the universities and the change in title from 'sister' to 'registered nurse' consolidated this move. Nurses have become more willing to challenge doctors directly on issues such as drug dosages, wound healing and palliative care (Wicks, 1993). In addition, in many situations experienced nurses know far more than junior doctors (Miles, 1991).

For most of the twentieth century the division between medicine and nursing was perceived as a gender division rather than a class division, and it was gender that structured the particular tensions between women doctors and nurses. Women doctors have been drawn both to identify with nurses and to differentiate themselves, a process that has difficulties and also created moments of sisterhood and cooperation. In the past it was generally the doctors for whom this blurring created difficulties, kept at a distance both by fellow doctors and fellow women. A century later it is the nurses who are on the defensive. They now often find themselves portrayed as failed doctors, a representation that makes them extremely angry (Salvage, 1985: 8). But women GPs and gynaecologists, in particular, have been able to claim that they combine the roles of doctor, nurse, midwife.

Tensions have arisen in the ways in which these similarities and differences are marked out. Women doctors have been perceived, by male doctors, hospital managers and by patients, either as not real doctors (and hence confused with nurses) or as needing to be reminded of their womanhood by being associated with nurses. Neither of these makes for an easy relationship with the nurses who represent that from which they must differentiate in order to assert their medical status, but must identify with in order to be perceived as 'real women'.

In the reminiscences of the older women doctors a set of instances emerged when a shared identity with the nurses was imposed. Two that were regularly reported were the absence of separate changing rooms and the fact that as residents they had often been forced to live in nurses' homes. These experiences gave them a message that they did not fit in. Neither doctors' spaces nor nurses' spaces were 'rightfully' theirs. Interestingly the nurses never, ever, mentioned that having the women doctors in their changing rooms was a problem and male nurses had no difficulty sharing with male doctors. But the older doctors retain a sense of awkwardness and humiliation associated with these memories. At times their discomfort was on behalf of the nurses who were differentiated from them in ways that seemed unfair. Though living in nurses' homes, for example, the doctors had the same freedom as the men to come and go at night while nurses were still denied their own key. In the 1950s they still had to have a late pass and be escorted to their quarters: 'I used to think, here I am, 22, and I can come and go but these women of 45 were still being let in with a key.'

Matrons were not at all happy to be landed with female doctors, whose private behaviour at least, was outside of their jurisdiction. Another doctor recalled that as an intern in the late 1960s:

> They housed three of us in the nurses' home and the nurses had a curfew. We had doors onto the verandah and could actually get in and out. There was a whole process where the nurses would come and tap on the window at 2 o'clock in the morning and say, can I come in? In the end I just used to leave the door open, and sometimes I'd wake up and they'd say, thank you, as they walked past. Eventually they moved me because they couldn't have all of that. Matron didn't like me. For lots of reasons.

Matrons tried to control the dress of all women whether they be nurses or doctors. A psychiatrist recalls 'being told by a sister that I shouldn't come to a ward round wearing a mini-skirt because it would outrage the consultant. I said to her, well I'm married to a consultant and he likes it! And I wouldn't go home and get changed, which she wanted me to do.'

I can well imagine the resentment about a woman who was able first, to ignore the dress codes imposed on nursing staff and second, appeal over their heads to the preferences of the male consultants to whom she had special access. Conflicts about whether doctors had to wear skirts and stockings or whether trousers were allowed continued until well into the 1970s, with some very bizarre justifications being produced:

> One of the nurses told me that women have perineal fallout! The germs fall down your legs, and . . . that was for many years why women had to wear pantyhose and skirts! (Doctor)

Since the 1980s a greater choice has prevailed, and female nurses as well as doctors are now free to wear either trousers or skirts.

It is in the years immediately after graduation that women doctors find their relations with nurses most difficult. Many claimed that nurses resented someone of the same sex being at a higher level and were reluctant to acknowledge their authority. As they grew older and more experienced there was a mellowing, and their relations with the nurses became easier and more rewarding. It was, by then, easier to appear confident, and to praise the others' skills.

The junior years are difficult for all doctors because they come into the hospital almost entirely lacking in practical skills. They do not know how to change dressings, put in drips effectively, or determine standard drug dosages. Registered nurses have to teach the interns but get virtually no recognition of their teaching function and they have to do it from a subordinate position in the hierarchy. Interns come into the wards thinking that their knowledge is superior only to find that the nurses have many sources of power. They may, for example, withhold crucial information about a consultant's likes or dislikes (Lublin & Gething, 1992). Registered nurses can make their lives a misery by waking them in the middle of the night to come down and make routine decisions which are formally the doctors' responsibility. For nurses this can be an awkward decision: they risk the doctor's wrath, but they could be in trouble for failing to call them soon enough.

Junior doctors live in fear of getting a 'bollocking' from the consultants, if they give the wrong drug or telephone them unnecessarily and they look to the nurses for protection. A lot of nurses expressed sympathy for junior doctors because they were aware of the dreadful hours they worked: 'Often we have seen them working all day and then they have worked all night and they are still there the next morning'. They denied that they were less helpful to the women interns, claiming that if anything relationships were warmer because the women were generally more willing to ask questions and seek advice than the men. A few were sceptical, having observed doctors, more frequently women, adopt a strategy of deliberate helplessness, of saying 'I haven't a clue, would you show me' as a way of winning the nurses' sympathy. The nurses expect gratitude for the support that they give and are sensitive to being patronised in this way. Lurking behind such apparent humility, they think most doctors still regard the ideal nurse as one who 'takes responsibility' but does not undermine medical authority. Lublin and Gething (1992: 6) suggest that the traditional doctor–nurse game continues. Interns are still given information and supervision under the guise of suggestions.

The professionalisation of nursing, and the challenge to gender subordination, might suggest that more egalitarian relations are developing between medicine and nursing. But it may be argued that new and subtle forms of class domination are being mapped onto the older gender divisions. Nursing and medicine were once clearly gendered categories, each covering a variety of class locations; currently the relations between nursing and medicine are being perceived, at least by the nurses, as class relations, and gender and race divisions operate *within* each group (Bottero, 1992). In an interesting reversal, some nurses now express concern about being dominated by ambitious (working-class) male nurses rather than by doctors (Salvage, 1985: 9). There have always been working-class entrants to nursing, as recurrent shortages have forced hospitals to recruit uncredentialled assistants to perform 'basic' nursing work. This division was eventually formalised with the recognition of the enrolled nurse with a separate entry level and training path. In England a high proportion of these women are West Indian. Chua and Clegg suggest that this division may have enabled registered nurses to counter a potential proletarianisation of their work (1990: 153). However, as student labour is removed from hospitals, the RNs too have to pick up a lot of the menial tasks, a kind of deskilling that sits uneasily with their claims to professionalism.

While Chua and Clegg (1990) believe nursing has effected a professional closure, others, such as Hart (1994) note that nurses are leaving the system in larger numbers than ever and that in some colleges of education there has been a student reduction of 25–40 per cent (1994: 245). Where Chua and Clegg believe that since the Griffiths reforms of 1983 nurses have been able to incorporate themselves into NHS management structures, Hart comments that they are now 'more clearly than ever, excluded from the policy making process except on issues of clinical practice' and that 'just as nursing began to establish the possibility of a basis for itself beyond its traditional subordination to the medical model, it was subordinated ever more tightly to economic constraints' (1994: 242 and 258).

Male medical students from the working and lower-middle-classes have, to some extent, been displaced by women from upper-middle-class backgrounds. The fact that male doctors now marry doctors rather than nurses suggests that class divisions might be hardening rather than easing. Stegman found that nurses judge the clothes of women doctors as a visible sign of the disparities (1987: 210). The British nurses were in no doubt that a class wall existed between themselves and doctors of both sexes. In Australia, relations between doctors and nurses appear to be conducted more informally, but similar processes were happening. However, it must not be assumed that doctors are a homogeneous group.

In both the UK and Australia (to a lesser extent) hospitals are substantially staffed by immigrant doctors who return to their own countries when they have completed their training. For many of the nurses interviewed, race was an immediate issue as they reflected on their relationships with doctors. For all sorts of cultural reasons, their relations with Asian doctors, of both sexes, seemed to be less engaged, with a number of comments about the doctors being either passive or arrogant. In both countries doctors too are chafing under what they see as deteriorating working conditions and government assaults on their autonomy (Elston, 1993). Women doctors, concentrated in the more marginal positions, are the most vulnerable. Perhaps to compensate, they have begun to find ways of turning their gender into an advantage rather than a disadvantage. In doing so they have, in a sense, one-upped the nurses who may well perceive it as a class trick. Since the 1980s women doctors have confidently appropriated the ideal of a healer who combines the best of medicine and nursing and nurses have been placed on the defensive, being made to feel like failed doctors (Salvage, 1985: 8). The figure of the 'woman doctor' is fast taking from nurses their monopoly of the 'caring' functions.

There is a recognisable class discourse that now connects doing medicine with being 'bright' and doing nursing with being 'dumb'. When girls automatically became nurses, the distinction could not apply. As medicine has become more accessible to women, those who become nurses, whether registered or enrolled, may be seen as lacking the brains to be doctors. In fact, nurses rarely expressed any desire to be doctors, pointing to the difficulties, especially for women, of combining a medical career with any kind of civilised life.

Flirting with medicine

Theatres have the reputation of being the most sexualised area of the hospital and women doctors readily constructed them as places of sexual intensity. A female oncologist joked:

> Theatre nurses tend to be rather glamorous and sexy and wear lacy underwear and lots of mascara and they're there for the chaps, and because you're looking over masks, I mean, I'm sure people have mentioned that . . . theatres are sexy because there's eye contact . . . and pyjama-like clothing . . . and underwear very much on show.

I never observed theatre nurses who conformed to this description, but women who had trained as doctors during the 1930s right through to the current residents told similar stories. They were adamant that the nurses were not as helpful as they were to the young male doctors and in some cases were downright hostile and they attributed this directly to their being regarded as sexual competition. It is difficult to know how to interpret these stories, which are told with great animation and have the force of myth-making behind them. Given that the 'sexy nurse' is such a dominant cultural image it would be surprising if they did not buy into it. The nurses are almost always represented as young, white and single, though in fact nursing depends for its labour force very heavily on married and part-time workers and for a long time in the UK a high proportion of them have been black. The 'typical' nurse is invariably represented as a theatre nurse, but half the beds are actually occupied by people needing care in the less glamorous and long stay areas, especially the mentally ill (Salvage, 1985: 41–5).

Most nurses do not take the sexual discourse very seriously and denied any sexual interest in male doctors. While flirtation takes place, it is clearly age and time related (Stegman, 1987: 143–4). Some female nurses were aware that they could use sexuality for short-term ends, but also felt it trivialised their claims to professional status. They said they were more concerned with gaining recognition and respect than with flirtation. As far as they are concerned sexual jokes and flirtations are merely a way of getting through the day and defusing tensions. As Stegman reported in the United States, nurses experienced less humour with women doctors, in the form of kidding and joking, but viewed this positively, feeling that their relationships had more substance (1987: 150). Far from resenting women doctors as sexual rivals, female nurses said that their presence helped them deal with the unwanted advances of both doctors and patients. An Australian study has found that two in three registered nurses have experienced work-based sexual harassment (Weekes, 1995).

Nurses often enjoy the novelty of working with women surgeons. A theatre nurse described the atmosphere around a woman plastic surgeon as refreshing, with easier communication and less tension compared with 'your male patriarchs who walk in and think they are God off the streets'. Others said that the female doctors made you feel you were working as a team. Despite the talk of a bond, the nurses frequently experience male surgeons as both frightening and rude: 'to them you are just a nurse in the background'. In theatre they talk about themselves, cars, holidays, money, real estate or work movements and promotions and 'will mostly throw the conversation over the sisters' heads and aim for the anaesthetist'.

It is a cliché that nurses marry doctors, but fraternisation may also be interpreted as 'letting the side down' (Game & Pringle, 1983: 116). Tensions with male doctors were at least as evident as the dimension of storybook romance. These days it is far more likely that doctors will marry doctors. What is curiously absent when women doctors describe their supposed exclusion from doctor–nurse relationships is any account of their own sexuality. The implication is that they are desexed by the male doctors' preference for the nurses. To be seen to compete directly with the nurses would perhaps negate their authority and status as doctors, so when they describe their workplace relations they carefully place themselves 'above' and outside the world of sexual interactions. Presumably women doctors meet lovers and future husbands in the workplace but in conversation they barely acknowledge themselves as sexual beings.

Interestingly the *nurses* saw the sexual chemistry as operating most strongly among doctors. Where some of the older doctors recalled having once pretended to be nurses in order to get male doctors' attention, nurses insisted that the opposite was now more common. If you wanted to make a play for a male doctor, it was better if you could pass as a doctor. A theatre nurse had attended a party at which the male medical students, having sent out an open invitation to the nurses, then ignored them in favour of the female medical students. This links back to the issue of class and the perception of a divergence of class background which was not so obvious when gender determined who would be doctors and who would be nurses.

It is not only nurses who fuss around doctors or want to marry them. The nurses described how women doctors 'stake out their status' at social events and put energy into flirting with the men. They had many stories to tell of women registrars 'molly-coddling' their male colleagues, making them cups of tea, keeping an eye out for them when they are running late, and studiously avoiding conflict. Given the hierarchies of medicine, women hospital doctors may find themselves more directly in the position of handmaidens to the consultant than are the nurses. To some extent the old doctor–nurse game appears to have been replaced by a doctor–doctor game in which women doctors flirt and attract the attention of male doctors. Johnson and Elston's medical careers study found that 52 per cent of those women doctors who were married were married to doctors (Day, 1982) and Isabel Allen found that the same was true of nearly 60 per cent of the married 1981 qualifiers (1988: 34). In

Australia, Dennerstein et al. (1989) found a comparable figure of only 34 per cent, but their sample comprised all surviving women graduates of the University of Melbourne and is less likely to pick up current shifts. In my own sample (heavily biased towards consultants) the figure was 48 per cent. Male medical status may be reinforced more by the flirting behaviours of women doctors than that of the nurses. Women's medical authority is at times undermined by their own desire for male approval and fears of challenging men or being seen as man-haters.

What of relations between women doctors and male nurses? There has been much interest in the impact of male nurses on the status of nursing as they moved steadily into general hospital work in the 1970s to make up around 10 per cent of nursing staff. They seemed to have more sexual cachet than women doctors and their sexuality has been a subject of speculation. That such men were initially presumed, by hospital staff, by journalists and by the general public, to be gay is itself an indication of the dominance of discourses that construct the doctor–nurse relationship in sexual terms. The possibility of relationships between female doctors and male nurses was not taken seriously. Roland Littlewood suggests that while the relationship between a doctor and 'his' nurse is heavily charged with sexual significance, the notion of a female doctor having sex with a male nurse is 'incredible and bizarre' (1991: 155, following Cassell, 1986).

One registrar described a relationship she had for six months with a male nurse with whom she worked in intensive care. Two years later she remembered it positively enough but without long-term potential. Both disliked mixing work and private life and were careful not to let word get around at work. There is nothing unusual about this, particularly in the early stages of a relationship. But more than privacy was at stake here. She feared her tenuous medical authority would be undermined, and her professionalism questioned, while both feared ridicule. As word did get out the intensive care people were supportive but the other residents expressed discomfort. The double reversal both problematises the sexual dimension of doctor–nurse relations and upsets assumptions about doctor–nurse hierarchy. The gender reversal may have created space for a more equal exchange but it also created tensions. She said laughingly that: 'the male nurses that I've had anything to do with always think they're right . . . I have never met a male nurse who will admit he is wrong about something . . . Male nurses are always right. Remember that!' Tensions crept into the relationship when they argued the relative merits of medical and nursing knowledge:

Medical terminology tends to be precise. If you say grade 2 heart disease you know what it means whereas nursing terminology is very waffly. He was talking about normal daily activities. And I said, but does that include going up and down stairs or not? If I have to ring the cardiologist, he will know exactly what I mean. I was saying he would be better off describing the person's situation rather than using vague terminology. And he just refused to acknowledge my point. After that we never talked about medicine.

If heterosexual relations with nurses are difficult for women doctors, lesbian relations have another set of problems. Lesbian doctors (there were twenty in my sample) are wary that the nurses will not only resent the fact that they are doctors but presume that they are also mannish and aggressive. They felt it was easier for a nurse to say she was a lesbian because she is working in a feminine, caring job. Given the remaining problems women have in having their authority accepted it is crucial for them to create friendly relations with the nurses.

Beyond the doctor–nurse game

Is sexuality inevitably an obstacle for women doctors in their relations with nurses or can it be a positive force? I have elsewhere suggested in an analysis of boss–secretary relations that women bosses do use subtle forms of sexuality in their relations with secretaries – forms based on narcissism and mother–daughter symbolism (Pringle, 1988). I see fewer signs of this in the hospital setting. Nurses do not aspire to be doctors or generally see them as role models so the narcissistic possibilities are limited. Only in the nurse practitioner–doctor relationship are there occasional glimpses of the familial or apprenticeship dimensions.

Rather than looking to alternative expressions of sexuality that might be empowering, women doctors have increasingly criticised the dominant discourse as a form of sexual harassment which could easily extend to them. An anaesthetist commented that male doctors use their power to exploit the sexual feelings of female nurses and doctors too. The two groups of women increasingly share a rewriting of the doctor–nurse discourse in terms of sexual harassment. Women doctors often expressed relief that because they were outside the sexual discourse they were free to find other ways of managing the relationship. Sometimes they described this in terms of hard work and professionalism. Wherever possible they avoid exercising explicit authority or ordering nurses about: they ask rather than command. They also do a lot of things themselves that men would expect the nurses to do, like cleaning up dirty trolleys or taking patients to the toilet. The nurses almost universally appreciate this concern though they seem unaware of the effort that has gone into it. They are more likely to interpret it in terms of women doctors being, to quote a theatre nurse 'better organised and more obliging'.

Building relations of trust is important, and often involves tales of cooperation and sisterhood, of shared defiance of masculine, medical authority. A GP recalled her time as a registrar in England:

After the meeting the Professor of Cardiology came up and said to me, if you value your job here you will never, never speak against me in public again. And the nurse in charge of coronary care was a dragon, who absolutely terrified me. She ate residents for breakfast and spat interns out between times. But a week later there was a cardiology dinner and . . . the dragon came up to me and said, you're coming aren't you? WE want you to come. YOU will come . . . And she sat me down and she said, do you know when you came to the unit we thought you were a total wimp. And then you stood up to HIM! I didn't know he was considered in tremendous bad odour by almost everyone who counted. Standing up and refusing to be a little wimpish intern put my standing up the top somewhere.

Many had stories of crises which generated life-long bonding experiences. Here is one example:

The time that sticks in my mind is the time I was in intensive care. And intensive care sisters are the hardest women to break of all . . . There is this unit mentality: only *our* doctors know anything. Anyone who is not *our* intensive care doesn't know anything. And so you've got to really break through that. I got called in by the intensive care doctor one night . . . This patient was . . . getting harder and harder to ventilate and she was . . . having respiratory failure . . . She was dying. They had been resuscitating her after a cardiac arrest . . . and they'd punctured a lung.

I said, 'she needs two tubes in her chest right now'. And the sisters didn't know me because I wasn't one of their doctors and they wouldn't do what I told them. They wouldn't get it. Unfortunately my response to those situations is often to scream because I don't know what else to do. I always remember it because I hate it so much. I hate myself for a week after I've done it. I just had to yell at them. 'Do it now!' They put the tubes in and immediately the lady was retrieved from death to life.

And from then on you've won them. They'll do anything you say after that. But you tend to have to prove yourself like that before they will.

Rather than depending on hierarchical authority, women doctors must operate on the basis of reciprocity. Many conceptualised this in terms of creating 'friendships', although these rarely extend beyond the workplace. The popular doctors evinced considerable personal charm and interactive skills, which in turn are affected by age, experience and class background. A physician from the medical establishment denied she had ever been given a hard time by the nurses:

I think it is crap. I have never felt it. Certainly female nurses would call me Kathie much more than they would call male doctors by their first name . . .

and they would tell me things and share things with me that they would never share with the men. But I think all that is a plus.

A young West Indian GP was having more trouble. She recalled that:

> . . . your male partner will ask a nurse for something and she will rush and get it for him. You don't bother to ask, you just get it yourself, because, you know, they really don't feel that you should be on that level where you can have authority over them, and they find it very hard to deal with. It is simple things like, say, if you did some procedure on the patient and your trolley's dirty and it needs cleaning, the male doctor will just leave it and the nurses will clean it and not make a fuss, whereas if you, as a female doctor, left a dirty trolley, first of all, they wouldn't clean it, and if they did, you'd know about it.

For this doctor, vulnerable on racial as well as gender grounds, the dirty trolley encapsulated her problems in exercising authority. By contrast, a white, feminist, Cambridge-educated consultant took the nurses' side. She felt angry when the male doctors left a mess behind for the nurses to clean up and made sure that if she had to set up a drip or do a procedure at the bedside that she tidied things away.

Women doctors told many stories that celebrate their different ways of working and appear to embrace the nineteenth-century ideal of the 'female practitioner'. This was as true for the specialists and hospital doctors as it was for the GPs. An anaesthetist describes how, if someone is brought in from an accident covered in blood, she will 'automatically wash their face and hair because it seems self-evident that they will feel better waking up without blood caked all over their face'. The nursing staff will say, 'Oh, men would never do that'. A group of paediatric nurses agreed that women consultants were less patronising and more approachable than men. They will pick up the babies and cuddle them and change a dirty nappy if necessary. The men rarely do such a thing! An obstetrician recalls that as a resident she made tea and sandwiches for the nurses when they were busy. Women doctors in palliative care report working in a way that is more in tune with the nurses. It is usually the nurses who first feel that treatment should be stopped because they are the ones who are looking after the person and aware of his or her distress. Nothing infuriates them more than doctors who continue to perform tests and examinations on dying patients (Wicks, 1993: 19–20).

With the movement of women into medicine and men into nursing, gender is now less available as a means of propping up medical authority. The distinction between medical and nursing tasks in terms of 'cure' versus 'care' is not viable when doctors claim to be holistic and nurses stress their technical and managerial skills. Nursing has had its professional status acknowledged but has lost its monopoly on caring and has much to resolve about its future roles, particularly as it loses its independent management structure and is subject to increasing constraints in government spending. The ground continues to shift but the future relationship between nursing and medicine will need to be worked out around an ethos of mutual respect. This cannot be left to individual initiative alone. Care needs to be taken to identify areas of overlapping responsibility and devise better processes of consultative decision-making.

Women doctors have done much to indicate some of the new paths that can be taken. They have been more creative in finding ways of working with nurse practitioners, midwives and practice nurses, often teaching them a great deal. But there is fear there as well as a reluctance to hand over responsibility or recognise them as equals in the provision of health care. Midwives, for example, are unlikely to work with obstetricians on a subordinate basis. Women doctors symbolically stand between medicine and nursing, with a foot in both camps. At a time when jobs are scarce they have most to fear from nurses encroaching on their territory. Women doctors and nurses may be directly in competition in areas such as obstetrics and family planning. They fear that the appointment of nurse practitioners would undermine their own diagnostic abilities and counselling skills. On the positive side, the blurring of boundaries between women doctors and other health practitioners is already paving the way for more creative and egalitarian working relationships among health professionals.

9

Doctors and the Women's Health Movement

> Feminists seriously question physicians' technical expertise
> in many areas related to female sexuality and reproduction
> . . . some feminists believe that women's routine health needs
> cannot and should not be met by male professionals,
> regardless of their competence or humaneness. Instead,
> routine care should be deinstitutionalized,
> deprofessionalized, and reintegrated into female culture
>
> *(Ruzek, 1978: 14)*

Ruzek's words suggest something of the range of ideas that came together in the women's health movement. Feminists saw the male-dominated medical system as a microcosm of patriarchy and many believed that women should have nothing whatsoever to do with it. However, by concentrating their attack on 'male' professionals an opening was left for women doctors. Would they be considered, or consider themselves, a part of 'female culture' or would women doctors line up with their male colleagues? Would their presence provide the basis for a new dialogue between women's health activists and mainstream medicine? While not as a group renowned for radical political activism, some have been key participants in the women's health movement and made a major contribution to its achievements. And, despite the anti-doctor rhetoric, few feminists have seen it as a stark either/or choice. Increasing the number of women doctors and rethinking the place of medicine in relation to health go hand in hand.

The issue of women doctors has challenged feminists to explore their mixed feelings about western medicine and to work out new ways of addressing the issues around power and professionalism. As Foucault comments, 'it is necessary to pass over to the other side – the other side from the "good side" – in order to free oneself from those mechanisms which made two sides appear, in order to dissolve the false unity of this other side whose part one has taken' (quoted in Dews, 1987: 165).

The women's health movement began in the United States, fuelled by the struggle for abortion law reform and the realisation that men 'were making fateful decisions about women's bodies and their reproductive lives' (Ruzek, 1978: 18). In the spring of 1969 a group of women met in Boston to explore health issues and within two years self-help groups had sprung up across the country. These groups had both practical and theoretical concerns. Women sought to 'know' their own bodies, to take initiatives for their own health, and to understand the health care system in the context of a capitalist and patriarchal society (Frankfurt, 1972). The Boston Women's Health Collective produced a source book, *Our Bodies, Our Selves*, which became the bible of the movement internationally and has gone into many reprints since its first publication in 1973.

Women's health activists argued that, far from contributing to improvements in health over the last century, the male-controlled, technology-dominated health system had actually placed women's health in jeopardy. In particular they attacked childbirth practices which they said were tailored to the needs of doctors rather than patients, and the 'psy' therapies which were specifically directed towards ensuring that women conformed to traditional sex roles. They rejected 'the traditional medical view of women as inferior and "sickly" creatures' (Dwyer, 1992), as well as the traditional focus of the health system on women's reproductive role, and argued the importance of accepting and validating women's experiences and needs. A central focus was the preventable nature of much of the illness and disability experienced by women and the social, economic and environmental factors affecting their health. They also pointed to the growing inequalities in the delivery of health care with 'high quality service to the wealthy (and) shoddy, assembly line care for the poor' (Fee, 1983: 31). Against the fragmentation of health care services, and of heath care occupations, they held out an ideal of holistic care in which women were participants and not merely consumers in health.

The Boston group were not opposed to western medicine *per se* but criticised its failure to address the problems that affect women, the ways in which doctors trivialised and infantilised women patients, and the difficulties of participating in decision-making because of the inaccessibility of medical knowledge. There was a certain romanticism about how medical knowledge might be acquired and shared which is captured in the comments of one of its early members. In the early 1970s she was a high school teacher in Boston and she is now a senior registrar in community medicine in the East End of London. She recalled:

There was a real sense that non-medical people had to take over medical knowledge . . . It was very frustrating, as an outsider, trying to crack the medical books and actually find out what was going on . . . At some point I thought, why shouldn't I go to medical school and actually steal this knowledge for the people?

An Australian health centre doctor who, as a teenager had attended women's liberation meetings with her mother, has similar memories:

There was a whole group of young women who went back to school to do our HSC with the purpose of infiltrating the profession. There was a belief that a feminist transformation of society would occur by women going into specialist fields and creating change from the inside.

. . . I hated medical school. It was the most undermining experience I have ever had. I gained a lot of strength in surviving medical school by believing that there was a women's heath movement outside somewhere that I could be part of.

. . . I still see myself as an outside infiltrator. I've gone behind all those closed doors that say, do not enter, staff only . . . I feel that I am happy to be a guide and interpreter. And a lot of my work is like that. Reading medical reports and wading through the medical jargon and turning it into information that is useful to women.

The movement quickly spread internationally. British and Australian feminists had been similarly engaged in the struggle for abortion and contraceptive rights and had come up against the weight of the medical profession. In both countries women's health had emerged as a key feminist issue and self-help groups of all kinds were established. But the future of the women's health movement in the three countries, and the role of doctors within it, was to be very different. In the United States, women's health collectives operated on a volunteer basis. Despite their success in disseminating information, there was little possibility for institutional links with an organised health system. Their main achievement has been to ensure that abortion services became firmly entrenched in outpatient health services (Norsigian, 1996: 83–5).

In Britain, with its strong tradition of 'socialist medicine', feminists took it for granted that they should work within and transform the NHS. They established a network of Well Woman Clinics within the community health care services and also sought to transform the Family Planning Clinics which had been taken over by the NHS in 1974 (Pfeffer, 1993: 142). One of their publicly stated goals was to reach women who normally stay away from doctors for reasons of class or culture. The Well Woman Clinics aimed to provide patients with accessible literature on common women's health problems and bring women together in self-help groups to deal with shared issues such as tranquilliser addiction or menopausal problems. Feminists emphasised that women are the experts on their own bodies and that each must be listened to carefully with as much time and attention as she feels she needs.

The feminist-run clinics operated according to five broad principles that they believed should inform health care delivery (Foster, 1989: 341). These are:

1 All medical knowledge should be shared with the patient in a way that will give her greater control over her well-being.
2 Health care providers should work in open, egalitarian ways that facilitate the sharing of knowledge and expertise.
3 Health care should be holistic, treating the whole person rather than the disease.
4 Health care providers should empathise with patients rather than taking a detached 'professional' stance.
5 Health care should be equally accessible to all.

While they were attempting to provide a model of an alternative form of health care delivery it cannot be said that the Well Woman Clinics have had a huge impact on the NHS. Both clientele and workers have been predominantly white and middle-class and as a model it has not attracted much attention outside feminist circles (Foster, 1989: 344–50). Health service managers and some GPs were hostile to the clinics because their activity rates seemed unimpressive. By 1987 over one hundred health authorities claimed to have a Well Woman clinic in their area but many had simply renamed their Family Planning Clinics, and their main objective seems to have been to increase the number of women having Pap smears (Foster, 1989: 342–6). There was no special funding other than for Pap smears and the clinics effectively ran on volunteer labour. They relied heavily on feminist GPs working with local feminist groups to become anything more than Family Planning Clinics under another name. Tensions between doctors and other members of the health team were played down. It was claimed that problems arose not because feminist doctors were unwilling to relinquish their special status but rather because volunteer workers had difficulty in valuing their own skills and knowledge 'as highly as those of the high status professional' (Foster, 1989: 342–3).

In Australia, by contrast, women's health centres and feminist controlled family planning clinics have received public funding since the years of the Whitlam Labor Government and had a powerful impact on the health system. As Dwyer sums it up:

The Australian women's health movement has been one of the more visible and successful forces for change in the broad health system . . . An extensive network of special women's health services has been developed, as well as a range of advisory and advocacy structures within health authorities. There are hundreds of community-based groups of women organised around particular health issues. (Dwyer, 1992: 211)

The Australian network of funded women's health centres is *unique*: there is nothing remotely like it in Britain or North America.

The Australian women's health movement, like the British, originated in struggles with the family planning movement. The Family Planning Association of Australia, which previously existed only in New South Wales, had a reputation as a right wing, judgmental organisation which refused to treat single women or to refer anyone for abortion. Women's liberationists set out to change its middle-class, conservative image and to take it in a more radical direction. In the mid-1970s, under their influence, the Association became involved, with a variety of other organisations, in taking sex education programs into schools, and it came into bitter conflict with an existing team of women doctors who visited private girls schools, for not taking a high enough moral approach (Siedlecky & Wyndham, 1990: 173–81). It generated further conflict with the medical profession in 1976 when it introduced trained nurse practitioners to take over some of the work previously carried out by doctors. The Australian Medical Association attacked what it saw as 'deprofessionalisation' and criticised its links with the women's health centres. The RACGP was also fearful that the FPA was taking business away from GPs, particularly women. In the 1960s, the introduction of the pill and the new IUDs, both of which required a medical consultation, had created almost overnight an important new source of income for GPs and they did not want to lose it.

While many women doctors were hostile to feminist-run health centres, a few embraced them wholeheartedly. Dorothy Nolan and Stefania Siedlecky were a mainstay of the Family Planning Association while Dr Siedlecky also became the first doctor at Leichhardt Women's Health Centre and later a women's health policy adviser to the federal government. Dr Margie Taylor, now an Adelaide GP, as a student was an active participant in the feminist movement and the struggle against the Vietnam war. She recalled:

> I had nothing to do with the medical school if I could possibly help it and spent most of my time across the road . . . In my intern year I came back from Sydney, where I'd been to visit Leichhardt, and I rang up my friends and said, call a meeting. We're going to set up a women's health centre here. So we did. We put in a submission. And eventually we got the money.

Taylor worked there for a time, took the same wages as everyone else and was accepted as a full member of the collective.

The emerging women's health movement developed quickly from organising small self-help groups to demanding separate services controlled by women and based on feminist principles. By 1990 there were around thirty women's health centres in Australia with the strongest concentration in New South Wales. Because they are publicly funded they have been able to reach out to more women and offer a wider range of services than the Well Woman Clinics. Typically these centres began by focusing on basic gynaecology, reproductive health and psychosocial health issues and then expanded to include occupational and environmental health, services related to sexual and physical violence against women, and provision for groups with special needs – women of non-English-speaking backgrounds, lesbians, women with disabilities, women in rural areas, older women and what the National Women's Health Policy described as 'the health effects of sex-role stereotyping, including weight and body image problems' (Dwyer, 1992: 13–14).

The place of doctors in the health team had to be addressed not only abstractly but in relation to concrete decisions about budget priorities. This chapter will focus on the unique Australian experience, drawing on interviews with health centre workers in two states, with doctors presently working in the centres, and with members of the extensive 'old girls network' who have worked in them in the past.

Women doctors and the feminist habitus

Women doctors have been perceived by feminists as both heroines and ogres. The entry of women into medicine was the feminist *cause célèbre* of the late nineteenth century, and contemporary liberal feminists have welcomed the increasing numbers of women doctors believing, like their predecessors, that the social subordination of women is reflected in the organisation of medicine and that the reform of medicine requires that women take their place as equals within it. But radical feminists have been explicitly anti-doctor. They have stressed the need to get back in touch with a women's culture and a healing tradition that is critical of contemporary medicine. To the medical model they counterpoise a more social view of health and illness as embedded in the conditions under which women live and work. Women doctors obviously occupy an awkward relation to this tradition which celebrates 'women healers' precisely because they are *not* doctors (Ruzek, 1978). If doctors are thought to be acting on behalf of men to consolidate patriarchal relations, women doctors might be regarded as traitors to their sex. While exceptions were made for individuals who shared feminist ideals and were prepared to forgo their professional privilege, 'women doctors' as a category were regarded by many as 'honorary men' or even as 'worse than the men'.

In Australia the hostility of some women doctors to the women's health centres appeared to support this view. In 1976, five women doctors, claiming to represent the Medical Women's Society, sent a deputation to the Prime Minister to protest against funding for the first Women's Health Centre at Leichhardt in Sydney and for the Family Planning Association which had recently come under feminist control. They were opposed to abortion, sex education and the open discussion of lesbianism (Siedlecky & Wyndham, 1990: 173–81). Another group, led by Dr Margaret Raphael, attempted to undermine the work and philosophy of the feminist centres by establishing what they called an 'orthodox' medical women's centre staffed by fully trained personnel and not subject to 'political bias' (Stevens, 1995: 112). This centre still exists and is frequently cited by the media as an authority on women's health.

Women doctors who choose to work in women's health centres generally share a kind of equal opportunity feminism but have not had much contact with radical feminism. As subaltern figures they represent medical authority but from a weak position within the field. Many come with an interest in alternative health and/or preventative medicine, a desire to learn more about women's health issues and a commitment to egalitarian working relations both with clients and colleagues. Often they are preparing to set up in general practice or gain extra qualifications in public health. Some are ambivalent about medicine and are contemplating alternative careers in law, journalism or the bureaucracy. A number are lesbians or single parents who welcome the opportunity to be more open about their personal lives than they can be in most other parts of the health system. Jobs in women's health centres are often attractive because they are convenient, or close to home, or provide part-time work. In all these ways they are not so far removed from many of their co-workers. But where doctors are used to taking the medical field as their primary reference point, most of their colleagues are constituted through a field that is defined largely by its hostility to medicine and its links with a broad-based women's movement.

When they work in a women's health centre, doctors encounter an explicitly 'feminist' habitus which rests on a sense of shared sisterhood, a presumed equality of each woman's contribution and a rejection of hierarchy. In the field of feminism, cultural capital is built up by affirming the common identity of all women as oppressed, working collectively to articulate women's needs and to challenge male domination, treating professionals with suspicion as power-seeking, and insisting that all skills can and must be shared. The first workers at Leichhardt Women's Health Centre described themselves as a collective. The Centre had a management committee comprising staff and elected members but no one was given the position of director and the doctor did not have authority over other workers (Stevens, 1995: 74). An ambivalent stance towards women doctors was evident in the following responses of a group of women's health workers to my question, are the doctors members of the collective?

> Well, um, yes they are . . . everyone who works here is a member of the collective . . . they can have input . . . but they are not full-time workers here and they don't have any obligation to come to collective meetings.

> . . . They are not actually part of the normal decision-making process and they'd . . . actually have to request to come . . .

> The value of doctors in this centre is . . . ah . . . that they are one of the major referral points to other clinical services. They are supposed to demystify the medical profession.

> Nearly all of them, when they first come here for interviews, ask about the medical supervision. And . . . ah . . . they have to understand very quickly that this centre is not medically supervised. People work independently.

> Occasionally I do period checks to see how they are doing case management . . . There is doctoring that overlays any . . . ah . . . overtly feminist ways of working.

Some health workers see little, if any, role at all for doctors:

> I would rather do without a doctor. It would be good to concentrate more on preventative work. A lot of women just come here to see a doctor because they think the atmosphere in the centre is nice. They wouldn't see our doctor any differently from how they would see the general practitioners. I think it is just a waste of our staff resources for they can get it elsewhere.

> I think doctors are technicians and women's health is all about empowering women and giving them information. Any worker can do that. You don't need someone as high paid as a doctor. I don't say there aren't any good doctors around. There are good technicians around and there are some good women who happen to be doctors who are even good counsellors. But I don't think it is necessary to employ doctors in a women's health centre.

While health workers experience women doctors as the bearers of medical power, feminist sociologists have argued that women are locked into the lowest paid and least challenging areas of medicine (Allen, 1988; Annandale, 1989; Dennerstein et al., 1989; Lorber, 1993). In earlier chapters I have presented women doctors as the subalterns of medicine, vertically integrated into a stratified system of cultural capital. For those who work in women's health centres the sense of vertical integration may be profoundly destabilised as they find themselves working in an environment in which the medical profession is routinely under attack:

It taught me a lot about how hated the medical profession is by a lot of people
. . . That was my strongest and bitterest experience of being discriminated
against, and it was by other women. But I think the medical profession has
done a lot to perpetuate it. That sense of always wanting to be the ones in
control has done so much damage.

When I hear women talking about how horrible doctors are, I'm not personally offended by that . . . because lots of doctors are. It is like the class struggle
isn't it? I can distinguish between the horrible crimes that the ruling class has
perpetrated and an individual that I might talk to. And I expect that level of
maturity amongst people I work closely with.

I have been badly treated but not appallingly. I am aware of other doctors who
have been treated appallingly. I'm very wary of 'feminist' health centre
scenarios and working there, yes. It's that whole thing, left over from the
seventies, of everyone being equal. Where I worked the person who had no
head for figures decided to liberate herself from that so she did the accounts.
It's the tall poppy syndrome . . . and god, women doctors are struggling too –
they have their own insecurities.

While some of the doctors remain highly critical of the ways in which
women's health centres operate, others have discovered a potential to
establish new horizontal ties with clients and co-workers, opening themselves to other influences and loyalties. The 'old girls' invariably say that
their experience of the centres has had a lasting impact on the way they
choose to practise medicine. Women doctors who identify with the goals
of feminism often speak an anti-medical discourse in a way that implies
an explicit rejection of their subaltern role. They have been on the
receiving end of a lot of hostility from the Australian medical elites who
have regularly accused them of circulating 'bad doctor' lists through the
centres. Those who stay have effectively stepped off any career ladder
and their incomes, while higher than those of other health workers, are
well below those of most doctors. They may surrender their illusions of
upward mobility within the medical hierarchy, call into question their
reliance on these elites for their status and authority and discover other
kinds of cultural capital in terms of credibility within the different field
of organised feminism.

Women doctors have been vital to the establishment, high profile and
ongoing legitimacy of women's health centres. Their contribution has
been understated and undervalued, partly because of the anti-doctor
ideologies embodied in the centres and partly because those who have
written about women's health centres have, understandably, not wished
to draw too much public attention to divisions (Broom, 1991; Stevens,
1995). But doctors cannot afford to feel sorry for themselves or plead
powerlessness. As Anna Yeatman (1993) has argued in relation to feminist academics and bureaucrats, they cannot continue to plead that they

are marginalised but must acknowledge their power as gatekeepers of certain kinds of knowledge and start to engage in a politics of representation. Doctors have been forced to accept that they represent medical power and absorb the flak, recognising that their own sense of obligation and responsibility, while crucial to the viability of the centre, is likely to be resented by those not in a position to share it. When criticised, they cannot simply walk away but have to enter into an explicitly political domain and engage with the criticisms. This means spending time explaining, reporting, arguing about what they do, and endeavouring to work as part of a team in which everyone's skills are respected, challenged and developed. The articulation and working through of the tensions between doctors and other workers has also meant that feminist assumptions about medical expertise, effective health care delivery and the workings of collectives have been challenged and modified.

Doctors have at times felt under attack when they were not. A woman who had been a centre administrator commented that the doctors thought she hated them as a group when she had merely treated them like everybody else and in fact encouraged them to take up leadership roles. She went on to describe her 'hammock theory of organisation':

> The doctors were one pole of power and I was the other and everyone else was arranged in the hammock. They complained about being stuck in service delivery but the more you tried to encourage them out the more unsure they felt about what the hell they were doing and why. My concern was that women's health centres must impact on the health system generally. A women's health centre has go to be out there in the world . . . trying to get things to change. The doctors felt very uncomfortable about that I think.

In her view it was not their medical status but their political naivety that was often the problem. Health workers value the doctors who know how to operate politically. There have been many instances of warm and trusting relationships developing between doctors and other workers. Dr L.'s colleagues appreciated the fact that she was a 'rugged campaigner' who was prepared to 'go on state-wide committees and stick it right up them!' They admired her feminist philosophy and strong political sense and would not have dreamed of trying to reduce her to a technician. For Dr L.: 'It is a privilege to work here. I get opportunities that I would not get in general practice. I don't want to be in private medicine. We have a huge number of conflicts, and lots of unresolved issues, but at least we can have them.'

Creative tensions

In all the women's health centres similar issues have surfaced concerning the role that doctors should play, how much they should be paid, the

extent of their clinical autonomy, and how to ensure that their specialised knowledge and medical socialisation do not allow them to dominate.
Should doctors be restricted to consultations or involved in group work?
Should they take their turn on the child care roster? Does it make sense
to use them for education or counselling when they are more expensive
than other health workers?

When Leichhardt opened, salaries were the same for all except the
doctor and the cleaner. While the status of the cleaner does not seem to
have generated much concern, that of the doctor clearly did. Some
argued that it is only because of medical dominance that doctors get
higher pay, and therefore they should be prepared to work collectively
and receive the same wages (Davey, 1991). Others see a trade-off between
higher pay and membership of the collective and in some centres
doctors were given a choice between the two. Dr B. said cheerfully:

> On paper I got more but I donated down to the same level as everyone else . . .
> Money is power and if doctors won't take less money then you have to give
> them less power . . . none of us had ever worked in a collective before.

Taking the lower rate became something of a badge of honour, evidence
of the doctor's political commitment. Dr T. recalled:

> I used to get paid collective rates as well as doctor rates. But I wasn't as good
> as J. She took collective rates all the time. I figured I needed the money.

Health centres put a lot of time and energy into selecting their doctors. Doctors who may not previously have experienced anything more
than the most cursory of job interviews will be hit with a battery of questions concerning their views on abortion and tranquillisers, HRT and
Depo-provera, and have to establish that they are willing to work with
nurses as independent practitioners. For some centres the ultimate test
was whether, if a woman came in saying she needed a day off work, the
doctor would give her a medical certificate. 'One of the local women
was very firm about that. She said, women know if they need a break and
you have got to give it to them!' Doctors will 'fail' an interview if they
insist too strongly on their legal obligations or their rights to clinical
autonomy.

Collectives have often been reluctant to trust doctors with clinical
judgments, believing that they should be the ones to determine broad
policy about acceptable treatments. Health care workers tend to have
strong views about the merits of conventional drugs versus alternative
treatments, with issues such as HRT and Depo-provera being highly
contentious. They said:

We actually don't know what the doctors are doing in the surgery on their own and how to assess that. It is very, very difficult.

I have a concern that there is one particular doctor that is putting nearly every women on hormone replacement therapy. She hadn't actually read my notes where I had already put them on a calcium supplement which was addressing osteoporosis. I feel like I am working an uphill battle to convince doctors that naturopathy has a place. It is not scientific therefore it does not have worth.

Mental health is a difficult one because a lot of doctors . . . think mental health is a chemical imbalance and chemical interventions can fix it . . . So there are a few issues that other workers in women's health centres probably watch doctors on.

A doctor with very similar views about the social bases of mental illness expressed her frustration with collectives that rigidly enforced such policies without understanding the underlying medical conditions:

It became policy that anti-depressants would not be prescribed. People who came to Leichhardt had to come off everything. I agree with them about the use of anti-psychotic medications because their husband was bashing them. But a woman who had terrible ear damage leading to dizziness was told to stop her Stematil . . . and I was really hurt by their lack of faith. I also disagreed with them about Depo-provera and said there was a place for it: well, this is anathema to the feminist creed, the equivalent to committing treason.

This doctor was struggling to convince her co-workers that the centre could intervene more effectively if it did not revert to a blanket rejection of medical expertise. Several doctors pointed to the contradiction that while health workers treated medical knowledge with suspicion, they enthusiastically embraced alternative treatments for which there was often no verification:

There was a woman at a conference giving a paper about monilial infections. There was a big thing at the time that everything that is wrong with you is due to a monilia infection and you've to give huge doses of anti-monilial drugs. I saw all these feminists writing down 'correct' doses and I thought, this is just nonsense, she's just picked up these ideas from a couple of articles. I don't think women, just because they're feminists, should accept something just because it's put forward by women.

A number of doctors made it clear that they were prepared to respect alternative health practices but in turn wanted to be respected for what they could offer:

I don't like being in a situation where I'm not given equal respect. I'm happy to give respect to naturopathy . . . but I want an equal, reciprocal relationship instead of western medicine always being the naughty one.

They contested attempts by the workers to treat them as narrow technicians:

> I was explaining that if someone has a lot of social problems or is feeling very depressed, it takes longer. And they were saying, basically you shouldn't be doing that, we have counsellors here. I am happy to send people to counsellors but I need to see them once or twice first. I have been seeing a lot of women with severe PMT. And you need to establish if that is the problem or if they have other stresses that are making it worse. I don't think anyone who goes to a women's health centre wants to have the doctor not listen to what they are saying, or saying, well you can tell that to a counsellor.

> Medicine is an institution so obviously it can function to reinforce the status quo. But like anything else, it depends what you do with it. A lot of women doctors working in health centres and female GPs are not doing that at all. They are helping women to learn more about their own bodies, maybe teaching them negotiating skills for safer sex and things which I think are quite empowering.

They threw back at the women's health workers their own criticisms of fragmented practice:

> We are supposed to be about primary health and holistic care but we segment everyone into body parts. It is really personified by the body parts nurse. There is your breast screening nurse, and your stomal therapy nurse and so on. I am not meant to have an ongoing role so in some sense I have a lot of ambivalence about the work I do. How do I ignore someone's asthma which is obviously out of control when they have come in for their smear?

Unlike GPs, the centres do not see long-term patients and have to rely on referrals. But this doctor wanted to 'treat the whole person' even if she could not possibly be 'the whole treatment'.

Doctors argued not only that they had a wide range of skills but that these skills were of great importance if women's health was to be taken seriously.

> I'd been doing a lot of work on communication and I was talking about it at a meeting. They got a bit upset and they thought it was the doctor talking down to them. In fact I'd done a lot more of this sort of work than they had. And I'd done a lot of work on sexuality which few doctors had done at that time. It would be hard not to be in a position of being an expert.

Health care workers have over time come to recognise the value of professional skills but it has involved a struggle. For them, political concerns often jostle with unexamined feelings of envy or resentment about doctors' status and privilege. The treatment of doctors as 'technicians' is also often accompanied by a refusal to provide them with back-up support. Several workers complained about how frequently the doctors ask the person at reception to put their files away. One said proudly, 'They never dare ask me! I am very busy here too.' A doctor complained:

> I would say to somebody, look, I have been talking to Mrs X for half an hour and I have another patient waiting, will you take her over and explain where she can get this and this. And they'd say, oh I'm just going to the post office or, no, I'm going home. They would leave at 5 o'clock. I might work till seven.

While this doctor was appealing to fairness in the allocation of time, it is fairly obvious that 'somebody' experienced this as a repetition of the master–servant relationship and a reaffirmation of the superior value of the doctor's time.

For many doctors, one of the attractions of coming to a women's health centre is precisely the possibility of working in teams and doing preventative work. One had been preoccupied with how to reach the victims of domestic violence:

> There is such a stigma that people will not come to meetings and workshops. We do a fair bit of work with the Central and South American community. We couldn't run a group for these women on domestic violence but we are contemplating one on food and nutrition. They'll come to that and then we can talk about domestic violence.

Doctors who try to work democratically may be experienced as no less threatening than those who seem more demanding. Those who come to the centres with a social view of health often find that attempts are made to keep them away from counselling and educational work. They argue, forcefully, that this merely perpetuates the medical model.

Doctors have also pointed to the many practical difficulties of collectively running a health centre. Many complained that they had worked longer hours and been forced to carry both legal and financial responsibility. Several referred to the impotence of collectives and management committees in dealing with issues like financial malpractice:

> There was a case of embezzlement and I think because it was by a woman from a non-English-speaking background they did not want to do anything about it. I finally said, you have to do something or I will go to the police. And I got phoned back that night and they did do something about it.

In this case, the doctor had stepped in, rather like a governor with reserve powers, to resolve the situation. But resentments ran high and she left shortly afterwards. Feminists did not take kindly to this assumption of responsibility but they have had to take on board some of the criticisms of the workings of collectivities. As Stevens (1995: 71–94) acknowledges in her history of Leichhardt Women's Health Centre, collectives have not always been effective even at ensuring that basic housekeeping tasks like cleaning get done, let alone supervising staff adequately.

There have been ongoing tensions about how time is best used. Doctors (and nurses too) often experience a conflict between medical time and the much slower pace of 'feminist' time:

> I find, coming back, that my ideas of efficiency and output, and what I expect of myself in an ordinary working day, are totally different to the culture of this organisation. And that is a tension. I find it hard to tolerate the expectation that I will spend half a day a week out of three in staff meetings. There is still an expectation of a flat management structure and it means everyone has a right to an opinion on every decision. I find it incredibly inefficient and boring.

This woman considered herself to be a committed feminist who was more than willing to be involved in the running of the organisation. But she considered that the collective ran in a way that was wasteful of everybody's time and that her colleagues were being politically inept in refusing to address the issues of productivity and accountability.

Relations between doctors and health workers have shifted somewhat as both have struggled to come to terms with new political realities. Originally the centres were funded directly by the Commonwealth but after 1981 responsibility was passed to the states. The need for separate services for women, and the value of preventive activities, has not been universally accepted. Health authorities, with an orientation to direct service delivery and a preoccupation with quantifiable productivity have begun to scrutinise their activities more closely. Tensions arise from the dual roles of direct delivery of feminist health services and advocacy for system change. Some states have refused to include doctors' salaries in the grants, thereby forcing the federal government to fund doctors through Medicare bulk billing. Where this has happened, centres do not have the luxury of debating how they will use their doctors and whether they can be part of the collective, because there is very little leeway. If doctors can only be employed on a sessional basis, perhaps for seven hours a week, it makes no sense for them to spend three or four of those hours at a collective meeting but neither is there much scope for them to do anything other than one-to-one consultations. Centres come to rely on doctors for some of their resources creating new tensions and dependencies:

> Because we have to bulk bill, they are now earning their own money . . . they are actually bringing income into the centre . . . which they like to point out.

The shift from one-hour to thirty-minute appointments has put huge pressure on the doctors, who are usually dealing with people they do not already know, who come in with complex problems. The expectation that they will do their own paperwork may be egalitarian but it cuts severely into the time available for patients. Doctors complained that 'GPs rarely do any of those things themselves. But there is this feeling that if someone else did that it would be making doctors special.' They feel that by denying their specific skills and failing to put them to best usage, the health centres are denying their own feminist principles and restricting their capacity for effective service delivery.

Despite their criticisms, the current group of women doctors say they and co-workers experience mutual respect and are often surprised when told of past battles. It is hard to know whether the issues have been resolved or whether the centres themselves are less intensely political than they used to be. One doctor observed that feminism was barely discussed any more while others commented:

> I was appalled at the level of feminist consciousness there. I thought I'd be out of my depth and way behind and that they would all be more sophisticated politically. And they weren't!

> They seem to be frightened of new blood and are employing fairly conservative suburban women now . . . Recently they decided not to give a job to someone who was young, forceful and articulate because she would be too threatening to some of the other women working there.

Workers are often no better informed than doctors about current feminist debate and many work in women's health centres not out of feminist zeal but because the pay and conditions are better than they are outside. The concerns of clients have also changed. Where they once came in with horror stories about appalling medical treatment, they are now more likely to come for second opinions, or to deal with sexual abuse or domestic violence. And, while they are referred to other workers in the centre, it is the doctor that they generally want to see. With the passage of time the meanings attached to being 'a feminist' have become more varied and complex and, it would seem, there has been a considerable blending of the subaltern habitus with the habitus of feminism.

Making some difference

Women doctors have played an important part in the women's health movement internationally. Without their presence the movement could not have had the influence on mainstream health care that it has. They have navigated a turbulent field and both transformed and been transformed by it. Women doctors may be understood as structuring agents in restructuring the field. They have had much to learn from women's health activists about why doctors have been so strongly disliked and in turn they have challenged the feminist habitus with its easy acceptance of collective decision-making, its denigration of professional skills and its assumptions about sisterhood. There has been a strengthening of links with female GPs, many of whom have been drawn into the centres to do sessional work, often on aspects of preventative health. The working through of the tensions has contributed significantly to concepts of democratic medicine and implemented them at a local level.

The Australian women's health centres not only provide services but constitute a base from which to influence policy. Women's health advisers were appointed both federally and in most of the states and in 1989 a national women's health policy was launched by the Prime Minister. Feminist doctors have also had a direct influence on the medical curriculum. The New South Wales Health Department, for example, funded the RACGP to produce a course on women's health as part of the family medicine program, and the tender was given to a group of women who had worked in women's health centres. The course has provided a base for lobbying the college which, as one doctor commented, still finds it hard to see what the problems are. 'They say, "what's this women's health? I do Pap smears! I examine breasts! What's the problem!"' The course is a voluntary one, and still taken by very few men, but it does mark an attempt to articulate 'best practice' in a way that is sensitive to gender inequalities.

Worcester and Whatley (1988) have argued, with reference to the United States, that the 'discovery' of women's health has meant the medicalising of new areas of women's lives, hooking women more tightly into a system which does not meet their needs. They offer PMS and osteoporosis as prime examples, with pervasive cancer fears just waiting to be encouraged and exploited. In this view women doctors are implicated in the further commodification of health. But 'medicalisation' is double-edged. While it permits the expansion of medical power it also enables problems to be recognised and treated. It provides here and now solutions rather than waiting for revolutionary social change in some idealised future. Greer (1992) might claim, in relation to menopause, that doctors are medicalising a natural process but it is equally possible to argue they are improving the quality of life. Pap smears and mammograms may not be the last word on women's health but they have undoubtedly lengthened lives, improved their quality and provided women with choices. While they have created new anxieties they have provided opportunities for empowerment not only for doctors but for patients.

No one group can claim the high moral ground about what constitutes health and how it is best achieved. Critics of 'the medical model' often appeal all-knowingly to forms of truth about health and what is good for us. But in a pluralist society differences have to be respected and compromises worked out. Feminism itself and the conditions that gave rise to it in the 1960s and 1970s have changed. The women's health movement could not remain permanently on the margins and the transformation of many of its demands into funded services has involved a considerable degree of professionalisation. In this new context women doctors seem less like 'the enemy' and are merely one of a number of professional groups seeking to work together in relations of mutual respect.

While there have been good reasons to criticise doctors, they are often held responsible for too much. They did not invent the health system by themselves and it is not entirely their fault that people have unrealistic expectations of them to 'fix' things. Feminist historians have begun to view medicine as 'more complicated and less villainous' than previously assumed (Theriot, 1993) while the British sociologist Mary Ann Elston (1991) suggests that we are on the threshold of a decline in medical dominance.

The last decade has seen a turning away from attempts to integrate the monolithic structures of capitalism and patriarchy and a new emphasis on the need to address instances of gender domination in their specific contexts. Medical interventions have not simply been imposed on a reluctant population. Medical technologies may be seen as potentially neutral, their meanings coming from the discursive practices in which they are situated. They may be used in ways that give women greater control over their lives or they may turn women passive recipients.

David Silverman suggests that 'medical dominance' is an inappropriate model for understanding doctor–patient relations since power is not simply a finite quality to be fought over in battles. Both doctors and patients may speak through a variety of discourses including 'medical dominance' and 'patient control'. None is intrinsically more liberating than any other and it is always a question of the relation between discourses and the context within which they are invoked (Silverman, 1987: 231–2). A patient can interrupt a discourse on the virtue of high-tech births by demanding natural birth. But she can also disrupt discourses of patient power by demanding advice rather than self-expression, or pain relief rather than autonomy. Similarly, a doctor might dominate not only by prescribing HRT or Depo-provera but by refusing them to women who have decided they are appropriate to their needs. Rather than assuming that doctors have total power, and that they are wrong whatever they do, it is important to think about how relationships might be renegotiated. The experiment of the women's health centres indicates that it is possible to reposition doctors as valued members of health teams which they do not control.

10

Conclusion

Do women doctors make a difference to the practice of medicine and to women's health? The answer must be a resounding 'yes', not only in Britain and Australia, where this study is based, but throughout the Western world. Women now account for around 50 per cent of medical graduates and the proportion continues to increase. Arguably this is one of the most significant occupational shifts of the last twenty years. It will ensure the continued feminisation of general practice and higher proportions of women in most of the specialties. Feminist sociologists in the UK continue to argue that medicine 'celebrates and sustains a masculinist vision' (Davies, 1996: 669). Davies points to the heroic individual effort involved in successfully completing the training and also the ways in which medical autonomy is sustained by the preparatory and follow-up work of others, mostly women. Direct masculine exclusionary practices are still widespread, especially in the surgical specialties (Allen, 1994) and, as Crompton observes, the Distinction Awards, which enhance average salaries in the UK by an average of 18 per cent are concentrated on the male-dominated specialties (1997: 11). But they draw similar conclusions to those presented in this book, suggesting that while 'in the relatively short run' masculine dominance is likely to persist, in the longer run the medical profession will be dramatically different. Davies predicts that as more women enter the profession there may be a 'transformation from within' (1996: 673). Crompton is more cautious, reminding us that women doctors' 'family friendly' career choices have left little space for a challenge to men's professional hegemony (Crompton, 1997: 10). Yet, as governments are now aware, these choices have major implications for 'manpower' planning and have brought pressure for a major rethinking of training programs and work schedules. As women accumulate cultural and symbolic capital they are in a position to create new visions of how medicine should be practised.

They already talk about medicine in ways that differ from the conventional masculine approaches.

I have not been concerned in this book to try and quantify 'how much' difference women make but have preferred to play with difference in a more Deleuzian sense, as force, action, effectivity. As Elizabeth Grosz has put it, Deleuze's project involves 'the re-energization of thought, the affirmation of life and change, and an attempt to work around those forces of anti-production that aim to restrict innovation and prevent change: to free lines, points, concepts, events from the structures and constraints which bind them to the same, to the one, to the self-identical' (Grosz, 1995: 129). Rather than treating gender as a binary and locking women into the position of 'the other' it is possible to emphasise the diversity of 'masculinities' and 'femininities' that exist both in the medical world and more widely (Crompton, 1997). More interesting than any absolute truths about the differences between men and women is the discursive production of difference and the subjectivities that get constructed in relation to these meanings. Therefore the issue is not whether women doctors are truly more caring than men but what can now be done with such claims. Can they be used to fracture the associations between medicine and masculine authority, to open the ground for a rethinking of what we want medicine to be?

I have made no attempt to claim that women doctors have any kind of advanced feminist consciousness, or that this is necessary to bring about change. While they share a great deal with their male colleagues, women doctors are very differently positioned in the medical field and different speaking positions are available to them. When women doctors talk about medicine it quickly begins to seem more accessible to women than the usual stereotypes allow. Women doctors are also forced to practise differently, regardless of their own attitudes and beliefs. Patients and co-workers impose different expectations on them and even the most brilliant women doctors are likely to have come up against the power of the medical establishment at some stage.

The rapid movement of women into medicine is redolent with meanings that go far beyond equal employment issues. The demand that they be accepted on equal terms with men points towards a world in which work, medicine and gender relations are dramatically repositioned, as we discover what 'equal terms' might actually mean. Their presence is unsettling. On the one hand it appears to complete the 'modern' phase of medicine but, on the other, it ends the association between masculinity and medical 'modernity' which has generated glamour and status.

This cannot be a story of women triumphantly taking an equal place in a transformed 'human' medicine, although such aspirations will be present. It is more like a kaleidoscope which makes it possible to view the variety of ways in which women doctors have operated in a world in which masculine authority, even in surgery, has been challenged. Beyond the broad sweep, struggles go on at a local level and outcomes vary. Chance factors come into play. Opportunities briefly open up for women in certain areas and then just as suddenly shut down again. It is a world in which women clear one set of hurdles only to find another set looming; a world in which they both gain from and feel imprisoned in the 'human face' metaphor; and a world in which demands for greater flexibility may simply recast the old male full-time and female part-time work patterns.

There remains a large gap between the 'feminism' embraced by women doctors and that of women's health activists but the groups are drawing closer together. Doctors have more training in women's health issues and are more aware of the critiques, while at the same time feminist approaches are becoming more diverse and less overtly hostile to medicine. Some feminists are also beginning to concede that such characteristics as expertise, impartiality and impersonality may, as doctors have always claimed, be necessary to practice medicine effectively and should not be regarded as inherently masculine (Crompton, 1997). Where medical women's organisations once concentrated their attention on demands for part-time work and training, and assumed that most women would prioritise family over work, they are beginning to call for a much more flexible system which would enable both men and women to contribute to their full potential without sacrificing their personal lives. They are now challenging discrimination and the medical hierarchy, the haphazard nature of training programs, the quality of doctor–patient relationships, and the inappropriate behaviour of many of their male colleagues. The fact that so many women doctors are prepared to work part-time, and in jobs that are not well paid, constitutes an enormous threat to the profession. Women appear to be less concerned with power and income, less likely to stand on ceremony, and more willing to cooperate with a range of health care practitioners.

It has become a sociological cliché that when women move into an occupation its status falls. While feminists have challenged such simplistic assumptions about the relation between gender and status, in this case we might want actually to celebrate any links we can find between the rising proportion of women and a profession that has begun to step off its pedestal and become more democratic. We have moved closer to a level playing-field and, from the consumers' point of view, one that is more responsive than it used to be. The presence of growing numbers of women doctors has contributed subtly to these changes, interrupting the smooth flows of medical power, creating the possibility of greater movement around the field, and even sharing the field with other practitioners. Women did not self-consciously or as a unified group set out to transform medicine but their presence is producing changes beyond what any but a tiny minority may have ever visualised.

References

Abel-Smith, B. 1960. *A History of the Nursing Profession*. London: Heinemann
Adam, B. 1994/5. Time for feminist approaches to technology, 'Nature' and work. *Arena Journal* (new series), 4: 91–104
Adam, B. 1995. *Timewatch: The Social Analysis of Time*. Cambridge: Polity
Adlam, D. & Rose, N. 1981. The politics of psychiatry. *Politics and Power*, 4: 165–202
AIHW 1996. *Medical Labour Force Survey 1994*. Canberra: AIHW National Health Labour Force series no. 6
Allen, H. 1986. Psychiatry and the construction of the feminine. In Miller & Rose: 85–110
Allen, I. 1988. *Any Room at the Top? A Study of Doctors and their Careers*. London: Policy Studies Institute
Allen, I. 1994. *Doctors and Their Careers: A New Generation*. London: Policy Studies Institute
Allen, I. 1996. Career preferences of doctors. *British Medical Journal*, 313: 2
Alterkruse, J. M. & McDermott, S. W. 1988. Contemporary concerns of women in medicine. In Rosser: 65–90
AMWAC 1996. *Annual Report 1995–96*. Sydney: Australian Medical Workforce Advisory Committee Report 1996.4
AMWAC & AIHW 1996. *Female Participation in the Australian Medical Workforce*. Sydney: Australian Medical Workforce Advisory Committee & Australian Institute of Health and Welfare Report 1996.7
ANZCA 1994. Female Anaesthetists – ASA Questionnaire 1993: Does gender matter in the pursuit of a career in anaesthesia? Preliminary Report. *ANZCA Bulletin*, March: 14–15
Anderson, N. A., Bridges-Webb, C. & Chancellor, A. H. B. (eds) 1986. *General Practice in Australia*. Sydney: Sydney University Press
Ang, I. 1996. *Living Room Wars: Rethinking Media Audiences for a Postmodern World*. London: Routledge
Annandale, E. 1989. Proletarianization or restratification of the medical profession? The case of obstetrics. *International Journal of Health Services*, 19(4): 611–34
Areskog-Wijma, B. 1987. The gynaecological examination – women's experiences

and preferences and the role of the gynaecologist. *Journal of Psychosomatic Obstetrics and Gynaecology*, 6: 59–69

Armstrong, D. 1976. The emancipation of biographical medicine. *Social Science and Medicine*, 13A: 1–8

Arnold, P. 1996. The womanpower that matters. *Australian Medicine*, 2 September: 10

Arnold, P. 1992. Much ado about mothers. *Australian Medicine*, 18 May: 7

Atkinson, P. & Delamont, S. 1990. Professions and powerlessness: Female marginality in the learned occupations *Sociological Review*, 38(1): 90–110

Bagnall, D. 1987. Caps off to the lady doctors. *Vogue Australia*, November: 181–3

Balint, E. & Norell, J. S. (eds). 1973. *Six Minutes for the Patient: Interactions in General Consultation*. London: Tavistock

Balint, M. 1964. *The Doctor, his Patient and the Illness*. London: Pitman

Baly, M. E. 1980. *Nursing and Social Change*. London: Heinemann

Baly, M. E. 1987. The Nightingale nurses: The myth and the reality. In *Nursing History: The State of the Art*, ed. C. Maggs. London: Croom Helm

Bartky, S. L. 1988. Foucault, femininity and patriarchal power. In *Feminism and Foucault*, eds I. Diamond & L. Quinby. Boston: Northeastern University Press

Bashford, A. 1994. Nursing bodies: The gendered politics of health in Australia and England, 1860–1910. PhD Thesis, History Department, University of Sydney

Battersby, C. 1989. *Gender and Genius: Towards a Feminist Aesthetics*. London: The Women's Press

Baume, P. E. 1994. *A Cutting Edge: Australia's Surgical Workforce*. Report to the Inquiry into the Supply of, and Recruitment for, Medical Specialist Services in Australia. Canberra: AGPS

Becker, H., Geer, B., Hughes, E. & Strauss, A. 1961. *Boys in White: Student Culture in Medical School*. Chicago: University of Chicago Press

Begley, Y. 1987. Personal view. *British Medical Journal*, 295: 604

Belgrave, M. 1990. In *Women Doctors in New Zealand: An Historical Perspective 1921–1986*, ed. M. M. Maxwell, pp. 203–16. Auckland: IMS NZ Ltd

Bell, G. 1994. Doctors get better. *SMH Good Weekend*, 26 February: 26–31

Bem, S. 1974. The measurement of psychological androgyny. *Journal of Consulting and Clinical Psychology*, 42(2): 155–62

Benson, J. R. 1992. Surgical careers and female students. *Lancet*, 339: 1361

Benson, W. S. 1988. The history of the college examination. In *To Follow Knowledge: A History of Examinations, Continuing Education and Specialist Affiliations of the Royal Australasian College of Practitioners*, ed. J. C. Wiseman. Sydney: RACP

Best, J. 1988. *Portraits in Australian Health*. Sydney: MacLennan & Petty

Bewley, S. 1991. The future obstetrician/gynaecologist. *British Journal of Obstetrics and Gynaecology*, 98: 237–40

Blake, C. 1990. *The Charge of the Parasols: Women's Entry to the Medical Profession*. London: The Women's Press

Bottero, W. 1992. The changing face of the professions: Gender and explanations of women's entry to pharmacy. *Work, Employment and Society*, 6(3): 329–46

Bourdieu, P. 1989. For a socio-analysis of intellectuals: On homo academicus. An interview with Pierre Bourdieu. Introduced by Lois J. D. Wacquant. *Berkeley Journal of Sociology*, 24: 1–29

Bourdieu, P. 1990. *The Logic of Practice*, trans. R. Nice. Cambridge: Polity Press

Bourdieu, P. 1993a. The properties of fields. In *Sociology in Question*, pp. 72–7. London: Sage

Bourdieu, P. 1993b. *The Field of Cultural Production: Essays on Art and Literature*, ed. and introduced by R. Johnson. Cambridge: Polity Press

Bretos, C. 1984. Women doctors need flexible training and work schedules. *Australian Doctor*, 21 September: 18–19

Britt, H. 1990. What do general practitioners do? In *Towards Evaluation in General Practice: A Workshop on Vocational Registration*, ed. D. P. Doessel, pp. 45–51. Canberra: Department of Community Services and Health

Britt, H., Bhasale, A., Miles, D. A., Meza, A., Sayer, G. P. & Angelis, M. 1996. *The Gender of the General Practitioner: A Comparison of GP Characteristics, Their Patients and the Morbidity Managed.* Family Medicine Research Unit, Department of General Practice, University of Sydney: 1–22

Broom, D. H. 1991. *Damned if We Do: Contradictions in Women's Health Care.* Sydney: Allen & Unwin

Buchan, J. & Stock, J. 1990. *Early Careers of General Practitioners.* Institute of Manpower Studies, Brighton: University of Sussex

Busfield, J. 1986. *Managing Madness: Changing Ideas and Practice.* London: Unwin Hyman

Byrne, E. 1984. A natural place in the community . . .? *Australian Doctor*, 8 October: 22–3

Calhoun, C. 1993. Habitus, field, and capital: The question of historical specificity. In *Bourdieu: Critical Perspectives*, eds C. Calhoun, E. LiPuma & M. Postone, pp. 60–88. Cambridge: Polity Press

Calnan, M. 1988. Images of general practice: The perceptions of the doctor. *Social Science and Medicine*, 27: 579–86

Calnan, M. & Gabe, J. 1991. Recent developments in general practice: A sociological analysis. In *The Sociology of the Health Service*, eds J. Gabe, M. Calnan & M. Bury. London: Routledge

Cartwright, F. F. 1967. *The Development of Modern Surgery.* London: Barker

Cassell, J. 1986. Dismembering the images of God: Surgeons, heroes, wimps and miracles. *Anthropology Today* 2(2): 13–15

Castel, R., Castel, F. & Lovell, A. 1982. *The Psychiatric Society.* New York: Columbia University Press

Central Sydney Area Health Service 1993. *Review of Recruitment and Selection Practices for Registrar and Fellow Positions at King George V Hospital.* March: 1–23

Chalmers, J. 1992. Women in medicine. *Medical Journal of Australia*, 157: 726–7

Chesler, P. 1972. *Women and Madness.* New York: Avon

Chua, T. & Clegg, S. 1990. Professional closure: the case of British nursing. *Theory and Society*, 19(2): 135–72

Clark, G. 1964. *A History of the Royal College of Physicians of London*, Vol. 1, Oxford: Clarendon Press

Clark, G. 1966. *A History of the Royal College of Physicians of London*, Vol. 2, Oxford: Clarendon Press

Clarke, P. J. 1992. Surgical careers and female students. *Lancet*, 339: 994–5

Coney, S. 1988. *The Unfortunate Experiment.* Auckland: Penguin Books

Connell, R. W. 1991. Live fast and die young: The construction of masculinity among young working class men on the margin of the labour market. *ANZ Journal of Sociology*, 27(2): 141–71

Connell, R. W. 1987. *Gender and Power.* London: Polity

Cook, A. M. 1972. *A History of the Royal College of Physicians of London*, Vol. 3. Oxford: Clarendon Press

Cooke, M. & Ronalds, C. 1985. Women doctors in urban general practice: the patients. *British Medical Journal*, 290: 753–5

Cox, D. 1991. Health service management – a sociological view: Griffiths and the non-negotiated order of the hospital. In *The Sociology of the Health Service*, eds J. Gabe, M. Calman & M. Bury. London: Routledge

Crompton, R. 1990. Professions in the current context. *Work, Employment and Society*, Special Issue: 147–66

Crompton, R. 1987. Gender, status and professionalism. *Sociology*, 21: 413–28

Crompton, R. & Le Feuvre, N. 1997. The feminisation of the medical profession: Theoretical and empirical implications. *University of Bergen*, 25–26 April (Draft MS): 1–17

Crompton, R. & Sanderson, K. 1990. *Gendered Jobs and Social Change*. London: Unwin Hyman

Crouch, M. & Manderson, L. 1993. *New Motherhood: Cultural and Personal Transitions in the 1980s*. Amsterdam: Gordon & Breach

Dally, A. 1991. *Women under the Knife*. London: Hutchinson

Dally, A. 1990. *A Doctor's Story*. London: Macmillan

Daly, M. 1978. *Gyn/Ecology*. Boston: Beacon Press

Daniel, A. 1990. *Medicine and the State*. Sydney: Allen & Unwin

Davey, M. 1991. The role of doctors in women's and community health centres. University of Tasmania: MSc Primary Health Care thesis

Davies, C. 1996. The sociology of the professions and the profession of gender. *Sociology*, 30: 661–78

Davies, C. (ed.). 1980. *Rewriting Nursing History*. London: Croom Helm

Day, P. 1982. *Women Doctors: Choice and Constraints in Policies for Medical Manpower*. London: King's Fund Centre

Dennerstein, L., Lehert, P., Orams, R., Ewing, J. & Burrows, G. 1989. Practice patterns and family life – a survey of Melbourne medical graduates. *Medical Journal of Australia*, 151(7): 386–90

Dent, O. 1989. *Clinical Workforce in Internal Medicine and Paediatrics in Australia – 1988*. Sydney: RACP

Department of Health UK 1992. Maternity Services: Government Response to the Second Report from the Health Committee, Session 1991–92. London: HMSO

Dews, P. 1987. *Logics of Disintegration: Post-structuralist Thought and the Claims of Critical Theory*. London: Verso

Diamond, I. & Quinby, L. (eds). 1988. *Feminism and Foucault*. Boston: Northeastern University Press

Dillner, L. 1991. WIST-ful thinking. *British Medical Journal*, 303: 734

Dingwall, R. & McIntosh, J. (eds). 1978. *Readings in the Sociology of Nursing*. London: Churchill Livingstone

Dingwall, R., Rafferty, A. M. & Webster, C. 1988. *An Introduction to the Social History of Nursing*. London: Routledge

Dohler, M. 1993. Comparing national patterns of medical specialization: a contribution to the theory of the professions. In *Social Science Information*, pp. 185–231. London: Sage

Donnison, J. 1977. *Midwives and Medical Men*. London: Heinemann

Dowling, S. & Barrett, S. 1991. *Doctors in the Making: The experience of the preregistration year*. Bristol: SAUS Publications, University of Bristol

Ducker, D. G. 1980. The effect of two sources of role strain on women physicians. *Sex Roles*, 64: 549–59

Dudley, H. 1990. Stress in junior doctors. *British Medical Journal*, 301: 75–6

Durham, G., Salmond, C. & Eberley, J. 1989. *Women and Men in Medicine: The Career Experiences*. Wellington: Department of Health

Dwyer, J. 1992. Women's health in Australia. In *Community Health: Policy and Practice in Australia*, eds F. Baume, D. Fry & I. Lennie. Sydney: Pluto

Ehrenreich, B. & Ehrenreich, J. 1977. The professional managerial class. *Radical America*, 11(2): 12–17

Ehrenreich, B. & English, D. 1972. *Witches, Midwives and Nurses: A History of Women Healers*. New York: Feminist Press

Ehrenreich, B. & English, D. 1978. *For Her Own Good: A Hundred and Fifty Years of the Experts' Advice to Women*. New York: Anchor Press

Eisner, M. & Wright, M. 1986. A feminist approach to general practice. In *Feminist Practice in Women's Health Care*, ed. C. Webb, pp. 113–45. Chester: John Wiley & Sons

Elliott, P. 1972. *The Sociology of the Professions*. London: Macmillan

Ellis, N. 1991. What is happening to general practice in the UK? *Medical Journal of Australia*, 154: 333–6

Elston, M. A. 1977. Women in the medical profession: Whose problem? In *Health and the Division of Labour*, eds M. Stacey et al. London: Croom Helm

Elston, M. A. 1980. Medicine: half our future doctors. In R. Silverstone & A. Ward (eds), pp. 99–139

Elston, M. A. 1991. The politics of professional power: Medicine in a changing health service. In *The Sociology of the Health Service*, eds. J. Gabe, M. Calnan & M. Bury, pp. 58–88. London: Routledge

Elston, M. A. 1993. Women doctors in a changing profession: The case of Britain. In Riska & Wegar (eds), pp. 27–61

Elston, M. A. & Lee, D. W. 1996. *The Impact on Increasing Numbers of Women Doctors on the Medical Workforce A Report for the Medical Workforce Standing Advisory Committee*. London

Fairclough, N. 1992. *Discourse and Social Change*. Cambridge: Polity Press

Fee, E. (ed.). 1983. *The Politics of Sex in Medicine*. New York: Baywood

Ferrari, J. 1996. Major cities have too many GPs. *Weekend Australian*, 13–14 April: 4

Fett, I. 1974. Australian medical graduates in 1972. *Medical Journal of Australia*, XX: 689–98

Fett, I. 1976. The future of women in Australian medicine. *Medical Journal of Australia*, Special Supplement November: 33–9

Fiander, A. 1991. Part time training in obstetrics and gynaecology. Letter, *British Medical Journal*, 303: 60

Firth-Cozens, J. 1990. Sources of stress in women junior house officers. *British Medical Journal*, 301: 89–91

Firth-Cozens, J. 1991. Women doctors. In *Women at Work*, eds J. Firth-Cozens & M. A. West, pp. 131–42. Milton Keynes: Open University Press

Flax, J. 1990. *Thinking Fragments: Psychoanalysis, Feminism, and Postmodernism in the Contemporary West*. Berkeley: University of California Press

Flynn, C. A. & Gardner, F. 1969. The careers of women graduates from the Royal Free Hospital School of Medicine, London. *British Journal of Medical Education*, 3: 28–42

Forman, F. J. 1989. Feminizing time: An introduction. In Forman & Sowton (eds), pp. 1–9

Forman, F. J. & Sowton, C. (eds). 1989. *Taking Our Time.* Oxford: Pergamon Press

Foster, P. 1989. Improving the doctor/patient relationship: A feminist perspective. *Journal of Social Policy,* 18(3): 337–61

Foucault, M. 1972. *Madness and Civilisation: A History of Insanity in the Age of Reason.* London: Tavistock

Foucault, M. 1973. *The Birth of the Clinic.* London: Tavistock

Foucault, M. 1977. *Discipline and Punish.* London: Tavistock

Foucault, M. 1980. *Power/Knowledge: Selected Interviews and Other Writings,* ed. C. Gordon. New York: Harvester Press

Fox, M. 1989. Unreliable allies: Subjective and objective time in childbirth. In Forman & Sowton (eds), pp. 123–34

Fox, N. 1992. *The Social Meaning of Surgery.* Milton Keynes: Open University Press

Frankenberg, R. 1992. 'Your time or mine': Temporal contradictions of biomedical practice. In R. Frankenberg (ed.), pp. 1–30

Frankenberg, R. (ed.). 1992. *Time, Health and Medicine.* London: Sage

Frankfurt, E. 1972. *Vaginal Politics.* New York: Quadrangle

Freidson, E. 1970a. *Profession of Medicine, a Study of the Sociology of Applied Knowledge.* New York: Harper & Row

Freidson, E. 1970b. *Professional Dominance: The Social Structure of Medical Care.* Chicago: Aldine

Gamarnikov, E. 1978. Sexual division of labour: The case of nursing. In *Feminism and Materialism,* eds A. Kuhn & A. Wolpe, pp. 96–123. London: Routledge

Gamarnikov, E. 1991. Nurse or woman: Gender and professionalism in reformed nursing 1860–1923. In *Anthropology and Nursing,* eds P. Holden & J. Littlewood. London: Routledge

Game, A. & Pringle, R. 1983. *Gender at Work.* Sydney: Allen & Unwin

Garton, S. 1988. *Medicine and Madness: A Social History of Insanity in New South Wales 1880–1940.* Sydney: University of NSW Press

Gathorne-Hardy, J. 1984. *Doctors: The Lives and Work of GPs in London.* London: Weidenfeld & Nicolson

Gilbert, R. 1993. Problems encountered by women GPs. Letter, *British Journal of Hospital Medicine,* 49(1): 67

Godlee, F. 1990. Stress in junior doctors – stress in women doctors. *British Medical Journal,* 301: 76

Goldberg, V. 1984. Women doctors: The office temps of medicine. *Australian Doctor,* 6 September: 16–17

Graffy, J. 1990. Patient choice in a practice with men and women general practitioners. *British Journal of General Practice,* 40

Gray, J. 1982. The effect of the doctor's sex on the doctor–patient relationship. *Journal of the Royal College of General Practitioners,* 32: 167–9

Greer, G. 1992. *The Change.* London: Penguin

Grosz, E. 1995. *Space, Time and Perversion: The Politics of Bodies.* Sydney: Allen & Unwin

Hage, G. 1994. Anglo-Celtics today: Cosmo-multiculturalism and the phase of the fading phallus. In *Community/Plural,* eds G. Hage, J. Lloyd & L. Johnson, 4: 41–77

Hantrais, L. 1993. The gender of time in professional occupations. *Time and Society,* 2(2): 139–57

Harrison, B. 1981. Women's health and the women's movement in Britain: 1840–1940. In *Biology, Medicine and Society 1840–1940,* ed. C. Webster, pp. 15–71. Cambridge: Cambridge University Press

Hart, C. 1994. *Behind the Mask: Nurses, Their Unions and Nursing Policy*. London: Baillière Tindall

Hart, J. T. 1988. *A New Kind of Doctor: The General Practitioner's Part in the Health of the Community*. London: Merlin Press

Hellstedt, L. M. 1979. *Women Physicians of the World: Autobiographies of Medical Pioneers*. Washington: McGraw-Hill

Hinde, F. C. 1990. The training of the obstetrician-gynaecologist for the 21st century. *Obstetrics and Gynaecology*, 30(2): 93–7

Hirvela, E. R. Surgery 2001: Twilight of the gods. *Archives of Surgery*, 128: 658–62

Hooper, J., Millar, J., Schofield, P. & Ward, G. 1989. Part-time women general practitioners – workload and remuneration. *Journal of the Royal College of General Practitioners*, 39: 327, 400–3

Illich, I. 1976. *Medical Nemesis: The Expropriation of Health*. New York: Random House

Irigaray, L. 1985. *Speculum of the Other Woman*. Ithaca: Cornell University Press

Jacob, J. 1988. *Doctors and Rules: A Sociology of Professional Values*. London: Routledge

Jacobus, M., Keller, E. F. & Shuttleworth, S. (eds). 1990. *Body/Politics: Women and the Discourses of Science*. New York: Routledge

Jefferys, M. & Sachs, H. 1983. *Rethinking General Practice*. London: Tavistock

Johnson, L. 1993. *The Modern Girl*. Sydney: Allen & Unwin

Johnson, R. 1993. Editor's introduction. In Bourdieu 1993b.

Johnson, T. J. 1972. *Professions and Power*. London: Macmillan

Joint Working Party 1991. *Women Doctors and their Careers*. London: Department of Health

Jordanova, L. 1989. *Sexual Visions: Images of Gender and Medicine Between the Eighteenth and Twentieth Centuries*. New York: Harvester Wheatsheaf

Khursandi, D. C. 1994. Female anaesthetists – ASA questionnaire 1993: Does gender matter in the pursuit of a career in anaesthesia? Preliminary report. *ANZCA Bulletin*, March: 14–15

Kincaid-Smith, P. 1995. Where are the women specialists? *Australian Medicine*, 10

Kinnersley, P. 1990. The ashes of general practice. *Medical Journal of Australia*, 153: 54–6

Komesaroff, P. 1995. Sexuality and ethics in the medical encounter. Conference paper, Baker Medical Research Institute, Melbourne

Konner, M. 1993. *The Trouble with Medicine*. London: BBC Books

Koutroulis, G. 1990. The orifice revisited: Women in gynaecological texts. *Community Health Studies*, XIV(1): 73–84

Kristeva, J. 1982. *Powers of Horror: An Essay on Abjection*. New York: Columbia University Press

Lambert, T. W., Goldacre, M. J., Edwards C. & Parkhouse, J. 1996. Career preferences of doctors who qualified in the United Kingdom in 1993 compared with those of doctors qualifying in 1974, 1977, 1980, and 1983. *British Medical Journal*, 313: 19–24

Laurance, J. 1993. Women step back from the cutting edge. *Times*, 27 May. London

Lawler, J. 1991. *Behind the Screens: Nursing, Somology, and the Problem of the Body*. London: Churchill Livingstone

Lawrence, B. 1987. The fifth dimension – gender and general practice. In *In a Man's World. Essays on Women in Male-Dominated Professions*, eds A. Spencer & D. Podmore. London: Tavistock

Leabeater, C. 1992. Australian women and the Medicare schedule of benefits: A discussion paper. May, Sydney: Medical Women's Society of NSW

Leavitt, J. W. 1980. Birthing and anaesthesia: The debate over twilight sleep. *Signs*, 147–65

Leeson, J. & Gray, J. 1978. *Women and Medicine*. London: Tavistock

Lefford, F. 1987. Women doctors: A quarter-century track record. *Lancet*, 1: 1254–6

Lester, E. 1986. A personal view. *British Medical Journal*, 293: 331

Levin, B. 1988. *Women and Medicine*. Lincoln, Nebraska: Media Publishing

Lewis, M. 1988. *Managing Madness: Psychiatry and Society in Australia 1788–1980*. Australian Institute of Health Canberra: AGPS

Lipton, G. 1993. 2020: A clinician's perspective. Paper to Council of RANZCP, 23 October: 1–10

Littlewood, R. 1991. Gender, role, and sickness: The ritual psychopathologies of the nurse. In *Anthropology and Nursing*, P. Holden & J. Littlewood. London: Routledge

Littlewood, R. & Lipsedge, M. 1982. *Aliens and Alienists: Ethnic Minorities and Psychiatry*. London: Penguin

Lorber, J. 1984. *Women Physicians: Careers, Status, Power*. New York: Tavistock

Lorber, J. 1993. Why women physicians will never be true equals in the American medical profession. In Riska & Wegar (eds), pp. 62–76

Lublin, J. & Gething, L. 1992. RNs as teachers of junior doctors. *Australian Journal of Advanced Nursing*, 10(2): 3–9

Lupton, G. M. & Najman, J. M. 1989. *Sociology of Health and Illness. Australian Readings*. Sydney: Macmillan

Macintyre, S. 1977. Childbirth: The myth of the Golden Age. *World Medicine*, 15 June, 17–22

Mackay, L. 1989. *Nursing a Problem*. Milton Keynes: Open University Press

Mackinnon, A. 1986. *The New Women: Adelaide's Early Women Graduates*. Adelaide: Wakefield Press

Mackinnon, A. 1997. *Love and Freedom: Professional Women and the Reshaping of Personal Life*. Melbourne: Cambridge University Press

Maggs, C. J. *The Origins of General Nursing*. London: Croom Helm

Magner, L. N. 1992. *A History of Medicine*. New York: Dekker

Mansfield, F. 1991. General practice in the nineties: Cottage industry or academic speciality? *Medical Journal of Australia*, 154: 29–32

Markus, M. 1987. Women, success and civil society: Submission to, or subversion of, the achievement principle. In *Feminism as Critique: On the Politics of Gender*, eds S. Benhabib & D. Cornell. Minneapolis: University of Minnesota

Martin, B. 1988. Feminism, criticism, and Foucault. In *Feminism and Foucault*, eds I. Diamond & L. Quinby. Boston: Northeastern University Press

Maulitz, R. C. 1988. Grand rounds: An introduction to the history of internal medicine. In Maulitz & Long (eds), pp. 3–14

Maulitz, R. C. & Long D. E. (eds). 1988. *Grand Rounds: One Hundred Years of Internal Medicine*. Philadelphia: University of Pennsylvania Press

McBride, M. 1993. Problems encountered by women GPs. Letter, *British Journal of Hospital Medicine*, 49(1): 67

McCall, L. 1992. Does gender fit? Bourdieu, feminism, and conceptions of social order. *Theory and Society*, 21: 837–67

McCormick, J. S. 1989. What is a good doctor? *Family Practice*, 6(4): 247–8

McDonald, I. A., Cope, I. & Forster, F. M. C. 1981. *Super Ardua*. Melbourne: RACOG

McKeigue, P. M., Richards, J. D. M. & Richards, P. 1990. Effects of discrimination by sex and race on the early careers of British medical graduates during 1981–87. *British Medical Journal*, 301: 961–4

McKinnon, S. E. et al. 1995. Women surgeons: Career and lifestyle comparisons among surgical subspecialties. *Plastic and Reconstructive Surgery*, 95(2): 321–9

McNay, L. 1992. *Foucault and Feminism*. Cambridge: Polity

Mies, M. Why do we need all this? A call against genetic engineering and reproductive technology. In Spallone & Steinberg, pp. 34–47

Miles, A. 1991. *Women, Health and Medicine*. Milton Keynes: Open University Press

Miller, P. & Rose, N. (eds). 1986. *The Power of Psychiatry*. Cambridge: Polity

Minden, S. 1987. Patriarchal designs: The genetic engineering of human embryos. In Spallone & Steinberg, pp. 102–9

Mizgala, C. et al. Women surgeons: Results of the Canadian Population Study. *Annals of Surgery*, 218(1): 37–46

Mohan, J. 1991. Privatization in the British health sector: a challenge to the NHS? In *The Sociology of the Health Service*, eds J. Gabe, M. Calnan & M. Bury. London: Routledge

Moldow, G. 1987. *Women Doctors in Gilded-Age Washington*. Urbana and Chicago: University of Illinois Press

Morantz-Santchez, R. M. 1985. *Sympathy and Science: Women Physicians in American Medicine*. New York: Oxford University Press

More, E. S. & Milligan, M. A. 1994. *The Empathic Practitioner: Empathy, Gender and Medicine*. New Brunswick: Rutgers University Press

Morris, M. 1988. *The Pirate's Fiancée: feminism, reading, postmodernism*. London: Verso

Mulvey, M. 1982. History of women in medicine. *Royal Prince Alfred Journal*, Winter Issue: 30–3

Murray, K. D. S. 1993. Frère Jacques dormez-vous? *Arena Magazine*, February–March: 37–40

Nelkin, D. & Lindee, S. 1995. *The DNA Mystique: The Gene as a Cultural Icon*. New York: W. H. Greeman & Co.

Neumayer, L. et al. 1993. Female surgeons in the 1990s: Academic role models. *Archives of Surgery*, 128: 669–72

Neve, M. H. 1980. *This Mad Folly! The History of Australia's Pioneer Women Doctors*. Sydney: Library of Australian History

Newman, L. 1991. Second among equals. *British Journal of General Practice*, 42: 71–4

Nolan, W. 1970. *The Making of a Surgeon*. New York: Random House

NSW Health Department 1991. *Profile of the Medical Workforce in NSW, 1990* Workforce Planning Unit Human Resources Branch, August. Sydney: NSW Health Department

Norsigian, J. 1996. The women's health movement in the United States. In *Man-Made Medicine: Women's Heath, Public Policy and Reform*, ed. K. L. Moss, pp. 79–98. Durham: Duke Univerity Press

Oakley, A. 1980. *Women Confined: Toward a Sociology of Childbirth*. Oxford: Martin Robertson

Oakley, A. 1984. *The Captured Womb*. Oxford: Blackwell

Osborne, T. 1993. On liberalism, neo-liberalism and the 'liberal profession' of medicine. *Economy and Society*, 22(3): 345–56

Osler, K. 1991. Employment experiences of vocationally trained doctors. *British Medical Journal*, 303: 762–4

Palmer, G. R. & Short, S. D. 1989. *Health Care and Public Policy: An Australian Analysis*. Melbourne: Macmillan

Parkhouse, H. F. & Parkhouse, J. 1989. Women, life and medicine – achieving the balance. An account of 1974 women medical graduates in 1987. *Community Medicine*, 11: 1–16

Parkhouse, J. 1979. *Medical Manpower in Britain*. Edinburgh: Churchill Livingstone

Parkhouse, J. 1991. *Doctors' Careers. Aims and Experiences of Medical Graduates*. London: Routledge

Parry, N. & Parry, J. 1976. *The Rise of the Medical Profession*. London: Croom Helm

Parsons, T. 1968. Professions. *International Encyclopedia of the Social Sciences*, Vol. 12, ed. D. L. Sills. London: Macmillan

Pfeffer, N. 1987. Artificial insemination, in-vitro fertilisation and the stigma of infertility. In Stanworth

Pfeffer, N. 1993. *The Stork and the Syringe. A Political History of Reproductive Medicine*. Cambridge: Polity Press

Phillips, A. 1987. *Divided Loyalties: Dilemmas of Sex and Class*. London: Virago

Pringle, R. 1988. *Secretaries Talk*. London: Verso

Pringle, R. & Collings, S. 1993. Women and butchery: Some cultural taboos. *Australian Feminist Studies*, 17: 29–46

Pringle, R. 1995. Destabilising patriarchy. In *Transitions*, eds R. Pringle & B. Caine. Sydney: Allen & Unwin

Pritchard, P. 1992. Doctors, patients and time. In R. Frankenberg (ed.), pp. 74–93

Procter, S. & Roberts, S. 1987. Hard times – hard choices: Positive decision-making for part-time women doctors. *Medical Education*, 21(3): 260–4

Quadrio, C. 1989. Reflections on RANZCP Congress 1988. Letters to the Editor. *ANZ Journal of Psychiatry*, 22: 340–4

Quadrio, C. 1991. Women in Australian and New Zealand psychiatry: the fat lady sings. *ANZ Journal of Psychiatry*, 25: 95–110

Quadrio, C. 1992. Sex and gender and the impaired therapist. *ANZ Journal of Psychiatry*, 26: 346–63

Quadrio, C. 1997. Women and men and the medical workforce in Australia. Editorial, *Medical Journal of Australia*, 166: 7–8

Ragg, M. 1993. Blinded with science. *Bulletin*, 30 March: 4–20

Ragg, M. 1994. GPs in terminal decline. *Bulletin*, 4 October: 28–32

Ragg, M. 1996. Is there a boofhead in the house? *Australian Magazine*, 13–14 April: 52–7

RCOG. 1987. *Memorandum of Council on the Role of Women Doctors in Obstetrics and Gynaecology*. May, London: RCOG

Rees, L. & van Somerin, V. 1984. Personal view. *British Medical Journal*, 289: 827

Relman, A. S. 1990. The changing demography of the medical profession. *New England Journal of Medicine*, 321(22): 1540–1

Rhodes, P. J. 1989. The career aspirations of women doctors who qualified in 1974 and 1977 from a United Kingdom medical school. *Medical Education*, 23: 125–35

Rice, S, 1988. *Some Doctors Make You Sick*. Sydney: Angus & Robertson

Rich, A. 1976. *Of Woman Born: Motherhood as Experience and Institution*. New York: W. W. Norton

Riessman, C. K. 1983. Women and medicalization: A new perspective. *Social Policy*, Summer: 3–18

Riska, E. & Wegar, K. 1993. Women physicians: A new force in medicine? In Riska & Wegar (eds), pp. 77–94

Riska, E. & Wegar, K. (eds). 1993. *Gender, Work and Medicine: Women and the Medical Division of Labour*. London: Sage

Riviere, J. 1986. Womanliness as a masquerade [1929]. In *Formations of Fantasy*, eds V. Burgin, J. Donald & C. Kaplan, pp. 35–44. London and New York: Methuen

Roberts, H. (ed.) 1981. *Women, Health and Reproduction*. London: Routledge & Kegan Paul

Roberts, H. 1985. *The Patient Patients: Women and their Doctors*. London: Pandora

Roberts, J. 1991a. Junior doctors' years: Training, not education. *British Medical Journal*, 302: 225–6

Roberts, J. 1991b. General practice: Feeling fine, getting better. *British Medical Journal*, 302: 97–100

Rose, N. 1993. Medicine, history and the present. In *Reassessing Foucault*, eds C. Jones & R. Porter. London: Routledge

Rose, N. 1986. Psychiatry: The discipline of mental health. In Miller & Rose, pp. 43–84

Rosen, G. 1944. *The Specialization of Medicine with Particular Reference to Ophthalmology*. New York: Froben

Rosser, S. V. (ed.). 1988. *Feminism within the Science and Health Care Professions: Overcoming Resistance*. Oxford: Pergamon

Rothfield, L. 1992. *Vital Signs: Medical Realism in Nineteenth Century Fiction*. Princeton, NJ: Princeton University Press

Rothman, B. K. 1989. *Recreating Motherhood: Ideology and Technology in a Patriarchal Society*. New York: W. W. Norton

Rothwell, H. 1995. Medicalisation of childbearing. *British Journal of Midwifery*, 3(9): 318–23

Rowland, R. 1987. Of woman born, but for how long? The relationship of women to the new reproductive technologies and the issue of choice. In Spallone & Steinberg, pp. 67–83

Rue, R. 1992. Women in medicine [editorial]. *British Journal of Hospital Medicine*, 48(6): 287–9

Russell, D. 1995. *Women, Madness and Medicine*. Cambridge: Polity Press

Ruzek, S. B. 1978. *The Women's Health Movement: Feminist Alternatives to Medical Control*. New York: Praeger

Salvage, J. 1985. *The Politics of Nursing*. London: Heinemann

Saul, A. 1994. Theoretical and political implications of the management of childbirth. *Issues in Contemporary Sociology Conference*, School of Behavioural Sciences, Macquarie University: 1–9

Savage, W. 1986. *A Savage Enquiry*. London: Virago

Sax, S. 1989. The politics of health in Australia. In Lupton & Najman (eds)

Schlicht, S. M. & Dunt, D. R. 1987. Women's perceptions of female general practitioners. *Community Health Studies*, xi(3): 176–82

Schofield, T. 1993. Medical technology and childbirth. Paper delivered at Making Bodies: Women and Technology Seminar, Sydney University, 29 May

Scully, D. & Bart, P. 1973. A funny thing happened on the way to the orifice: Women in gynaecology textbooks. *American Journal of Sociology*, 78(4): 1045–9

Shapiro, M. 1978. *Getting Doctored: Critical Reflections on Becoming a Physician.* Kitchener: Between the Lines

Shapiro, M. 1989. Challenging the doctrine of idealism: The long-term consequences of medical training. In Lupton & Najman (eds)

Shapiro, M. C., Western, J. S. & Anderson, D. S. 1988. Career preferences and career outcomes of Australian medical students. *Medical Education,* 22: 214–16

Sharpe, S. 1995. A geography of the birthing moment: Space and social practice at the RHW Birth Centre. Honours Thesis: Dept of Human Geography, Macquarie University

Shaw, H. 1979. The careers of women graduates from St Mary's Hospital Medical School, London, 1961–72. *Medical Education,* 13: 275–83

Shorter, E. 1984. *A History of Women's Bodies.* London: Penguin Books

Shorter, E. 1985. *Bedside Manners: The Troubled History of Doctors and Patients.* New York: Simon & Schuster

Showalter, E. 1987. *The Female Malady: Women, Madness and English Culture, 1830–1980.* London: Virago

Siedlecky, S. 1979. Reactions to the Leichhardt Women's Health Centre. *New Doctor,* 5: 29–32

Siedlecky, S. & Wyndham, D. 1990. *Populate and Perish: Australian Women's Fight for Birth Control.* Sydney: Allen & Unwin

Silverman, David 1987. *Communication and Medical Practice.* London: Sage

Silverstone, R. & Ward, A. (eds). 1980. *Careers of Professional Women.* London: Croom Helm

South Australian Medical Women's Society. 1994. *The Hands of a Woman: Stories of South Australian Medical Women and Their Society.* Adelaide: Wakefield Press

Spallone, P. & Steinberg, D. L. (eds). 1987. *Made to Order: The Myth of Reproductive and Genetic Progress.* Oxford: Pergamon Press

Spencer, A. & Podmore, D. (eds). 1987. *In a Man's World. Essays on Women in Male-Dominated Professions.* London: Tavistock

Stanworth, M. 1990. Birth pangs: Conceptive technologies and the threat to motherhood. In *Conflicts in Feminism,* eds M. Hirsch & E. F. Keller, pp. 288–304. New York: Routledge

Stanworth, M. (ed.). 1987. *Reproductive Technologies: Gender, Motherhood and Medicine.* Cambridge: Polity Press

Stegman, C. B. 1987. *The Effects of Social and Environmental Factors on Informal Teaching–Learning Transactions Between Female Nurses and Female Physicians.* Doctor of Education Thesis Maryland: Nova University

Stein, L. I. 1967. The doctor–nurse game. *Archives of General Psychiatry,* 16 June: 699–703

Stein, L. I., Watts, D. T. & Howell, T. 1990. The doctor–nurse game revisited. *Nursing Outlook,* 38(6): 264–8

Stephen, P. J. 1987. Career patterns of women medical graduates 1974–84. *Medical Education,* 21(3): 255–9

Stevens, J. 1995. *Healing Women: A History of Leichhardt Women's Community Health Centre.* Sydney: First Ten Years History Project

Stoeckle, J. D. (ed.). 1987. *Encounters between Patients and Doctors: An Anthology.* Cambridge, MA: MIT Press

Street, A. F. 1992. *Inside Nursing: A Critical Ethnography of Clinical Nursing Practice.* Albany: State University of New York

Summey, P. S. & Hurst, M. 1986a. Ob/Gyn on the rise: The evolution of professional ideology in the twentieth century. Part 1. *Women and Health*, 11(1): 133–45

Summey, P. S. & Hurst, M. 1986b. Ob/Gyn on the rise: The evolution of professional ideology in the twentieth century. Part 2. *Women and Health*, 11(2): 103–22

Szasz, T. 1961. *The Myth of Mental Illness*. New York: Harper & Row

Tatlock, L. 1992. Speculum feminarum: Gendered perspectives on obstetrics and gynecology in early modern Germany. *Signs*, 17(4): 725–60

Taylor, A. D. 1993. *How to Choose a Medical Specialty*. 2nd ed. Philadelphia: W. B. Saunders

Theriot, N. 1993. Women's voices in nineteenth century medical discourse: A step toward deconstructing science. *Signs*, 19(1): 1–31

Thompson, E. P. 1967. Time, work-discipline, and industrial capitalism. *Past and Present*, 38: 56–97

Tindall, G. 1991. Medicalizing the menopause: Hormone replacement therapy – solution or problem? *Journal of the Royal Society of Medicine*, 84: 569

Tolhurst, H. 1996. The art of being a female rural GP. Paper presented to the Victorian Rural Divisions Coordinating Unit Conference

Treichler, P. A. 1990. Feminism, medicine, and the meaning of childbirth. In M. Jacobus, E. F. Keller & S. Shuttleworth (eds)

Turner, B. S. 1987. *Medical Power and Social Knowledge*. London: Sage

Turner, J., Tippett, V. & Raphael, B. 1994. Women in medicine – socialization, stereotypes and self perceptions. *ANZ Journal of Psychiatry*, 28: 129–35

Van Someren, V. 1991. Part time working and job sharing in the NHS. *British Medical Journal*, 5 December: 1377–8

Van Someren, V. 1992. Women in medicine: A feeling of futility. *British Medical Journal*, 26 January: 226–7

Vanek, J. 1974. Time spent in housework. *Scientific American*, 231(5): 116–20

Vincent, L. 1985. Women doctors in Western Australia 1895–1950. *Royal Western Australian Historical Society*, 30–44

Wajcman, J. 1991. *Feminism Confronts Technology*. Sydney: Allen & Unwin

Wacquant, L. J. D. 1988. Towards a reflexive sociology: A workshop with Pierre Bourdieu. *Sociological Theory*, 7(1): 26–63

Walby, S. 1986. *Patriarchy at Work*. Oxford: Blackwell

Walby, S. & Greenwell, J. 1994. *Medicine and Nursing: Professions in a Changing Health Service*. London: Sage

Walkowitz, J. 1992. *City of Dreadful Delight: Narratives of Sexual Danger in Late-Victorian London*. Chicago: University of Chicago Press

Waller, K. 1988. Women doctors for women patients? *British Journal of Medical Psychology*, 61(2): 125–35

Walsh, M. & Willcox, S. 1992. The future of general practice. Issues Paper No. 3, National Health Strategy, March

Walsh, M. R. 1979. The rediscovery of the need for a feminist medical education. *Harvard Educational Review*, 49(4): 447–66

Walsh, M. R. 1977. *'Doctors Wanted: No Women Need Apply'. Sexual Barriers in the Medical Profession 1835–1975*. New Haven: Yale University Press

Ward, A. W. M. Careers of medical women. *British Medical Journal*, 284: 31–3

Webb, C. (ed.). 1986. *Feminist Practice in Women's Health Care*, Chichester: John Wiley

Webb, N. 1984. Women and the medical school. In *Centenary Book of the University of Sydney Faculty of Medicine*, eds J. A. Young, A. J. Sefton & N. Webb, pp. 218–37. Sydney: Sydney University Press

Webster, C. (ed.). 1981. *Biology, Medicine and Society 1840–1940*. Cambridge: Cambridge University Press

Weekes, P. 1995. Nurses face sex harassment. *Australian*, 18 May

Welford, H. 1993. Birth's labour's lost. *Guardian Weekly*, 2 May p. 25

West, C. 1984. When the doctor is a 'lady': Power, status and gender in physician–doctor dialogues. In *Women, Health and Medicine*, ed. A. Stromberg. Palo Alto: Mayfield

White, B., Cox, C. & Cooper, C. 1992. *Women's Career Development: A Study of High Flyers*. Oxford: Blackwell

Wicks, D. 1993. Nurses and doctors at work: Theorising the sexual division of labour. *Working Paper No. 1, Psychosocial Health Papers*, University of Newcastle, NSW

Williams, A., Whitfield, M., Bucks, R. & St Claire, L. 1991. Differences in the attitudes of men and women practitioners to responsibility and competence. *British Journal of General Practice*, 41: 27–9

Williams, L. 1990. Feminine frontiers: Queensland's early medical women. In *Fevers and Frontiers*, eds J. Pearn and M. Cobcroft, pp. 134–58. Brisbane: Amphion Press

Williams, L. 1992. Two of a kind: Pioneer medical women in country practice in Australia. In *Health, History and Horizons*, ed. J. Pearn. Brisbane: Amphion Press

Willis, E. 1983. *Medical Dominance*. Sydney: Allen & Unwin

Wilson, G. 1995. *One Grand Chain – A History of Anaesthesia in Australia 1846–1934*. Sydney

Wilson, R. & Allen, P. 1994. Medical and dental staffing prospects in the NHS in England and Wales 1993. *Health Trends*, 26(3): 70–9

Winton, R. 1988. *Why the Pomegranate? A History of the Royal Australian College of Physicians*. Sydney: RACP

Witz, A. 1992. *Professions and Patriarchy*. London: Routledge

Women in Medicine 1992a. *Careers for Women in Medicine: Planning and Pitfalls*, 3rd ed. London: Women in Medicine

Women in Medicine 1992b. *Job Sharing and Part-Time Work in General Practice*. London: Women in Medicine

Worcester, N. & Whatley, M. H. 1988. The response of the health care system to the women's health movement: The selling of women's health centres. In Rosser

Working Group on Specialist Medical Training. 1993. *Report 1992–93*. London: HMSO Calman Report

Wright, S. 1985. New nurses: New boundaries. *Nursing Practice*, (1): 1

Wyndham, D. 1986. Medical men rule, OK for women? *Healthright*, 5(2): 23–6

Yeatman, A. 1993. Voice and representation in the politics of difference. In *Feminism and the Politics of Difference*, eds. A. Yeatman & S. Gunew, pp. 228–45. Sydney: Allen & Unwin

Young, G. 1981. A woman in medicine: Reflections from the inside. In *Women, Health and Reproduction*, ed. H. Roberts. London: Routledge & Kegan Paul

Zola, I. K. 1972. Medicine as an institution of social control: The medicalizing of society. *Sociological Review*, 20(4): 487–504

Index